AF479190

Christianity and democratisation

Manchester University Press

PERSPECTIVES ON DEMOCRATIC PRACTICE

series editors: SHIRIN M. RAI and WYN GRANT

With the ebbing away of the "third wave" of democratisation, democratic practice is unfolding and consolidating in different ways. While state based representative democracy remains central to our understanding of the concept, we are also conscious of the importance of social movements, non-governmental organisations and governance institutions. New mechanisms of accountability are being developed, together with new political vocabularies to address these elements in democratic practice. The books published in this series focus on three aspects of democratic practice: analytical and normative democratic theory, including processes by which democratic practice can be explained and achieved; new social and protest movements, especially work with a comparative and international focus; and institution-building and practice, including transformations in democratic institutions in response to social and democratic forces. Their importance arises from the fact that they are concerned with key questions about how power can be more fairly distributed and how people can be empowered to have a greater influence on decisions that affect their lives.

This series takes forward the intellectual project of the earlier MUP series, *Perspectives on Democratization*.

Already published

Susan Buckingham and Geraldine Lievesley (eds) *In the hands of women: paradigms of citizenship*

Bart Cammaerts *Mind the gap: internet mediated policy processes beyond the nation state*

Francesco Cavatorta *The international dimension of the failed Algerian transition: democracy betrayed?*

Katherine Fierlbeck *Globalizing democracy: power, legitimacy and the interpretation of democratic ideas (2nd edn)*

Carina Gunnarson *Cultural warfare and trust: fighting the Mafia in Palermo*

Jennifer S. Holmes *Terrorism and democratic stability revisited (2nd edn)*

Anca Pusca *Revolution, democratic transition and disillusionment: the case of Romania*

Christianity and democratisation

From pious subjects to critical participants

JOHN ANDERSON

Manchester University Press
Manchester and New York

distributed in the United States exclusively by Palgrave Macmillan

Published by Manchester University Press
Oxford Road, Manchester M13 9NR, UK
and Room 400, 175 Fifth Avenue, New York, NY 10010, USA
www. manchesteruniversitypress.co.uk

Distributed in the United States exclusively by
Palgrave Macmillan, 175 Fifth Avenue, New York,
NY 10010, USA

Distributed in Canada exclusively by
UBC Press, University of British Columbia, 2029 West Mall,
Vancouver, BC, Canada V6T 1Z2

British Library Cataloguing-in-Publication Data
A catalogue record for this book is available from the British Library

Library of Congress Cataloging-in-Publication Data applied for

ISBN 978 0 7190 7738 8 *hardback*

First published 2009

18 17 16 15 14 13 12 11 10 09   10 9 8 7 6 5 4 3 2 1

Typeset
by Action Publishing Technology Ltd, Gloucester
Printed in Great Britain
by MPG Books Ltd, Bodmin, Cornwall

For Jill

Contents

Preface and acknowledgements

This book falls into the category of a research-based text that is aimed primarily at a senior undergraduate and postgraduate audience interested in questions related to religion and politics. Though at one level a textbook, it is rooted in my own researches into religion and politics, in particular in the former communist world. In offering a new synthesis on the relationship of democracy to different strands within the Christian tradition it covers a large amount of ground and inevitably relies heavily on the work of many other specialists. It is impossible to thank all those authors by name – though they can be found in the bibliography – but I can at least apologise where I have misunderstood, misinterpreted or grossly over-simplified developments within the traditions and countries about which they write. Several people, however, can be mentioned because in various ways they contributed to my understanding by organising conferences and seminars where the complex relationship of religion and democracy has been discussed, or by commenting on my attempts to analyse this subject. These include Zsolt Enyedi, Jeffrey Haynes, John Madeley, Joan O'Mahony and Phillip Walters, and other participants in European Consortium on Political Research conferences that took place in Copenhagen and Budapest. Thanks also go to successive generations of students who have taken my 'Religion and World Politics' class at St Andrews, as well as colleagues in the School of International Relations who have offered useful insights into a diverse range of topics. Special thanks must go to Tony Lang who read the manuscript in draft form and offered useful comments and advice, particularly in those areas where my own knowledge was deficient. The writing up of the project was delayed by periods of ill-health and I am truly grateful to several doctors and consultants who helped me deal with these and reinforced my belief in a strong public health system. Above all I owe thanks to my family: to Joseph and Caitlin whose teenage demands for chauffering, concert tickets, driving lessons and hard cash, together with their wit and good company, kept this peculiar academic pursuit in proper perspective; and to Jill who has put up with much over the last couple of years but has (mostly) kept smiling throughout.

1

Introduction

Christianity and democracy have had a long and sometimes troubled relationship. The roots of political pluralism are often seen as embedded within the Protestant historical experience of Northern Europe and North America, though whether this was a direct consequence of Reformed Christianity is contested. Conversely, the Roman Catholic Church has been depicted as a social institution that sought to halt the development of democracy from the late eighteenth to the early twentieth century in Europe and Latin America. Very little attention was paid to the neglected third branch of Christianity, Eastern Orthodoxy, and the underlying assumption in this case was that close ties to nation-states and the long history of oppression under Ottomans, fascists and communists meant that these churches were not in a position to contribute towards democratic development. With the collapse of communism the democracy–Orthodox nexus has come under the spotlight, but since the end of the twentieth century we have also seen renewed attention being paid to the Protestant connection. In the 'developing world' questions have been raised anew about the political implications of religion in the light of the rapid expansion of Pentecostalism, whilst in the United States Samuel Huntington asked whether Protestantism was in some sense essential to maintaining the quality of American democracy, if not to the future survival of American 'civilisation'. Equally significant has been the fact that religious voices have joined the debate over what we actually mean by democracy. Religious 'conservatives' have expressed concern at the assumption that the acceptance of democracy requires an uncritical embrace of a heavily individualistic liberalism, whilst religious 'liberals' have recognised that whilst achieving the vote is important this tells us nothing about whether the new political orders genuinely empower the voiceless or serve the common good. And whilst these debates continue within religious traditions, more sceptical political scientists might respond with 'So what?' for, even if religious communities have changed their attitude to democracy over the years, it doesn't matter that much. In most circumstances the churches are relatively insignificant politically speaking, and in many processes of political change short-term outcomes have more to do with the contingent choices of politicians whilst long-term trends are heavily dependent upon the cultural, socio-economic and international context within which democratisation takes place.

★ ★ ★ ★ ★

This book picks up on many of these themes, aiming to provide a synthesis of existing work and to offer new insights into the engagement of Christian traditions with the democratic experiment. In particular it focuses on countries in the process of transition to a democratic order or those which might be prospective candidates for democratisation in the future. For that reason it has little to say about religion's role in established democracies, with the single exception of the USA – which is exceptional in so many ways when it comes to religion – and does not look, for example, at the role of Christian Democratic movements in Europe or at Christian social movements that have periodically appeared to combat the perceived social and morals ills of society. But these experiences are important, above all in pointing to the religion–democracy relationship as a dynamic affair, one subject to continued evolution and development, and subject to constant re-negotiation in democratic political orders. Here we need look no further than Prime Minister Gordon Brown's proposal to end his role in the appointment of Anglican bishops or the often agonised debates about how mature democracies should handle the relatively new challenge of a religious pluralism that goes way beyond historical experiences of variety within a broad Christian tradition.

So here the focus, with the exception of the next chapter, is on new democracies or countries in a process of transition. At one level we simply want to tell a story, to provide an overview of the religion–democracy relationship. Here we can identity three broad periods, each one shorter than its predecessor. The first, covered very briefly in Chapter 2, starts with the advent of Christianity and runs through to the 1960s, as there gradually emerged within Christian thought and practice an engagement with ideas about human equality, about consultation, about tolerance and about participation. Traces of this can be found in the Old Testament's prophetic commitments to social justice, in Christ's promotion of the notion of equality before God, in the activities of 'heretical' sects who sought freedom to worship as they pleased, and in late medieval Conciliar movements with their discussions of participation in both the secular and religious realms. These ideas were developed much further after the Reformation, with the focus on individual judgement, the reading of scripture, congregational church life and, however reluctantly, the gradual acceptance of the idea that individual believers and believing communities might legitimately see things differently. It was only a short step to extending these ideas to the political realm and a variety of groups, from the English Levellers to the American revolutionaries, further developed the idea of political participation – some influenced by Christianity, but also by the ideas emerging from the Enlightenment. Whilst Protestants gradually came to terms with these new ideas, the experience of the French Revolution turned the Roman Catholic Church firmly against what it saw as the anarchical and amoral style of democratic politics, and transformed it into a major opponent of democracy until well into the twentieth century. Only the experience of communism and theological change within led to its transformation into a (sometimes) enthusiastic supporter of democratic governance.

The second period we are concerned with covers the so-called 'third wave' of democratisation, generally deemed to have started in the mid-1970s and perhaps to have stalled in the mid-1990s as some of the new democracies struggled to consolidate and others failed to get beyond a formal 'electoralism' that did little to transform power relationships. During this period many scholars noted the ways in which religious groups, especially Catholic ones, helped to undermine authoritarianism through public critique, defence of human rights, support for civil society, and involvement in the negotiation of political change. In many countries the churches made a contribution to democratisation and in a few countries religious organisations were major players in effecting change. At the same time, as democracy in some shape or form was achieved, religious communities did not always find it easy to adapt to aspects of new political orders where their status and role often declined, where they faced competition for influence from other religious and secular groups, and where the 'moral atmosphere' of the new societies did not always sit comfortably with their traditional teachings (Chapters 3–4).

This was particularly evident in the Orthodox post-communist countries where religious communities had no experience of democratic governance and no substantial tradition of thinking about social and political issues. As the 'third wave' began to stall, it was in this third period and in these same countries that the establishment of truly 'liberal' democracies often appeared problematic. Their traditionally dominant Eastern Christian churches struggled to come to terms with the realities of democratic governance, and all too often found it hard to resist the temptation of preferring historic alliances with State and nation over engagement in the sphere of civil society (Chapters 5–6). Meanwhile, in the North American 'home of democracy' the question of the 'proper' relationship between religion and politics came to the fore again, in part as a consequence of the rise of the Christian Right and its revitalisation during the presidency of George W. Bush. In 2004 Samuel Huntington raised the question of whether America's Anglo-Protestant culture was being undermined by multiculturalism and whether her democratic 'civilisation' could survive once these ideological roots were knocked away (Chapter 7). Simultaneously, new challenges for democracy were being raised by the rapid expansion of Pentecostalism in many parts of the globe, with some suggesting that the essential conservatism of this religious tradition would militate against any further democratisation by promoting political passivity and acceptance of the status quo, however authoritarian that might be. Against this, other scholars argued that this phenomenon might create a new Weberian effect, leading to both economic development and political democratisation (Chapter 8). All this suggested that, even in the early twenty-first century, the question of the relationship between democracy and Christianity remained a live issue.

★ ★ ★ ★ ★

In telling this story, what quickly becomes apparent is that when Christian churches respond to democracy, they are reacting to different aspects of the democratic paradigm, some of which cause them more problems of adaptation than others. Our assumption is that democracy can take a variety of forms and that these are very much shaped by historical, cultural, economic, social and political context. Nonetheless, whilst this is not the place to explore the huge literature on the subject, we might suggest that there are some core defining features of what we call 'democracy', and that these include the basic notions that:

- the people should be included in the political process and in some sense they should rule, though definitions of who are to be included as the people and how they are to rule will always remain contested;
- the rulers should in some sense be accountable to ruled, and that should they forfeit popular trust there are mechanisms in place that permit the peaceful removal and replacement of the rulers;
- politics is essentially a competitive process, with mechanisms in place to permit us as citizens to compete with others for power or to choose between a variety of groups or individuals competing for popular support;
- all citizens are endowed with rights as well as obligations, and that the definition of the rights usually incline to the permissive, i.e. we are free to act as we wish so long as our actions do not harm others. They also include some basic protections such as freedom to associate, freedom of expression, freedom from arbitrary arrest etc.

At the most basic level few modern Christian communities would offer a fundamental opposition to any of these propositions, but most would add qualifications and elaboration.

At the theological level many would remind believers and non-believers alike that human sovereignty at the political level does not negate the role of divine sovereignty or the fact that human rulers are also accountable before God for the ways in which they govern. More difficult for religious leaders might be the notion of popular rule as permitting all matters to be decided by majority vote with all the churches, but perhaps most explicitly the Roman Catholic Church, expressing doubts about the suggestion that majorities can decide everything, especially when it comes to 'moral' or 'theological' issues. Some concern has also been expressed about the notion of 'competition', with the Eastern Christian traditions preferring to stress the wholeness of Christian societies and to be wary of parties and groups which encourage division. Perhaps most problematic for virtually all the churches has been the notion of rights, for whilst the majority of Protestants and Catholics, and some Orthodox, have bought into the general discourse of human rights, not surprisingly all would seek to limit their understanding of rights with reference to their basic teachings and moral understandings, and many would claim that the corresponding notion of obligation to the community has been under-emphasised in modern rights discourse.

Many religious communities have also expressed concern that the requirement that they accept democracy should not mean that they have to uncritically accept all the liberal assumptions that sometimes go with it. Some Christian groups would raise questions about the necessary separation of Church and State, often described as essential for democratic governance despite the fact that many European states have proved able to reconcile democracy and establishment. Doubts might be expressed about any understanding of secularism as central to democracy, and the notion that in some sense religious interventions in politics are illegitimate in a democratic society.[1] They might also reject the suggestion that religious believers should not utilise religious language in public debate and should adhere to some ostensibly neutral, secular language when they enter the public arena. Whilst there may be prudential reasons for so doing, religious leaders would argue that to exclude them from making reference to their value systems is essentially asking them to be dishonest about their motives and that additionally it would be discriminatory in a truly democratic order.[2] Finally there is a wariness of those visions of democracy which root pluralist politics in individual autonomy without reference to some notion of obligation, moral restraint or concern for 'traditional' or communal understandings of public life – a concern that, as we shall see, is shared in different ways by the Vatican, the Russian Orthodox hierarchy and the Christian Right. All this points us towards the inevitability of a certain tension between the religious and political order, even where religious organisations do in broad measure accept the structures and modus operandi of political democracy. For in promoting absolute values and particular evaluations of moral behaviour – whether it relates to issues of sexuality, social justice, or war and peace – there will, as we shall see, almost certainly be occasions when the teachings of the churches come into conflict with the political or societal consensus.

* * * * *

Beyond telling this story, we also raise a number of analytical questions that will enable us to shed further light on the relationship, in particular asking what is it that makes religious organisations choose to oppose or support democratisation at different times and in a variety of contexts. The opposition is easier to explain historically, and in part this simply reflects the dominant view until the nineteenth century – and even beyond in many places – that democracy was simply undesirable and unacceptable, associated with anarchy and mob rule. In this sense the churches were accepting the view of a wider society. Equally, once constitutional governance and liberal democracy did begin to spread, those churches with a hierarchical disposition could see some obvious challenges to their ideological and institutional hegemony within society. For Pius IX and his successors the very notion of 'freedom of conscience' and the 'sovereignty of the people' was anathema, a violation of natural law and good order. But many Protestants also remained wary of the moral and ideological pluralism that came with democratic governance and feared that mob rule might ensue. More practically, as republican governments started to criticise and even persecute religious institutions, the latter acquired an additional reason to be sceptical of political pluralism. In such circumstances it was hardly surprising to find Catholic leaders in Central Europe, Iberia or Latin America favouring authoritarian regimes that shared a hierarchical vision of religious and political order, and often acted to defend the institutional interests of the dominant churches. Equally, after the collapse of communism, churches fearful of change, unused to religious and political pluralism, and in some cases struggling to find legitimacy after their compromises with the old regimes, often appealed to the State for protection against competitors rather than acting in ways supportive of more liberal political development.

Given that authoritarian regimes, communists excepted, often prove supportive of religious organisations, why should Christian churches have in many cases shifted towards a pro-democracy position? In the Protestant case Steve Bruce has made the argument that there is a relationship between the religious tradition and democracy, but that the links are 'unintended consequences'. We shall return to his argument later but the basic point is that individualism, lay activism, perpetual fragmentation, privatisation, egalitarianism and social inclusion all helped to 'undermine the organic and communal basis for religion' and lay the foundation for congregational and then political democracy. This may not have been the intention of the reformers of the sixteenth century and their later followers, but it was a natural, and almost inevitable, consequence of their activities.[3]

A second type of explanation might be described with reference to 'altruism', that is, the suggestion that from the 1950s onwards the churches in general, and the Roman Catholic Church in particular, adopted an attitude towards the temporal order that proved more supportive of democratic values and practices. Samuel Huntington noted that the 'third wave' was very much a Catholic wave and he argued that this was (a) because most of the Protestant countries were already democratic, (b) because these democratising countries were at a middle income level and thus now ready for political change, and (c) because of changes in the Catholic relationship to the secular world. For Huntington the key factor explaining Catholic support for democratisation lay in the changes within the Church following Vatican II which brought a powerful social institution into opposition with authoritarianism. This was reinforced by a new generation of priests less inclined to an uncritical relationship with political power and influenced by liberal ideas prevalent in the West from the 1960s onwards, which emphasised individual rights and concepts of social justice. As hierarchically organised churches tied into a wider transnational religious organisation, national Catholic hierarchies enjoyed considerable institutional resources in their struggle against authoritarianism, as well as legitimacy within their home countries, and thus posed major dilemmas for governments in traditionally Catholic countries. All this was reinforced by the election of John Paul II whose very first encyclical addressed the issue of human rights and whose pastoral visits sometimes served to undermine authoritarianism as an acceptable form of government.[4] In sum, the reasons for the changing Catholic attitude towards democracy lay in religious change that affected the ideas and actions of national hierarchies. For example, in Latin America and Iberia it might be argued that, whereas once the religious focus on hierarchy, paternalism and authority reinforced these traits in the wide society, the changing orientation of the churches helped to shift the political culture in a more participatory and individually oriented direction that laid the basis for democratisation – though this was only one, often minor factor in the process. But there was also another, perhaps implicit, strand to the argument, which was to suggest that in changing thus the Catholic Church was actually becoming more 'Protestant' (as members adopted the more individualistic, 'pick and mix' approach to the Church's teaching that was sometimes seen as characteristic of Protestantism) and only for that reason was it beginning to contribute to political change. In essence what Huntington offered was a slight revision of the traditional assumption of a Protestant/democracy relationship by positing a Western Christianity/democracy relationship.

Not all authors would have accepted this implication, though many would have agreed with the notion that the churches' changing position on democracy had a lot to do with Vatican II and that it was essentially altruistic, rooted in a theological and very genuine concern with the treatment of individual human beings. After the Second World War most Western churchmen came to accept the principle that states did not have the right to treat individuals as they chose in pursuit of some 'greater good' and, after Vatican II, most gradually came to accept that defending human rights was a legitimate activity for church leaders. In response to this 'new thinking' national hierarchies in many countries began to adopt a more pro-active role that served to undermine the legitimacy of authoritarianism and, in consequence, to promote democratisation. Such openness to the world did not preclude wariness of political actors or presume common interests between churches and the secular order, but did mean that the old uncritical relationship with political authority was no longer acceptable.

A further strand in this argument is to be found in the writings of George Weigel, whose book *The Final Revolution* essentially attributes the downfall of the Soviet system to the 'moral and cultural revolution' that preceded 1989 and argues that this can in part be explained by the activities of Pope John Paul II. In Weigel's words, 'What Lenin started at Petrograd's Finland station on April 16, 1917 ... Pope John Paul II began to dismantle at the Jasna Góra monastery in Częstochowa, the shrine of the Black Madonna, Queen of Poland, on June 4, 1979.'[5] He rejects accounts of Soviet collapse that focus on the role of Gorbachev, Reagan, the Helsinki Final Act or economics, instead preferring to see 1989 as a 'revolution of the human spirit' and arguing that the West has 'often forgotten that politics is a function of culture, and that at the heart of culture is religion'.[6] Above all, however, Weigel focuses on 'the Wojtyła difference'. Pope John Paul II's prime vision of himself was as a pastor, as a defender of humanity in the broadest sense, and as such he was strongly influenced by the post-Vatican II vision of a Church acting in the political arena under the influence of a commitment to the defence of human dignity.[7] At the same time Pope John Paul II was an astute political actor and, as we shall see, once democracy had been achieved in his own country and elsewhere, was more than capable of standing up for the interests of the institutional Church as well as pursuing his broader concern with human dignity as understood by that Church. In this sense Weigel reinforced an explanatory framework that stressed both theological change and the role of a religious leadership now convinced that the Church or churches should seek to defend human dignity wherever it was subject to abuse.

Whilst Bruce stressed inadvertency in the Protestant case and Huntington theological change in the Catholic case, others are more sceptical. For Jeffrey Haynes, writing about Africa, it is true that in some contexts the Christian churches adopted leadership roles within democratisation processes, but he argues that they did so in partnership with the State 'to achieve a hegemonic ideology that stresses the desirability of stability rather than progressive change'. Haynes accepts that the claim of a key religious role in African democratisation processes is 'superficially plausible' yet is wary of giving religious organisations too much credit.[8] Looking at the Roman Catholic Church he notes that at the beginning of the post-colonial period it was often viewed with considerable suspicion by the new political elites but that the gradual Africanisation of religious leadership helped to moderate this attitude, whilst the social conservatism of many bishops led to their reintegration into the governing social elite. In consequence, Haynes suggests that once the 'third wave' began, though individual religious leaders may have had genuine democratic credentials, they, like other members of the socio-political elite, represented part of the status quo, concerned 'to keep political and social change within manageable proportions – to seek to ensure that events do not spiral out of control'.[9]

In his study of religion and politics in Africa, Haynes explores why the churches tended to adopt this position, generally supportive of the existing order but willing to jump on the democratisation bandwagon. He notes that their position reflected the fact that 'they themselves benefited materially from the status quo because they were inherently conservative; they believed that governments, however bad, were exercising authority ordained by God; and, finally, they recognised that their church's corporate position in a country was in part dependent upon state acquiescence or support'.[10] From a Gramscian perspective Haynes argues that even where successful democratisations have occurred in Africa they have essentially been 'passive revolutions' rather than fundamental political changes involving the redistribution of power from one group to another. Here religious leaderships continue to play a hegemonic role, ensuring that change does not challenge 'stability' and even utilising their access to international funding and support to promote this essentially conservative position. Like other 'big men' in Africa religious leaders used this access to funds to enrich themselves, develop patronage and ensure their own position in any new order.[11] To simplify, the argument is that the preservation of their social and political hegemony requires religious leaders to support existing regimes in Africa, and that only when domestic and international pressures make change possible do religious leaders tend to support democratisation, in some individual cases for perfectly altruistic and theological reasons, but also in an effort to preserve their corporate and ideological position in the new, post-authoritarian order.

A similar conclusion appears to emerge from Sabrina Ramet's analysis of the role of the Polish Catholic Church during the transition process, albeit without the explicitly Gramscian framework. Briefly reviewing the Church's difficult relationship with the communist regime, she notes that during the martial law period the hierarchy adopted a somewhat ambiguous position. While individual priests and lay people adopted a strongly critical position, 'the Church, headed by Glemp, counselled against confrontation, participated ever more actively in negotiation forums with the State, and concentrated much of its energy on extracting concessions for itself'. This position was noted by the public, with a 1983 survey reporting that 24.2% of the population believed the Church to be more supportive of the government than the opposition, whilst only 6.5% thought it was more supportive of the opposition. Ramet, drawing on Bohdan Cywiński, tends to see the Polish Church as 'Julianic', as inherently in opposition to states but also concerned to ensure its ideological dominance of society. When such a 'Church is given access to power, it is apt to become a *theocratic Church*, meaning that it will try to use state mechanisms to impose the rules and religious values of its own faith on everyone living in the territory of the given society, including those believers who subscribe to other faiths'.[12] By 1988 it was clear to the Church that a new era of opportunity was dawning and, once it had achieved its first priority, sweeping the communists from power, it formulated a 'precise game plan, pushing for the restoration of Catholicism as the official state religion of Poland, the introduction of Catholic religious instruction in public schools, the tightening of divorce laws, the proscription of abortion ... guarantees that "Christian values" ... not be offended on the broadcast media, the redrafting of the constitution along lines pleasing to the Church, and the conclusion of a new concordat ...'. Yet despite all this, Pope John Paul II during his fifth visit to Poland was able to claim that Polish Catholics were the victims of intolerance, prejudice and marginalisation, a view that contrasts very strongly with the position developed by Ramet.[13] In common with Haynes, the essence of her argument appears to be that Vatican II may have had a less significant effect than some commentators suggest and that for all the commendable rhetoric, the Catholic Church's – and probably other churches' – primary concern had remained with their own institutional and ideological interests. Given this, they would find it hard to resist the temptation to pursue their hegemonic position once the old anti-religious regime had been overthrown and democracy established.

A fourth approach to explaining religious activism lies in rational choice theory and is perhaps best developed in Anthony Gill's *Rendering unto Caesar*, a study of Catholicism and the State in Latin America. Gill explores the religious contribution to political change in South America and in particular is concerned with explaining why some religious hierarchies supported political change, others supported authoritarian regimes and yet others simply stood aside – and in effect supported the status quo. This difference, he suggests, cannot adequately be explained by the mainstream literature with its focus on the growing awareness of social injustice and major changes introduced by Vatican II, because these ostensibly impacted upon the whole Catholic Church yet only some national hierarchies adopted a 'progressive' position. Instead he posits a market explanation rooted in a number of key propositions focusing on the role of competition. Put crudely, 'where the Church faces greater competition for members, bishops will be under pressure to defend the interests of the poor, thereby breaking their traditional alliance with the elite. Not doing so would lead to a greater loss of poorer parishioners to competing groups . . .'. Equally where there is no competition 'an episcopacy can ignore parishioner complaints . . . and continue an alliance with the political elite'.[14] Using statistical data Gill suggests that levels of competition offer better predictive results than an analysis of poverty, the level of repression or internal church reform, and notes that the two countries with the highest levels of competition – Brazil and Chile – witnessed the emergence of reform-minded episcopacies even before Vatican II.

To back up his argument he develops case studies of Chile

and Argentina which are similar in many respects, yet are countries whose bishops responded very differently to authoritarian and repressive rule. Though Gill offers a much more nuanced approach than we can do justice to at this stage, his case studies initially appear to support his general hypothesis. Looking at the Chilean case he notes that even before the Second Vatican Council the Catholic Church faced extensive competition from both Pentecostals and communist activists. One way of defeating them was to rely on traditional state alliances that would eliminate or at least restrict the activities of challengers, but when this 'proved unsuccessful' the option of seeking popular support began to appear more attractive. When the Christian Democrats were in power, and even the socialists, the Church found it easier to maintain good relations with the State, but the military regime targeted the poor both politically, through its campaign for order, and economically, as they were the first group to suffer from the imposition of neo-liberal economics. Having gained some public credibility the Church had no option but respond to popular interests if it was to retain influence within society, and Gill concludes that 'faced with a growing Pentecostal population among the popular classes, any support for a right wing authoritarian regime meant betraying the interests of those the Church most needed to win. In the final analysis the episcopacy opted for the poor'.[15] By way of contrast the Argentine hierarchy, facing no serious ideological or religious competition, 'found no trouble in legitimating the military governments that came to power in the 1960s and 1970s'.[16]

The attraction of this approach is two-fold. Firstly, it allows us to take account of the fact that religious organisations, like other groups, have institutional interests that they cannot ignore in making political choices. They may prefer to focus on their primary 'spiritual' goals, but they function in the real world and have to respond when the State acts in ways that may threaten their position – whether on moral issues connected to matters of individual behaviour, sexuality, life and death, or economic issues that may relate to their tax status or legal restrictions on their right to build churches, open charitable institutions etc. Secondly, this approach does offer an explanation of why different religious organisations subordinate to the rulings of a larger, transnational religious tradition, nonetheless responded in different ways to similar challenges. Gill's case of Chile and Argentina appear to back up this argument, though it remains to be seen how convincing the claim is when investigated in more detail and whether it might work when applied to other parts of the world and other religious traditions.

* * * * *

Beyond explaining why religious communities opposed or supported democratisation, at various points in the book we address a series of other issues, raising questions about the nature of the relationship between Christian churches and 'actually existing' democracy, and about the problems that emerge when religion and nationalism fuse and the impact this may have on the possibility or quality of democracy. And we end by briefly returning to the 'big questions' about religion, civilisation, political culture and the nature of democracy, questions implicit in Max Weber's writings on religion and resurrected in more explicit, if less sophisticated fashion, in Samuel Huntington's persistence in focusing on the religious basis of political communities and larger civilisations. Here we avoid the sort of religious determinism that is sometimes read out of Huntington and take on board the arguments of authors such as Alfred Stepan who suggests that all religious traditions are multi-vocal and capable of providing intellectual and practical resources for democratic development.[17] Nonetheless, we do develop an argument that at particular points in history religious traditions do have 'centres of gravity', sets of orientations that are likely to make churches, religious leaderships, their followers and even the political cultures in part shaped by those traditions more or less sympathetic to democratic development. For all this, there remains the nagging doubt that even if religious traditions have engaged in a variety of ways with democracy and have tended to act in support of or in opposition to democratisation, does it really matter given the centrality of other more temporal factors in explaining democratisation? In this book we cannot promise a definitive answer to this question, but hopefully can offer a resource for those interested in exploring and thinking more about the complex relationship between Christianity and democracy, and point to some of the ways that at least some churches have encouraged their communities to move from being passive political subjects to engaged and critical participants.

Notes

1 J. Keane, 'Secularism?', in D. Marquand and R. Nettler (ed.), *Religion and Democracy* (Oxford: Blackwell Publishers, 2000), pp. 5–19.

2 On this debate see R. Audi and N. Wolterstorff, *Religion in the Public Square: The Place of Religious Convictions in Political Debate* (Lanham: Rowman and Littlefield, 1997); and the chapters by J. Stout, C. Eberle and R. Mouw, in T. Cuneo (ed.), *Religion in the Liberal Polity* (Notre Dame: Notre Dame University Press, 2005), pp. 157–216.

3 S. Bruce, 'Did Protestantism create democracy?', in J. Anderson (ed.), *Religion, Democracy and Democratization* (London: Routledge, 2005), pp. 3–20.

4 S. Huntington, *The Third Wave: Democratization in the Twentieth Century* (Norman: University of Oklhoma Press, 1991), pp. 73–80.

5 G. Weigel, *The Final Revolution: The Resistance Church and the Collapse of Communism* (Oxford: Oxford University Press, 1992), p. 16.

6 Ibid., p. 34.

7 Weigel, *The Final Revolution*.

8 J. Haynes, *Religion and Politics in Africa* (London: Zed Books, 1996), p. 104.

9 Ibid., p. 109.

10 Ibid., p. 111.

11 Ibid., pp. 117–21.

12 S. Ramet, *Nihil Obstat: Religion, Politics and Social Change in East-Central Europe and Russia* (Durham: Duke University Press, 1998), p. 293; a Julianic Church is one that finds itself in opposition, and deprived of political power has only moral authority, but to the extent that this is recognised it perhaps gives the Church an inflated view of its position leading it to seek greater power when the old hostile regime is overthrown and perhaps become a 'Constantinian' Church where temporal and spiritual power are conflated.

13 Ibid., pp. 294–6, and then 296–306 for more detailed description of how these issues were handled; for details on the constitutional issue see J. Anderson, *Religious Liberty in Transitional Societies: The Politics of Religion* (Cambridge: Cambridge University Press, 2003), pp. 80–4.

14 A. Gill, *Rendering unto Caesar: The Catholic Church and the State in Latin America* (Chicago: University of Chicago Press, 1998), pp. 7 and 48.

15 Ibid., p. 148.

16 Ibid., p. 171.

17 A. Stepan, 'The world's religious system and democracy: crafting the "twin tolerations"', in A. Stepan, *Arguing Comparative Politics* (Oxford: Oxford University Press, 2001), pp. 213–53.

2

Democracy and the Christian tradition

Historically Christianity's relationship with the democratic project has been ambiguous, as its theoretical commitment to the equality of all before God has often come up against an institutional and theological suspicion of a doctrine that appeared to locate sovereignty in the people. Though religious thinkers rarely discussed democracy as such prior to the modern era, from the fourth century onwards the Church's growing links to state power made it wary of a doctrine that fundamentally challenged existing (and thus God-given) forms of rule. Nonetheless, many writers have made a connection between Christian thought and democratic ideals. In De Gruchy's words:

> western Christendom undoubtedly provided the womb within which the democratic system, as we now know it, gestated, and it also contributed decisively to the shaping of the democratic vision through its witness, albeit ambiguous and severely compromised, to the message of the Hebrew prophets.[1]

And for De Gruchy it was the Old Testament critique of injustice and the New Testament promise of equality that offered at least some basis for the sort of just polity that democracy was seen to represent.

Graham Maddox elaborates this argument further in claiming that the Judeo-Christian tradition made significant contributions to the development of democratic politics. Amongst these were to be found an emphasis on the individual, most notably in the Protestant doctrine of the priesthood of all believers, an emphasis on freedom as liberating and on the equality of all before God, a stress on community bound together by covenant and contract, an emphasis on limited government, the notion of the separation of the political and religious realms, and a tradition of Prophetic opposition to evil rulers.[2] Others have been less convinced, with David Held noting that for much of its history the Christian Church sided with authoritarian powers, downplaying the notion of the active citizen and replacing it with the true believer directed to other-worldly concerns.[3] The aim of this chapter is less to resolve these arguments than to offer a brief overview – to tell the story – of some of the ways in which the Western Christian tradition engaged with the democratic idea up until the middle of the twentieth century. Particular emphasis will be placed on three elements in this story: the real and imagined Protestant contribution to the evolution of democratic politics; the post-revolutionary Roman Catholic reaction and opposition to democracy; and the mid-twentieth-century Vatican conversion to the merits of democracy. As noted in the introduction, we are concerned here to provide an account of key developments, but also to keep in mind the question of why these particular religious communities and traditions adopted the positions they did.

Christendom and participation

Within Western Christendom the issue of political democracy was not an issue for broad discussion in the early days of its imperial success. As the imperial mosaics in Ravenna and many contemporary churches make clear, the rule of a single emperor on earth was seen as a paler version of the sovereignty exercised by God over the wider creation. Though De Gruchy makes much of the prophetic tradition of Israel and suggests that participatory elements were present in its tribal structures, the Hebrew concern for justice was firmly located in an authoritarian communal context. Yet he is right to point out that in the Christian tradition it is this wider conception of a just community that has fed into contemporary religious critiques of authoritarian states, and of minimalist visions of democracy that limit the project to an extension of the suffrage whilst ignoring the claims of justice. Also interesting is his discussion of the word *ekklesia* which was taken from the political rather than the cultic language of the time and which had connotations of self-regulation on the part of the community.[4]

Yet whilst there remained strong counter-cultural currents within the Church, the period from the Constantian settlement to the Reformation was characterised by the emergence of the Church as a privileged institution closely allied to the existing political order and committed to a belief that strong political authority was essential to curb sinful human nature. During this period earlier practices such as the election of bishops quickly disappeared and senior clergy acquired status and wealth that often took them far from the vision of priests as servants of God and the people. At the same time the evolving intellectual understanding of the world tended to downplay the political, depicting earthly authority as ultimately relative and secondary. Only in the thirteenth century did there emerge a more nuanced discussion of politics which permitted at least some debate about the forms government might take.

Perhaps inevitably Thomas Aquinas (1224/5–74) provided much of the impetus for this, and he took a view of government that saw its role as more than merely providing a means of keeping human nature in check. Following Aristotle, he devoted at least some attention to the discussion of the forms of government and expressed fears that popular government was all too likely to lead to the tyranny of the majority. Aquinas viewed monarchy as in principle the best type of rule, but saw it as legitimate only to the extent that it upheld natural law and pursued the common good. Should it repeatedly violate the trust placed in it by God, then the people, or their noble leaders, might under certain circumstances have the right to rebel and overthrow a tyrant. There also seem to be hints of some notion of contract evident in the *Commentary on Romans* where Aquinas speaks of the origins of the State as lying 'in a kind of pact between king and people', though scholars have argued over the extent to which Aquinas was promoting a more participatory vision of the political order.[5] What is clear, however, is his preference for a mixed or balanced form of government that offered at least some check on tyrannical power. And in this at least he provided a basis of future discussions of the notion of limited government that was to be central to democratic political thought.

Across the water in England the first traces of participatory politics were emerging. In 1215 Magna Carta had, at least according to British popular mythology, established the principle that the king needed to consult his subjects before taking major decisions, especially on taxation, even though the subjects concerned were largely the rich and powerful. Then in 1295 Edward I summoned a model parliament which comprised representatives of all the shires with 'full and sufficient power from their communities' to conduct the necessary business. Such bodies in no way restricted the decision-making powers of kings, but did establish a precedent for a more consultative and even representative form of agreement between people and ruler. Moreover, in the later Middle Ages such bodies became more vocal as a forum for airing grievances and began to develop procedures and rules of conduct which established their role as a natural part of the governing process of the country.[6]

Debates over issues of consultation and participation became more extensive from the late thirteenth century onwards. Whilst Pope Innocent III and his successors developed the notion of the Vicar of Christ inheriting Christ's prerogatives on earth, John of Paris (d. 1306) developed a rather sceptical view rooted in a division of secular from religious authority. An advocate of what Ullman calls an 'ascending view of power', he saw papal authority as derived from the whole body of the faithful through election by their agents, the cardinals.[7] Such views were to re-emerge during the Conciliarist debates, and were more fully developed in the often controversial person of Marsiglio (1280–1343). In his writings we find an emphasis on law and political rule as validated by the will of the community – and he assumes the citizen body will be Christian – or the 'human legislator'. For Marsiglio God had invested authority in the people who expressed their will by empowering the king to rule their earthly lives and the Pope their spiritual lives, but at the end of the day secular authority was of greater import because it affected the daily lives of the citizen. Though he excluded slaves, aliens and women from citizenship, he did appear to allow some role to ordinary people within the political community.[8]

What is clear in many of the works of this period is a growing distinction between the spiritual and secular realm and, in William of Ockam and others, a tendency to desacralise the political realm.[9] In Jean Geerson (1362–1428?), Nicholas of

Cusa (1401–1464) and other Conciliar writers there is a growing emphasis on community involvement in both the Church and the secular political order, and on consent as a fundamental principle in both spheres. For Nicholas the Pope was simply one member of the Body of Christ subordinate to the Universal Church in the form of a Council, and a key condition of legitimacy was the consent of the community – though his own views shifted somewhat upon the attainment of clerical preferment. Nonetheless, increasingly the emphasis was on the need for a mixed form of government in Church and State alike, and one which gave at least some voice to the community at large.[10]

Democracy as a product of the Reformation?

John de Gruchy has suggested that democracy 'developed within the matrix of Christendom and the Enlightenment', and noted in particular the special role of the Reformation period in the genesis of democratic ideas.[11] Other writers have taken a similar line, with David Held arguing that:

> It was not until Western Christendom was under challenge, especially from the conflicts generated by the rise of nation states and by the Reformation, that the idea of the modern state was born, and the ground created for the general development of a new form of political regulation.[12]

Yet whilst arguing for this connection, many writers caution about overstating the causal notion of this relationship, with Steve Bruce describing the religious contribution to the spread of democracy as essentially 'accidental'. Discussing the Weber thesis regarding the relationship between the spirit of capitalism and Protestantism he notes Weber's argument that inadvertently the Reformation produced new attitudes towards work and money, and suggests that a similar 'accidental' relationship can be seen between Protestant religion and the emergence of liberal democracy.[13] Thus one of the products of the Reformation was religious fragmentation as the Universal Church was removed as a source of authority between God and man, and judgement of right and wrong put into the hands of the individual reading the Scriptures. One consequence of this was the creation of a host of communities each claiming the 'correct' version of the truth. This in turn made it much harder for states to impose religious uniformity and thus contributed to the emergence of the religiously neutral state and the growth of a religious tolerance to which few religious groups were genuinely committed. Therefore it was not surprising to find more 'democratic' forms of government emerging first in just those countries where the Reformation had the greatest impact.[14]

What is clear is that the contribution of the Reformation represented less of a sudden break with the past than is sometimes claimed. As we have seen, the previous century had seen extensive discussion of the issues of participation, consent, toleration and constrained government. During this period there had emerged in European towns an array of guilds and associations representing trades and interests in which consultative decision-making was the norm. And in England there had clearly developed an implicit understanding that monarchs required some form of consent from their subjects in order to legislate. Nonetheless, the radical intellectual and theological changes initiated by the reformers unintentionally promoted a more vigorous discussion of some of the ideas developing during the 'late middle ages'. For their part the reformers were often able to make use of the representative assemblies emerging in sixteenth-century Europe.[15]

Martin Luther's contribution to democratic evolution is most evident in his development of the notion of the priesthood of all believers, a theological doctrine that stressed the centrality of the individual, and his advocacy of a partial separation of Church and State. The former doctrine had a deeply egalitarian thrust in making no distinction between priest and layperson, prince or pauper when it came to one's relationship with God. Of course, in practice Luther was also stressing the 'naturalness' of ranks and relied heavily upon princes for the defence of his new teachings, but the seeds had been sown for a new vision of relations within the political community.[16] As Graham Maddox points out, 'whatever misgivings he might have had about human equality in the political sphere, nothing was going to stop the idea of a lordship of all the people ... from impinging mightily on the political structures of Europe'.[17]

Most accounts give a far more central place to Calvinism's

contribution to the emergence of democratic politics. Again, this was far from the intention of John Calvin who, like other reformers, placed far greater stress on the value of political stability than participation. In his ideal community pastors played a key role in regulating the life of the community and this potentially had authoritarian implications. We shall return to aspects of Calvinist thinking later, but it is worth noting that embryonic democratic forms tended to emerge first in countries influenced by Calvinism – England, Scotland, parts of Switzerland and the Low Countries – though this is to say nothing about causation. The basic arguments about its contribution to democracy centre in part at least on the views and political practice of Calvin himself, and the consequences of these in countries where Calvinism was influential. Hudson, for example, rejects the view that democracy was an 'accidental' consequence of this religious teaching and argues that Calvin's writings contained the seeds of subsequent democratic development. In particular he points to the notion of rulers as placed in power by God but dependent upon the support of the people for their position. Others are less convinced, noting that Calvinist practice in Geneva and elsewhere tended to place excessive power in the hands of the pastors or those dominated by them.[18] And Calvin's experience in Geneva, dependent as it was upon power struggles within the notionally representative assembly, made him less willing to commit himself to any one form of government.[19] For critics of the Genevan experience the true roots of democracy are to be found in the Anabaptist tradition, not in the excesses of Thomas Munzer but in the small groups of the faithful dotted around Europe. These communities established congregational democracies bound together by a covenant with one another, though in many countries persecution forced them to flee to the New World during the seventeenth century.

Throughout these discussions anything resembling a modern notion of democratic governance was simply not on the political agenda. Nonetheless, one can note in England the way in which the utility of parliamentary forms of government were quickly grasped by Puritan politicians who formed a lobby in Elizabeth I's first House of Commons to agitate for a more Protestant settlement than she might have favoured. Within the wider Reformation movement two ideas that were the subject of fierce debate can be seen as helping to advance a more pluralist political vision: the notions of resistance to tyrannical rulers and religious tolerance. The circumstances in which subjects might have the right to resist their rulers was discussed by the first wave of reformers but was developed much further by later writers, in part as a consequence of the St Bartholemew's Day massacre of 1572, when several thousand Protestants were murdered in Paris. Luther had flirted with the idea but his response to peasant uprisings made it clear that he saw this as a limited right and one not available to the hoi polloi. In England a number of works published during Queen Mary's reign and the years following addressed the question more systematically. Of these works one of the first to address this question was Bishop Ponet's *Short Treatise of Political Power* (1556),[20] which stressed that political power was conferred by the community and went on to suggest that in extreme cases it might be acceptable to depose and even kill tyrants, especially if they did not uphold true religion. Such views were taken further by Christopher Goodman who argued that 'we must obey God rather than man', but who shared John Knox's position that it was particularly problematic to allow women to rule. Others were cautious, with Peter Martyr following Calvin more closely in arguing that only the magistrates had the authority to depose an evil rule.

The massacre of 1572 encouraged Huguenots in France and Calvinist thinkers elsewhere to address more seriously the possibility of legitimate resistance to political authorities who had traditionally been thought of as placed in power by God. Theodore Beza maintained the traditional Calvinist view that whilst subjects could engage in passive resistance it remained up to magistrates to take the lead in more serious attempts to depose tyrants. The key work emerging from within the Calvinist tradition was the *Vindicae contra tyrannos* (1579) which developed more fully a theoretical justification of resistance. Here it was argued that the authority of rulers was rooted in a covenant with the community under which the prince promised to protect the people and defend true religion. Should the prince flout God's law then he in effect lost divine approval and the mutual obligation implicit in the contract was undermined. In such circumstances the leaders of the community had a duty to encourage a change in behaviour and, if that failed, to remove the erring ruler. Though most of these writers opted for a cautious approach which restrained the opportunities open to the wider citizen body, they laid the foundations for a view of governance as rooted in a contract between people and ruler, and one whose terms had to be observed by both sides.[21]

The second debate of significance for future democratic development was the issue of religious tolerance, the emergence of which can perhaps be seen as an 'accidental' but probably inevitable outcome of religious trends in this period. During the early stages of the Reformation few advocated tolerance, and understandings of religious liberty were generally narrow and theological in scope. For Calvinists it meant freedom in Christ or freedom from the 'mire of Catholicism';[22] for Catholics it was something of a concession arising from temporary political weakness rather than genuine commitment. Pope Clement VIII (1536–1605) reacted bitterly to the Edict of Nantes (1598) which gave some degree of freedom to French Protestants, describing it as 'the most cursed edict I could imagine … whereby liberty of conscience is granted to everyone which is the worst thing of all'.[23] In many cases tolerance was a product of political need or weakness,[24] with its keenest advocates in opposition sometimes becoming persecutors themselves once in power.[25] Part of the problem stemmed from the assumption of virtually all sixteenth-century thinkers that a state could not survive without a single faith, and that religious pluralism was likely to lead to political division. Yet despite these reservations, and despite discussions on this issue that continued into the seventeenth century, the Reformation led to a very gradual expansion of the realm of religious liberty for, as A. G. Dickens observed, once the European states took responsibility from the Church for religious order the old sanctions on religious difference began to fall away.[26] The reformers may not have been tolerant, but political necessity and religious fragmentation helped to create a commitment to some degree of religious freedom, even if in the early stages it was only extended to other types of Protestant. In the Scottish case, according to Bruce, 'only when each wave of dissent realized that it could not succeed in taking over the instruments of state coercion did it begin to find the use of such instruments offensive'.[27] In addition one should not neglect the gradual emergence of an enlightened scepticism about imposing religious truth nor the impact of free trade which required states to deal with others dominated by different religious traditions.

This religious opening to democracy was taken further during the seventeenth century, in particular as a consequence of developments in England. Though the motivations of the Puritans were primarily spiritual in nature, elements of their practice fed into a more participatory vision of political order. In particular, their understanding of the Church as a gathered community of believers, their view of churches as voluntary associations, and their tendency to decision-making by discussion rooted in exploration of the scripture had political implications. These may not have been clearly thought through, but if religious communities could function in this way, why not political institutions? In practice most ministers who advocated the 'rights of the people' in the church context made distinctions in defining who were the people and tended to give some a greater say than others, and most failed to accept the need to apply elective and consultative principles to national life.[28] Such reservations were also apparent in regard to the issue of religious toleration, with few Puritans willing to extend its scope beyond a small number of Protestant groups. Independents such as Oliver Cromwell and John Milton rejected any notion of the Commonwealth allowing Catholics to worship freely, and even more radical voices were generally muted when it came to permitting complete freedom. Partial exceptions included the Leveller movement, some of whose members combined a denunciation of Catholicism with a plea for tolerance. In several documents published in 1648–49 they contributed further to democratic development by promoting male suffrage, limited terms of office, the ending of cruel punishments, and the right of each congregation to choose their own ministers. More importantly for our purposes, they rejected the right of states of any type to dictate to human conscience.[29] Other advocates of religious tolerance included Roger Williams – whom we discuss later – and Henry Robinson who suggested that Turks had as much right to persecute Christians as Christians did Turks.[30]

One of the problems in assessing the 'religious' contribution to the evolution of democratic ideas stems from the nature of debates during the late sixteenth and early seventeenth centuries. Yes, it is possible to examine the discussions and literature of the period and trace numerous references to the Bible and divine inspiration utilised in defence of a more participatory politics but, as Christopher Hill points out in relation to the English Revolution, this tells us very little other than that the writers lived in a period when the Bible was the source of most ideas.[31] What the Reformation did, however, was to raise new questions about the nature of political obligation, assert the importance of individual judgement in spiritual and political matters, and introduce the notion of discussion and debate as central to decision-making within the gathered 'community of saints'. Protestantism thus contributed to democratic development through its promotion of small gathered religious communities based upon the principle of consent, through its promotion of education and literacy, and through its mostly reluctant acceptance of religious tolerance. Equally, radical reform led to a situation where states gradually came to separate out the religious and political sphere and to deny religion any formal political influence so as to avoid religious divisions fragmenting the new nation-states emerging in Europe. Yet, as many Catholics rightly predicted, this process had consequences rarely foreseen by the progenitors of change, with the growth of tolerance and individualism contributing to a process of gradual secularisation as the intellectual certainties of religion withered away, and belief was increasingly confined to the private sphere.[32] Over the next hundred years or so, this religious–political debate was to shift across the Atlantic and play a key role in shaping democratic development and thought.

Protestantism and the birth of American democracy

For many of those fleeing the violence of religious wars and intolerance in Europe, North America offered the promise of a freer environment in which to practise their faith or make their fortune. Whilst in practice few were committed to pluralistic politics or religious freedom in the abstract, the geographical, political and economic environment in which they found themselves was to play a major role in the further-ing of a democratic style of politics. At the same time the vast majority of the emerging townships preferred to describe their form of government as 'republican' rather than demo-cratic. The vision of political order emerging in the New World very much grew out of the changing nature of church governance. The Puritans had promoted a model of individ-ual congregations made up of committed believers who vested authority in elected elders and pastors. These churches were in turn united by common professions of faith but lacked any formal over-arching authority. For the early fathers of the American nation, the whole conception of America was rooted in a religious rhetoric that compared their voyage across the Atlantic to the Exodus of the Hebrews. Even at the political level some notion of pluralism was evident in the compact of the Pilgrim Fathers, just before they disembarked, where they promised to root government in the consent of the people – or adult males – and establish a 'civil body politic'.[33]

In practice the early American settlements varied consid-erably. The founders of many were settlers fleeing persecution, but Massachusetts was created by Puritans enjoying the blessing of the English king, and Maryland was originally a Catholic-dominated colony which in 1649 passed an Act of Toleration in an effort to preserve the right to prac-tise Catholicism.[34] In many the presence of governing assemblies, representative bodies and notions of consent did not entail any liberalism in dealing with those who failed to conform. Many of the Protestants who entered the New World to escape harassment firmly believed that they had come into the wilderness to preach true religion and deemed it sinful to allow any other form of worship.[35] And where participatory forms evolved, as in Massachusetts, the right to be involved in public affairs was initially limited to church members and the nonconformist was often subject to stiff punishment. Yet, as the century progressed, such restrictions proved difficult to maintain in the face of rising emigration, declining religious enthusiasm and the emergence of oligarchical rule in many colonies. Increasingly, religious institutions were restricted to imposing purely spiritual penalties upon dissenters, and increasingly a distinction emerged between secular and temporal power, though ministers often retained considerable social power as evident in Nathaniel Hawthorne's depiction of one such community in *The Scarlet Letter*.

From the beginning the issue of religious tolerance proved especially difficult to resolve, as the orthodox throughout the new territories sought to ensure conformity of belief and practice. One who fought against this trend and in many respects was to prove the father of religious freedom and American pluralism, was Roger Williams. Developing a very narrow view of the Church as a community of believers and virulently rejecting the errors of Catholicism and vacuity of nominal belief, Williams nonetheless believed that outside the Church those who differed should be left to their own devices. Fleeing from Britain and then from Massachusetts, he was to establish his own community in Rhode Island where tolerance would be the norm. Rejecting many of the ideas of covenant floating around in the 1630s and 1640s, Williams denied that some sort of contract had bestowed divine sanction on earthly government and suggested that all governments to some degree had God's approval. Equally insistent was his rejection of attempts by polities to enforce religious belief or conformity – though he did allow for the magistrate to enforce the norms of morality. But Williams was clear that no government could prevent an individual from worshipping as his conscience dictated and that government should protect freedom of religion.[36] In 1641 the more openly democratic implications of these ideas were given form when the townships of Portsmouth and Newport united and explicitly declared themselves 'a democracy or popular government'.[37]

Williams' advocacy of religious freedom had little direct impact upon the evolution of the American polity, and there has been considerable debate as to the precise contribution of religion to the American Revolution at the end of the following century. Some have stressed the importance of the Great Awakening, the religious revival of the mid-eighteenth century, as contributing to the development of the republic, in so far as it strengthened religious independence over the Anglican and Presbyterian dominance and reinforced the arguments of those like Thomas Jefferson who contested the right of any religious group to dominate the nation's political life. At the same time the emergence of a wide variety of churches in every town necessarily increased the degree of social pluralism in many communities, and made religious toleration a necessity if social conflict was to be avoided. Others have accepted this latter pragmatic interpretation but suggested that when looking at the inspiration for the American revolt the credit should not be given to the revivalist preachers, who by and large promoted political conformism. Instead they point to activities of more rationalist critics of the Awakening such as Revd Jonathan Mayhew, who used the pulpit to preach the right of resistance to arbitrary rule.[38]

Our focus on the religious roots of American democracy should not of course blind us to the important role of Enlightenment thinking in shaping the views of many of the intellectual advocates of political change. Nonetheless, it is worth noting that whereas in France democracy came to be associated with anticlericalism, in the United States republicanism was propagated by men claiming to be Christian or by people influenced by the radical dissenting tradition. Though increasingly leavened by Enlightenment thought, these people to some degree saw religion as essential to social stability and the well-being of the community. Simultaneously, the process of political upheaval had an impact upon the public role and status of religion in American life. In particular the revolution very quickly led to the promotion of religious tolerance as dissenters, Catholics and more secularist politicians such as Jefferson argued for a formal separation of Church and State. By the 1780s most of the states had removed any connection between religious adherence and civic capacity, and all of this was given nationwide recognition in the form of the First Amendment, which appeared to promote a vision of a state that favoured no religion – though in practice, the form of civil religion that emerged was to remain broadly Protestant until well into the twentieth century.[39]

In practice, of course, many states continued to maintain a de facto socially and politically privileged religious establishment, and it remained difficult for Catholics to achieve major political positions for many decades. At the same time the revolution did, as Nathan Hatch has pointed out, contribute to a democratisation of American religious life. The ninteeenth century was characterised by waves of religious populism and revivalism which took further the revolutionary challenge to notions of hierarchy and tradition. For Hatch the rise of evangelical Christianity in the first years of the republic represented 'a story of the success of the common people in shaping the culture after their own priorities rather than the priorities outlined by gentlemen such as the framers of the Constitution'. Though often internally authoritarian, such groups denied the distinctiveness of the clergy, recognised the spiritual experience of the ordinary person, and created the hope of a new, just order.[40] In this sense the revolution was both inspired by religious dreams, however secularised they had become for many political leaders, and in turn re-ordered the nature of Christianity within the new order.

As Alexis de Tocqueville was to suggest, religion continued to play a key role in ensuring the survival of the young republic and the maintenance of a civil polity. In his *Democracy in America* (1830) De Tocqueville placed great emphasis on the centrality of mores and values in preserving social stability, and in providing moral ties when long-observed political ties were being loosened. In this context he noted that even the closely knit Catholic community in America increasingly committed itself to pluralism and religious tolerance, a position that stemmed largely from its minority position within the new republic.[41] He also stressed the way in which religious institutions in all their variety of forms contributed to the development of the rich associational life that underlay the American democratic experiment and gave it its peculiar qualities. In particular he saw religion as coaxing citizens away from purely private concerns and into the public arena, where they sought to ensure that the developing polity operated within some form of moral framework.[42]

The impact of the Enlightenment and French Revolution: democracy as nightmare

Whereas the American Revolution convinced De Tocqueville of the basic compatibility of religion and democracy, the experience of 1789 suggested to him what might happen were irreligion to lie at the heart of political change. More importantly its consequences were to push Europe's most influential religious institution, the Roman Catholic Church, into a century and a half of hostility towards democratic politics.

On the eve of that revolution, Europe was in the throes of industrial and intellectual revolutions which challenged many traditional ways of thought and action. Events in America had shown that the old systems could be overthrown, whilst contemporary intellectuals were providing the justification for such actions. Though countries such as Britain, Poland and Switzerland had 'mixed' constitutions with elements of electivity built in, much of Europe was dominated by more or less enlightened despotisms, whose rulers sought to promote educational and economic reform but not at the expense of their own positions. Many of these rulers had taken on board elements of the critical thinking emerging from the Enlightenment. Writers such as Voltaire had mercilessly lampooned religious institutions and advocated religious tolerance for all. Across the water in Britain and America Tom Paine had strenuously argued for a secular state on the grounds that only thus could religious disagreements be kept within bounds and conflict averted. For Paine religion was a force that crushed the individuality and political life out of the would-be citizen, though in some writings he recognised that Christianity had helped to keep an ethical spirit alive.[43]

For all this, few rulers challenged the spiritual position of the Church, recognising all too well the utility of religion for preserving social stability, but they were often unwilling to back up religious claims with temporal powers.[44] For their part, religious institutions reacted to this challenge in various ways, with some more or less secularised clerics accepting much of the force of the Enlightenment critique. On the eve of the French Revolution the Church maintained a monopoly of public worship and the active persecution of Protestants had only recently ceased. Though many members of the elite were increasingly sceptical about the theological and institutional claims of the Catholic Church, few questioned its contribution to a social order in which roles and status were clearly defined. Nonetheless, amongst the masses there is some evidence of anticlericalism in parts of the country, and amongst the lower clergy an increasingly 'democratic' temper was apparent according to some observers, though few thought of extending pluralistic values to Protestants and Jews. Initially then, many of the lower clergy welcomed the assaults on privilege launched by the Estates General and many were to be elected to the increasingly revolutionary Constituent Assembly.[45]

The revolution brought fundamental changes in the position of the Catholic Church, as its assets were plundered and its public status much reduced. The new authorities moved rapidly to deprive the Church of its status as a privileged corporation, seeing the reduction of church wealth as in part a guarantee against the forces of reaction. The selling of church property and lands would create a new class of property owners with a stake in the changing political order and would increase state influence on the clergy by turning them into salaried employees. More overt conflict came when the Assembly sought to impose an oath to the Civil Constitution of the Clergy which effectively ignored the authority of Rome and vested the selection of religious authorities in secular electors. Whilst many clergy could accept some of the reforms, the question of the oath fundamentally divided the Church and pushed many religious into the hands of those opposed to the system. Tensions worsened as the more radical revolutionary leaders opted for an active campaign of de-Christianisation and pushed the cult of the Supreme Being. The rise of Napoleon brought an end to anti-religious excesses but not to the State's utilitarian view of religion, with the new emperor tending to see organised religion as good for others, notably women, and useful in preserving social peace.[46]

The impact of the French Revolution on European views of democracy, and in particular that adopted by the Roman Catholic Church, was generally negative. For many it was the religious question that had fundamentally undermined the high ideals of the revolution, with De Tocqueville seeing 'irreligion' as having 'produced the greatest public evil' in France.[47] In Britain Edmund Burke also emphasised 'religion as the basis of civil society', and as one of the great bonds that held society together. In similar vein, though often for instrumental reasons rather than through any commitment to organic views of society, many within the British political elite saw the establishment of religion as essential to the preservation of social order. Once the terror set in, most

British clergy, established and dissenting alike, expressed their distaste for revolutionary excess and, by implication, for democratic visions. Men like Wilberforce may have fought against slavery, but at home they remained paternalistic conservatives, suspicious of social reform and determined to preserve existing hierarchies.[48] As the century progressed Methodists and other evangelicals continued to campaign against specific social evils, but very few advocated political change of the type that would enfranchise more than a fraction of the 'lower orders'. In general dissenters were to be found on the liberal side of the political spectrum, initially in the Liberal Party and then, in some cases, the Labour Party at the beginning of the twentieth century, but in general only a small minority of Nonconformists were to be active champions of democracy.[49] More sceptical were Christians at the other end of the religious spectrum, with John Henry Newman arguing that episcopal Catholicism should provide leadership against democracy and the rights of man, and instil 'humility into the poor'.[50]

Similar patterns were evident elsewhere as the experience of 1789 rendered many religious activists sceptical about political change of any sort. What was less clear is how much this mattered, and Eric Hobsbawm has argued that the American and French revolutions led to a fundamental secularisation of the political order in which religious ideas and institutions counted for very little.[51] This may be the case but religious leaders remained influential figures in many societies and religious institutions affected the lives of many. In Germany, for example, Protestantism may have been encumbered by 'paternalism, and its identification with throne, altar and established order', but 'cultural Protestantism' remained a vital force amongst the educated middle classes.[52] Above all, however, it was in the Vatican and the Catholic countries where the experience of the French Revolution was to shape religious views of liberalism and democracy for the next 150 years.

Catholicism and democracy in the post-revolutionary era

Paul Sigmund has described the traditional Catholic attitude towards politics as emphasising the provisional nature of all political orders and their acceptability to the extent that they promoted public well-being. For the Church the prime concern was with the protection of its spiritual and institutional interests, and internally the institution had remained authoritarian and hierarchical, leading to a tendency to support political structures of a similar type. Moreover, prior to 1789 the notion of democracy had scarcely crossed Catholic consciousness, for representative institutions had largely, though not solely, emerged under Protestant auspices. The French Revolution in many respects placed the Church on the defensive and led to its identification of 'modernism', liberalism, democracy and nationalism with chaos and anti-religion, especially as all of these ideas were related to a conception of popular sovereignty which appeared to challenge that of the Creator. Pope Gregory XVI (1765–1846) reacted strongly to the new challenges and bitterly denounced 'the absurd and erroneous proposition which claims that liberty of conscience must be maintained for everyone'. The Syllabus of Errors published in 1860 firmly rejected the view that the Church should reconcile itself to 'progress, liberalism and modern civilisation', and the whole push towards declaring papal infallibility can be seen in part as a response to a modernity infected with democratic ideals.[53]

Some amendment of this hard line appeared evident in the commitment to social reform, albeit of a paternalistic kind, promoted by Leo XIII (1810–1903), most notably in the encyclical *Rerum Novarum* (1891) which built upon an emerging tradition of social Catholicism. This doctrine which developed in France and elsewhere during the mid-nineteenth century was often conservative in orientation, promoted by thinkers who espoused nostalgic visions of a semi-rural past where everyone knew their place.[54] Leo's encyclical very much fell into this type of thinking, and can be seen in part as a reaction to the attractions of the socialist movement to the new working classes. In this decree the Pope deplored the misery of the working class and attacked the exploitative nature of contemporary capitalism.

Attacking the false doctrines of materialism and class struggle, Leo called on Catholics to pay greater attention to the social question and to rebuild society on the basis of Catholic social principles. In practice this appeared to mean creating a type of corporate structure in which workers and employers collaborated to create a more humane form of socio-economic organisation.[55]

Though Leo XIII shifted the papal position on social issues, there is little evidence to suggest that he favoured any fundamental shifts on matters of liberalism, democracy or freedom of conscience. Though accepting that no form of government was absolute and that popular participation might be a good thing in some circumstances, he firmly rejected any notion that sovereignty resided in the people or that power was held by their consent. He was equally opposed to any attempts to separate Church and State or to permit freedom of worship in states where Catholicism dominated. And this position was essentially maintained by his successors well into the twentieth century. Pius X (1835–1914) argued that one of the chief aims of the State should be to 'favour religion' and, though he followed his predecessors in accepting de facto that there were separate spheres, he maintained the view that in certain areas (marriage, education, censorship) the Church's views should in some sense be privileged. He remained sceptical with regard to the errors of liberalism and fought strongly the advancement of the separation of Church and State in France which he saw as representing a divorce between the nation and the faith. At the same time he sustained papal criticisms of the notion of popular sovereignty with its emphasis on individual autonomy, something he saw as leading to the decline of traditional values.[56]

It was in this ideological and theological context that Christian Democratic parties began to emerge in Europe, albeit often enjoying a difficult relationship with the church authorities. Within Germany a Church under pressure from liberals, socialists and nationalists basically accepted much of the rhetoric of democracy and participation, including a formal commitment to freedom of conscience. This in turn led to the creation of the Centre Party which sought to hold the line against Bismarck's *Kulturkampf*, whilst not appearing dependent upon the clerical elite so despised by many politicians.[57] Here, as elsewhere, political organisation was for many Catholics an unpleasant necessity forced upon them by the anti-clerical campaigns of their opponents, yet the Vatican remained suspicious of political parties and in Italy turned a blind eye to the destruction of the Partito Popolare as a political force in the early 1920s, and increasingly threw its lot in with the rising fascist movement.[58]

From the early 1920s Catholic political attitudes were faced with a new challenge emanating from the rise of political movements, evincing extreme hostility towards religious institutions. In 1917 the Russian Revolution brought to power a movement overtly committed to the elimination of religious ideology and institutions, in theory through persuasion and social change but often in practice through the application of violence and repression. Other countries followed suit, with the Mexican authorities launching vicious attacks on the Church in the 1920s and 1930s, and radical elements of the Spanish republican movement executing several thousand religious personnel in 1936 as that country's crisis came to a head. All these movements, viewed in Rome as a product of an excessive mobilisation of the masses, helped to reinforce suspicion of democratic aspirations and promote a flirtation with the authoritarianism of the emerging fascist movement. Simultaneously the violent disruption of Europe that followed the rise of these latter movements, as well as their evident contempt for the Church's institutions and values, gradually helped to shift the Church towards supporting democratic politics.

Though Pius XII's (1876–1958) relationship with the fascists has been the subject of considerable controversy, it was he who rather tentatively pushed the Church towards an acceptance of democracy. In part he drew on the doctrines expounded in recent papal encyclicals, in particular the respect for the dignity of the individual regardless of class laid out in *Rerum Novarum*, which had democratic implications.[59] In part he was influenced by the political context in Europe following the defeat of Hitler, a situation where the Communist Party remained strong in a number of countries and where democracy seemed to offer the only viable political order in which the Church could defend its institutional interests and promote its values. Simultaneously there were other more intellectual influences at work, some more indirect stemming from Protestant thinking about democracy. In Germany the traditional Protestant suspicion of democracy had been challenged by Troeltsch and others, with the experience of the Nazi period and the division of the churches further reinforcing critiques of authoritarianism. And here the increasing level of political collaboration between Protestants and Catholics in the post-war German Christian Democratic movement meant that the ideas of such thinkers began to permeate Catholic thinking. Even more important, however, were Catholic thinkers such as Jacques Maritain (1882–1973) and John Courtney Murray (1904–67) whose ideas fed into the discussion that led up to Vatican II, though it is worth noting that the latter was writing within the context of America where Catholicism was still a minority faith, and thus it was easier to make the argument that religious liberty posed no threat to Catholic teaching or civil order.[60]

Vatican II and the Catholic conversion to democracy

This gradual evolution was effectively institutionalised in, and symbolised by, the decisions of the Second Vatican Council (1962–65) which nearly all sources agree had a major impact in shifting many national Catholic hierarchies away from unquestioning support of authoritarian regimes. Vatican I (1869–70) had reinforced a centralist, anti-modern and overwhelmingly negative vision of what the Roman Catholic Church was about. The effect of its successor council was to shift the Church in a more 'democratic' direction in which priests and bishops were no longer so clearly differentiated from laity, and in which the latter would be seen as participants rather than subjects in the Church's salvific mission. The fundamental notion of the *magisterium* finally deciding for the faithful was not abandoned, but the principle of participation by laity and lower clergy was established, and in turn symbolised in the shift towards vernacular liturgies in which the priest faced the people. Pope John XXIII (1881–1963) may have had no clear vision of where the Council would lead, but in his opening address he accepted that renewal would inevitably involve 'a change in mentalities, ways of thinking and prejudices, all of which have a long history'.[61] In the decree *Pacem in Terris*, released shortly before his death, the Pope effectively inspired the Church to shift its emphasis from one of confrontation/rejection to one of critical engagement with the modern world.

Two Council decrees were of particular importance for our purposes: *Dignitatis Humanae* (Declaration on Religious Freedom) and *Gaudium et Spes* (Pastoral Constitution of the Church in the Modern World). The first challenged the traditional view that 'error has no rights' and suggested that whilst natural law required all states to protect the rights of Catholics where they were a minority, the same duty was beholden on Catholic states vis-à-vis other minorities. Stressing that the right to religious freedom derives from the dignity of the human person the decree opens with the declaration that 'the human person has the right to religious freedom'.[62] In making this statement the Church was effectively defending religious pluralism, however reluctantly in some cases, and laying the basis for later church campaigns in defence of human rights more generally. For American theologian John Courtney Murray, one of the inspirers of this text, it meant that 'the Church does not deal with secular order in terms of a double standard – freedom for the Church when Catholics are a minority, privilege for the Church and intolerance for others when Catholics are a majority'.[63] At the same time, as critics suggested, it increasingly meant accepting that the constitutional democratic state would almost inevitably be a secular state which refused to take sides on religious matters.[64] The other important dimension of this degree was that it rooted the right to freedom of conscience in the dignity of the human individual, not the authority of the Church, and thus laid the basis for religious activists to get involved in wider campaigns for human rights, to defend those who were abused by the powerful regardless of their religious convictions.

Gaudium et Spes focused on the role of the Church in the modern world and looked at a variety of issues, including marriage, culture, economics, politics and international relations. On politics the emphasis was on the role of rights and civil liberties as means of achieving the 'common good', though this essentially traditional perception was reshaped in ways that tended to focus on democracy as probably the best political means available for achieving this end. Simultaneously, in recognising that the political community and the Church operated in different ways to achieve this same end, a further basis was laid for the acceptance of a less paternalistic political role for the Church – it would operate within the political order, often co-operatively, but occasionally more critically, rather than seek to control that order. Such conclusions were not unproblematic for a Church that internally remained hierarchical and authoritarian but nonetheless the decisions of Vatican II laid the theological and philosophical basis for a more critical engagement with the political order, even in states with notional Catholic majorities and regimes.

Not all Catholics were enthusiastic about the changes introduced by the Council, with the Spanish bishops in particular horrified by the willingness of the Vatican to 'compromise' with modernity. Most of the Spanish hierarchs fought a rearguard action at the Council to combat or modify the new positions, especially regarding the seeming acceptance of the separation of Church and State, and of religious liberty.[65] Nonetheless younger bishops and clergy in Spain and elsewhere, especially those who had been involved in social action, welcomed the decisions of the Council which they saw as justifying their attempts to defend the marginalised against repressive regimes and unjust socio-economic structures. In Latin America such clerics noted Vatican II's stress on human institutions as historically determined and therefore as contingent and open to criticism, whilst the more open attitude towards secular learning led many to engage with contemporary social scientific thinking, which by the late 1960s tended to be dominated by more 'progressive' positions. Above all, as Casanova has noted, the major consequence of Vatican II was 'the transformation of the Catholic Church from a state-centred to a society-centred institution'.[66]

★　★　★　★　★

In such a short amount of space it is impossible to do justice to Western Christianity's many engagements with the ideas and practices of democratic governance, but one can isolate a few clear lines of development. During the course of its early development from persecuted minority to the religion of an imperial order, the Christian Church tended to lose sight of its original egalitarian impulses and to take on board the hierarchical and monarchical characteristics of the temporal order with which it co-existed and which it came to legitimate. Throughout the 'middle ages' there were periodic challenges to this way of understanding political life, emanating from a variety of sects and radical thinkers within the Catholic Church, but only with the Reformation was the door opened to a more radical re-thinking of the religious and political order. Of course, the primary imperative of the reformers was religious in nature, but their promotion of individual judgement and their fragmentation of the religious scene ultimately, if often inadvertently, laid the ground roots for both religious pluralism and political democratisation. This process developed spasmodically over the next three hundred years, tending to move faster in the New World and the Protestant-dominated world whereas in the Catholic realm the experience of the French Revolution reinforced a suspicion of the very idea of democracy. Even in the Protestant world the emphasis was very much on a limited understanding of democracy that allowed sections of the population to vote but did not challenge the socio-economic conditions that might weaken the realisation of genuine popular rule. Nonetheless, by the mid-twentieth century, and following the defeat of fascism, democracy had become the predominant political form in the traditionally Western Christian world. With various degrees of enthusiasm the Roman Catholic Church came to accept democracy as a 'lesser evil', following their unhappy experiences with fascism and communism, but in the immediate aftermath of the Second World War there was little evidence to suggest that it was to become an active proponent of democratic change. Only with Vatican II did its embrace of pluralism become more whole-hearted and, whilst a rational choice approach might stress these changes as coming out of the Catholic Church's need to 'adapt to survive', one can also see it as a product of long-term changes in theological understandings within the institution. In consequence the Church in many developing countries shifted its position from defender of authoritarian rule to promoter of human rights and democracy. This adaptation is the subject of the next two chapters though, as we shall see, as authoritarian rulers tumbled and various degrees of democratisation became established, some of the older reservations about liberal democracy began to re-appear, voiced by both radical and conservative voices within the Catholic Church.

Notes

1 John W. de Gruchy, *Christianity and Democracy* (Cambridge: Cambridge University Press, 1995), p. 8.

2 Graham Maddox, *Religion and the Rise of Democracy* (London: Routledge, 1996), pp. 7–14.

3 David Held, *Models of Democracy*, 1st edition (Cambridge: Polity Press, 1987), p. 36.

4 De Gruchy, *Christianity and Democracy*, especially pp. 40–53.

5 Steven Ozment, *The Age of Reform 1250–1555: An Intellectual and Religious History of Late Medieval and Reformation Europe* (New Haven: Yale University Press, 1980), pp. 135ff.; J. Blythe, *Ideal Government and the Mixed Constitution in the Middle Ages* (Princeton: Princeton University Press, 1992).

6 J. B. Morall, *Political Thought in Medieval Times* (London: Hutchinson, 1971), pp. 62–3; R. Butt, *The Power of Parliament* (London: Constable, 1969), pp. 31–42.

7 Morall, *Political Thought in Medieval Times*, pp. 90–2.

8 Ibid., pp. 104–18; Ozment, *The Age of Reform*, pp. 155–9; Blythe, *Ideal Government*, pp. 193–202.

9 See the discussion in J. Canning, *A History of Medieval Political Thought* (London: Routledge, 1996), pp. 156ff.

10 Ozment, *The Age of Reform*, pp. 176–8; Blythe, *Ideal Government*, pp. 244–52.

11 De Gruchy, *Christianity and Democracy*, p. 57.

12 D. Held, *Models of Democracy*, 2nd edition (Cambridge: Polity Press, 1996), p. 39.

13 S. Bruce, *Religion in the Modern World* (Oxford: Oxford University Press, 1996), p. 13.

14 Ibid., p. 22; S. Bruce, 'Did Protestantism create democracy?', *Democratization*, 11:4 (2004), pp. 3–20.

15 J. H. Elliott, *Europe Divided* (London: Fontana, 1968), pp. 90–1.

16 Cf. Maddox, *Religion and the Rise of Democracy*, pp. 100–20; W. Cargill Thompson, *The Political Thought of Martin Luther* (Brighton: Harvester Press, 1984).

17 Maddox, *Religion and the Rise of Democracy*, p. 113.

18 For some of these debates see R. Kingdom and R. Linder (ed.), *Calvin and Calvinism: Sources of Democracy* (Lexington: D. C. Heath, 1970).

19 R. Wuthnow, *Communities of Discourse: Ideology and Social Structure in the Reformation, the Enlightenment and European Socialism* (London: Harvard University Press, 1989), pp. 126–8.

20 The text can be found at http://home. hiwaay.net/~pspoole/Ponet1.HTM (accessed 10 January 2005).

21 Maddox, *Religion and the Rise of Democracy*, chapter 5; A. G. Dickens, *The English Reformation* (London: Fontana, 1964), pp. 391–2; R. Kingdom, 'Calvinism and resistance theory, 1550–80', in J. H. Burns (ed.), *The Cambridge History of Political Thought, 1450–1700* (Cambridge: Cambridge University Press, 1991), pp. 193–218.

22 P. Benedict, '*Un roi, une loi, deux fois:* parameters for the history of the Catholic-Reformed co-existence in France, 1555–1685', in O. P. Grell and B. Scribner (ed.), *Tolerance and Intolerance in the European Reformation* (Cambridge: Cambridge University Press, 1996), pp. 65–93.

23 Quoted in O. Chadwick, *The Reformation* (London: Penguin 1970), p. 167.

24 See Andrew Pettegree's comment on tolerance in the Netherlands as 'a loser's creed', in Grell and Scribner, *Tolerance and Intolerance in the European Reformation*, p. 198.

25 This is brought out well in many of the essays in Grell and Scribner, *Tolerance and Intolerance in the European Reformation*.

26 Dickens, *The English Reformation*, p. 441.

27 S. Bruce, *Religion in the Modern World* (Oxford: Oxford University Press, 1996), p. 75.

28 B. Manning, 'Puritanism and Democracy, 1640–42', in D. Pennington and K. Thomas, (ed.), *Puritans and Revolutionaries* (Oxford: Oxford University Press , 1978), pp. 139–60.

29 J. Frank, *The Levellers* (Cambridge, Mass: Harvard University Press, 1955).

30 N. Carlin, 'Toleration for Catholics in the Puritan revolution', in Grell and Scribner, *Tolerance and Intolerance in the European Reformation*, pp. 216–30.

31 C. Hill, *The English Bible and the Seventeenth Century Revolution* (London: Allen Lane, 1993), p. 34.

32 Cf. Held, *Models of Democracy*, 2nd edn, pp. 72–5; Elliott, *Europe Divided*, pp. 391–6; D. Pennington, *17th Century Europe* (London: Fontana, 1970), p. 207.

33 B. Labaree, *Colonial Massachussetts – A History* (New York: 1979), p. 35.

34 M. Noll, *The Old Religion in a New World: The History of North American Christianity* (Grand Rapids: Wm. B. Eerdmans, 2002), p. 44.

35 M. A. Jones, *The Limits of Liberty: American History, 1607–1980* (Oxford: Oxford University Press, 1983), p. 8.

36 Ibid., p. 9; E. Morgan, *Roger Williams: the Church and State* (New York: Harcourt, Brace and World, 1967).

37 Maddox, *Religion and the Rise of Democracy*, pp. 160–1.

38 Cf. Jones, *The Limit of Liberty*, p. 29; M. Marty, *Pilgrims in their Own Land* (Boston: Little Brown, 1984), pp. 108–9.

39 T. Curry, *The First Freedoms: Church and State in America to the Passage of the First Amendment* (New York: Oxford University Press, 1986).

40 Nathan Hatch, *The Democratisation of American Christianity* (New Haven: Yale University Press, 1989), pp. 9ff.

41 Alexis de Tocqueville, *Democracy in America* (London: Collins, 1966), esp. pp. 355–85.

42 C. Hinchley, 'Tocqueville on religion and modernity: making Catholicism safe for liberal democracy', *Journal of Church and State*, 32:2 (1990), pp. 325–41.

43 G. Craig, *The Church and the Age of Reason, 1648–1789* (London: Penguin, 1970), chapter 15; John Keane, *Tom Paine: A Political Life* (London: Bloomsbury, 1995), pp. 19 and 394–6.

44 Cf. Craig, *The Church and the Age of Reason*, pp. 215ff.; G. Rude, *Revolutionary Europe, 1783–1815* (London: Collins, 1967), pp. 114–18.

45 J. McManners, *The French Revolution and the Church* (Westport: Greenwood Press, 1982), pp. 6–17.

46 This paragraph draws largely on McManners, *The French Revolution and the Church*; C. Geffre and J.-P. Jossua, *1789: The French Revolution and the Churches* (Edinburgh: T. and T. Clark, 1989) and N. Ravitch, *The Catholic Church and the French Nation, 1589–1989* (London: Routledge,1990), pp. 51–9.

47 Rude, *Revolutionary Europe*, pp. 68–74.

48 W. Gibson, *Church, State and Society, 1760–1850* (London: Macmillan, 1994), pp. 46–51.

49 Ibid., pp. 76–81; D. W. Bebbington, *The Non-Conformist Conscience: Chapel and Politics, 1870–1914* (London: George Allen and Unwin, 1982).

50 M. Cowling, *Religion and Public Doctrine in Modern England*, (Volume II (Cambridge: Cambridge University Press, 1985), p. 26.

51 E. Hobsbawm, *The Age of Revolution, 1789–1948* (London: Abacus, 1993), pp. 269–70.

52 D. Blackburn, *The Fontana History of Germany, 1780–1914* (London: Fontana, 1997), pp. 292–301.

53 P. Sigmund, 'The Catholic tradition and modern democracy', *Review of Politics*, 49:4 (1987), pp. 530–48.

54 R. Aubert, *The Christian Centuries, Vol. 5: The Church in A Secularised Society* (London: Darton, Longman and Todd, 1978), chapter 8.

55 Ibid.

56 Michael Schuck, *That They May Be One: The Social Teaching of the Papal Encyclicals, 1740–1989* (Washington: Georgeton University Press, 1991), pp. 1–44.

57 M. Fogarty, *Christian Democracy in Western Europe, 1820–1953* (London: Routledge and Kegan Paul, 1957), chapters 11–13.

58 T. Buchanan and M. Conway (ed.), *Political Catholicism in Europe, 1918–65* (Oxford: Clarendon Press, 1996), pp. 69–76; S. Kalyvas, *The Rise of Christian Democracy in Europe* (Ithaca: Cornell University Press, 1996).

59 J. Bryan Hehir, 'Catholicism and democracy: conflict, change and collaboration', in John Witte (ed.), *Christianity and Democracy in Global Context* (Boulder: Westview, 1993), p. 17–19.

60 Ibid., pp. 19–20.

61 A. Hastings (ed.), *Modern Catholicism: Vatican II and After* (London: SPCK, 1991), p. 29.

62 A. Stacpoole (ed.), *Vatican II By Those Who Were There* (London: Geoffrey Chapman, 1986), pp. 286–8.

63 Ibid., p. 289.

64 Hehir, 'Catholicism and democracy', p. 22.

65 N. Cooper, 'The Church: from crusade to Christianity', in P. Preston (ed.) *Spain in Crisis* (London, Harvester Press, 1976), pp. 60–2.

66 J. Casanova, *Public Religions in the Modern World* (Chicago: Chicago University Press, 1994), p. 71.

3

The Catholic 'third wave': undermining authoritarianism

In the first part of his 1991 book, *The Third Wave: Democratization in the Late Twentieth Century*, Samuel Huntington asks the question, 'What changes in plausible independent variables in most probably the 1960s and 1970s produced the dependent variable, democratizing regime changes in the 1970s and 1980s?' In response he suggests that there were essentially five key changes: the deepening legitimacy problems of authoritarian regimes, the unprecedented global economic growth of the 1960s which greatly expanded the middle class, changes in both doctrine and practice within the Roman Catholic Church, changes in the policies of important external actors, and what he calls 'snowballing' as one regime after another tumbled from the late 1970s onwards.[1] For our purposes it is his use of the religious argument that is most interesting, and in particular the focus upon change within one particular religious tradition.

The first stage of his argument here is simply to observe the strong correlation between Western Christianity and democracy and to note that of 46 democracies existing in 1988, 39 had a predominantly Protestant or Catholic tradition. Whilst he does not suggest a causal relationship, Huntington goes on to argue that:

> Western Christianity emphasizes, however, the dignity of the individual and the separate spheres of church and state. In many countries, Protestant and Catholic church leaders have been central in the struggle against repressive countries. It seems plausible to hypothesize that the expansion of Christianity encourages democratic development.[2]

The first 'wave' of democratisation was closely associated with the Puritan revolution and in the 1960s most studies still suggested a close correlation between Protestantism and democracy, whilst Catholicism was associated with 'the absence of democracy or late democratic development'.[3] This link to Protestantism was seen by Huntington as a product of the doctrinal emphasis on individual conscience and access to truth through the reading of Scripture, the democratic organisational principles of Protestant congregational life, and the linkage between Protestantism and capitalist development identified by Max Weber which had contributed to the emergence of democratic political orders. For Huntington there was an undeniable connection which he saw as still operating in the contemporary era, and he pointed to South Korea as a country where gradual liberalisation and democratisation had followed the growth of the Christian community in the post-war years from around 1% to 25% of the population (80% Protestant) with most of the converts to be found in the young, urban, middle class.[4]

Despite such cases, for Huntington the 'third wave' was primarily a Catholic wave, with around 75% of those countries democratising in the period 1974–89 having a predominantly Catholic tradition. In part this was simply a result of the fact that most Protestant countries were already democratic, whilst many Catholic countries had enjoyed particularly high rates of economic growth since the 1950s which brought them to a socio-economic level that might be seen as making them ready for democracy. Equally if not more important, however, was the fact that the Catholic Church had changed internally, and that a powerful social institution which hitherto had tended to support authoritarianism came to oppose dictatorial regimes. This was partly a product of change at the top, as Vatican II led to a fundamental rethinking within the Church about its relationship with society and the political order, and partly a product of a new generation of priests in both Europe and elsewhere, who were more attuned to popular needs and aware of the incursions of dictatorial regimes upon emerging Catholic understandings of human dignity. Whilst on occasions this led to a radicalisation of priests who subsequently turned to revolutionary activity, for most it was simply a restatement of the old idea of men and women as made 'in the image of God' and deserving of respect and proper treatment by political rulers. In consequence religious leaders and institutions increasingly found themselves in conflict with rulers whom they had hitherto supported, a role that was reinforced by the trans-national nature of the Catholic Church which reinforced the commitment to human rights and made it harder for regimes to appeal over the heads of local church leaders to what they hoped would be a more sympathetic Vatican. This commitment was further strengthened by the election of Pope John Paul II in 1978, whose very first encyclical forcefully restated the Church's commitment to human rights.[5]

These next two chapters focus primarily on this 'Catholic wave' though there will be occasional references to Protestant contributions which were sometimes influenced by the political theologies emerging within the Catholic tradition. In this first chapter, and after a brief digression on the traditional pro-authoritarian tendencies of the Catholic Church, the emphasis is very much on the ways in which a new activism served to undermine authoritarian regimes. It did so in the first instance by offering a series of critiques of social, economic and political injustice that challenged authoritarianism. This was backed up by practical measures aimed at supporting the development of 'civil society'. In the fourth chapter we build on this to explore the role of individual leaders and the peculiarly Catholic transnational dimension in bringing about change, as well as exploring some of the ways in which religious organisations contributed to the negotiation of transition. At the end of the latter chapter we shall also examine how Catholic hierarchies and churches have coped with the realities of democratic politics.

Running through these two chapters will remain the question of why (predominantly) Catholic religious institutions changed their political orientation so radically, and in many cases became enthusiastic supporters of democratisation. In the introduction we posited four broad types of explanation, though offered no conclusions on which, if any, was more helpful in explaining religious change. The first model, proposed by Bruce in relationship to the Protestant contribution to democracy, stressed inadvertency, that is, the notion that political change was a product of religious change but not an intended consequence. The second model, underlying Huntington's analysis, suggests that what I have called 'altruism' was at the heart of the new commitment to democratisation, as theological rethinking led to a new political orientation. The third and fourth models emerge in part to plug the gap in Huntington's theory which fails to explain why, given the change at the level of the international institution, some national hierarchies developed a critical position and others did not. They do so by pointing to religious self-interest, though neither require that this be a conscious objective of religious actors. In the Gramscian approach favoured by Jeffrey Haynes the argument is that churches jumped on the democratic bandwagon to preserve their ideological and institutional hegemony, whilst in the rational choice analysis developed by Anthony Gill the emphasis is on religious institutions seeking to preserve or enlarge their 'market share'. To these one might add a fifth approach developed by Daniel Philpott which accepts much of Huntington's argument but seeks to explain the gap in Huntington's approach by focusing on what might be called the structural situation of the different hierarchies. In particular he argues that much can be explained by their relationship with the State, their dealings with the transnational Church, their engagement with the wider society, and ties to national identity.[6]

Religious critiques of authoritarianism

Living with authoritarianism

Historically, religious organisations and individuals have often exercised prophetic roles, challenging the beliefs and lifestyles of political rulers, yet in practice, once religions became socially dominant or established, the predominant inclination has been to find a modus vivendi with the political order. In part this tendency arose out of self interest, for as religious communities acquired their own institutional and organisational structures they had more to lose by challenging the political order. Moreover, once they became the religion of the State they could rely on the protection of their position by that state in the face of challenges coming from within and outside the tradition. Equally, in many cases there were theological dimensions to this, with one strand of the Christian tradition stressing that rulers were put in place by God and that challenges to their position were rarely permissible. In the Catholic case it was clear that:

survival is the fundamental aim. Believing itself to be the unique means of human salvation, it must insist on its right to teach, proselytise and administer its sacraments. The exact nature of the temporal regime in any one country remains secondary to these basic objectives.[7]

Whilst this in theory allowed the Church to adapt to any political regime, prior to 1945 the predominant regime type in the world was authoritarian, so religious organisations in general, and the Catholic Church in particular, found themselves siding with such regimes despite occasional challenges from prophetic individuals. This attitude was reinforced in the inter-war years when the Vatican found itself adopting ambiguous positions with regard to fascism, a system church leaders often despised but which seemed the 'lesser evil' when contrasted with the rise of the explicitly anti-religious communist movement in the Soviet Union and beyond.[8]

This attitude undoubtedly influenced the Spanish Catholic hierarchy whose general suspicion of modernity and democracy was reinforced by considerable experience of struggle with anti-clericalism from the mid-nineteenth century and then by the struggle with radical republicanism in the 1930s. During the early years of the republican regime a series of measures had been passed aimed at curtailing the Church's privileges and secularising the Spanish state. This was often accompanied by physical attacks on religious personnel and the burning of religious property during the first half of the 1930s. The early stages of the civil war saw revolutionary propagandists promote a very harsh anti-clerical campaign that led to the deaths of around 7,000 priests, monks and nuns. In such circumstances it was hardly surprising that the majority of church activists supported the Nationalist cause, and in the late 1930s church publications often depicted Franco's army as fighting a religious crusade.[9] Many leading churchmen hoped that the Nationalist victory would not only see off the (as they saw it) communist inspired anti-clerical threat but that it would enable them to restore their privileged position within the country. The more idealistic hoped for a political context within which a new evangelisation of the country could take place and Catholic values be propagated. Optimistic campaigns were launched, and Franco's regime helped by trying to make attendance at Mass compulsory.

Simultaneously it restored many of the institutional privi-leges of the Church, providing generous support for the rebuilding of churches, reinstating religious education in schools, and colouring every public event with extravagant religious rituals. For its part the Church offered largely unquestioning support for the regime, using harsh language against political opponents of the Francoist order and gener-ally taking the side of the powerful in the new order. Not everything turned out as some churchmen had hoped – there was no breakthrough in evangelising the masses and the Concordat of 1953 gave Franco control over the appointment of diocesan bishops[10] – but by and large the generation who had lived through the civil war saw little reason to drop their support for Franco. After all, he had kept communism and disorder at bay, prevented the growing permissiveness of post-war Europe from reaching Spain, and guaranteed their position within post-civil war Spain.

Similar reasoning underlay the historic connection of Catholic hierarchies with the military-corporatist regimes emerging in Latin America during the mid-twentieth century. As in the Iberian peninsula, the nineteenth century had been characterised by a struggle between liberalism and conser-vatism in which the anti-clericalism of the former often drove the Church into the arms of reactionary political leaders. In Brazil, for example, Church and State were formally separated in 1891 and in consequence the church leadership adopted a defensive mentality in the struggle against modernity.[11] During the first half of the twentieth century the Catholic hierarchy's relationship with the State was subject to constant change, whilst they struggled to maintain their influence on the mass of the population experiencing massive social change under the impact of industrialisation and migration to the cities. By the middle of the century they had increasingly adapted to the corporatist style regimes emerging in various parts of the region, notably in Brazil where Getúlio Vargas, though personally agnostic, gained church support because of his support for order, stabil-ity and anti-communism. Though Vargas did not challenge the formal separation of Church and State he made it clear that the government would support the Church when it was in the 'collective interest', whilst for its part the Church as a political institution discouraged religious activists from developing a more critical stance.[12] This fear of communism was reinforced from the late 1950s and through the 1960s by the rise of radical movements within Latin America and the emergence of Castro's Cuba. In consequence Latin American hierarchies often welcomed the new wave of military take-overs that took place in the 1960s. In Brazil the bishops' conference initially described the 1964 coup as preventing a communist victory, though it did warn that the restoration of order should not be used to justify tyranny.[13]

A similar position was initially taken by the hierarchy in Chile though, as in Brazil, many churchmen were soon disillusioned by the brutal human rights abuses perpetrated by the new regime. In Argentina leading bishops appear to have been forewarned of the coup and been promised that the military would act to defend the values of Christian civilisation and further the Church's institutional position.[14] As Comblin puts it, for the new National Security States the primary role of the Church was to join the military in combating communism. In return they would be offered a renewal of their past privileges, with the promotion of religious teaching in schools, censorship, state defence of traditional morality and the support of Catholic worship.[15]

A rather unique collaboration of Protestant religious institutions with authoritarianism emerged in South Africa, which provided democracy for the white population whilst excluding the vast majority of the population from participating in politics. Here the defence of a particular type of government was less about promoting authoritarianism than justifying a political system based upon racial distinctions. As early as 1857 a Dutch Reformed Church (DRC) Synod had called for separate services for blacks and whites, and over subsequent decades this became the norm in most South African churches. Following the Second World War the doctrine of racial separation increasingly came to dominate South African society and a series of laws passed in 1949–53 served to institutionalise the apartheid system. This in turn was justified by the DRC with reference to the 'given-ness' of racial difference, with the notion of separation supported by reference to the biblical story of the Tower of Babel which told of God dividing people into races and tribes as a punishment for their presumption in seeking to reach heaven. Simultaneously, the real and imagined connections between the ANC and several communist states enabled state and church leaders to describe themselves as defending a unique 'White Christian civilization'.[16]

Though the predominant attitude of many Christian (especially Catholic) hierarchies during the mid-twentieth century was supportive of authoritarian regimes, sometimes seen as mirrors of the hierarchical and monolithic church model that had been promoted by the papacy since the late nineteenth century, there were always a minority of critical voices. Within the Catholic Church a number of priests and other religious personnel developed a social critique that implicitly indicted these regimes for failing to meet the needs of the people. In Spain intellectuals aware of debates in the wider Church began to argue for a more humane Catholicism open to the world and supportive of liberty. Simultaneously there was emerging here, as elsewhere, a Catholic workers' movement which sought to organise the working class in line with Catholic social teaching, often highly paternalistic, but which grew increasingly militant and ready to collaborate with Marxist and socialist unofficial trade unions. Similar concerns were also being raised in the late 1950s by a small minority of bishops who feared that over-reliance on ties to the State was costing the Church the support of the masses. Bishop Vicente Enrique y Tarancón of Solsona, later to be Spanish primate, published a series of pastoral letters castigating the authorities for their lack of interest in the poor.[17]

Across the Atlantic several priests and bishops were beginning to offer similar critiques in Latin America, with the already existing Catholic Action movements adopting more radical agendas as the 1950s progressed, albeit often as a defensive measure to prevent radical socialists from influencing the masses. In Brazil the National Bishops' Conference, founded in 1952 (i.e. before Vatican II made these more common), spoke up for the poor under the influence of Bishop Helder Camara, a man who was initially supportive of corporatist regimes but who by the 1970s had adopted a liberationist perspective.[18] For these activists the question was how those in poverty could be truly human and how an evangelisation programme might be developed that did not ignore human dignity and welfare. Yet by and large these early voices expressing criticism of authoritarian regimes were concerned primarily with ensuring that the interests and needs of the marginalised were met, rather than with regime change or democratisation as such. Only after Vatican II do we see these more critical agendas being taken up, often cautiously and with some reservation, by national hierarchies. And as we shall see, whilst the voices for social justice and human rights were strong, both religious 'radicals' and 'conservatives' were sometimes muted in their support for liberal democracy.

A voice for social and political justice

In much of the 'developing world' one of the major consequences of Vatican II was the emergence and reinforcement of a social critique of the economic inequality and injustice facing many of the world's poorest, a critique that drew on both theological insights and contemporary social science in leading some churchmen to promote a 'preferential option for the poor'. In the Latin American context this was worked out in what came to be known as 'liberation theology' which was probably supported by only a minority of priests and bishops but which for a decade or so became the most prominent discourse used to challenge authoritarian regimes and indeed the whole international economic order. At the Second Latin American Episcopal Conference held at Medellín in 1968 the bishops recognised that in Latin America there was a situation of injustice that could be recognised as institutionalised violence, because the existing structures violated people's basic rights. Though the bishops recognised the temptation to counter-violence they suggested that this might only lead to further injustices, and thus they refused to go down the road pursued by a tiny minority of priests who joined guerrillas fighting authoritarian regimes.[19] In shifting towards a 'preferential option for the poor' the bishops moved cautiously, acutely aware of the dangers of dividing churches where many hierarchs remained sceptical about the decisions of Vatican II.

Despite episcopal caution there gradually developed a new theological perspective, formally said to arise out of work with the marginalised but also heavily influenced by European ways of doing both social science and theology. The concept of 'liberation theology' was given currency following publication of Gustavo Gutiérriz's 1974 book *Theology of Liberation: Liberation and Faith*. Drawing heavily on 'dependency theory' which explained third world under-development in terms of structural inequalities in the world economy, rather than in terms of Latin American cultural failings, Gutiérriz also drew heavily on the Old Testament account of God bringing his people out of the wilderness and on the language of Vatican II. In particular he utilised John XXIII's rhetoric about the 'signs of the times' and the need for the Church to respond to and make use of modern ideas where appropriate. This, he argued, would lead the Church into 'prophetic denunciation' of oppressive regimes, and a rejection of the dehumanising effects of the currently dominant models of development. For Gutiérriz the work of Christ 'is a liberation from sin and all its consequences: despoilation, injustice, hatred' and sin is evident in 'unjust structures' as much as human failings: 'Sin demands a radical liberation, which in turn necessarily implies a political liberation.'[20]

Many of these ideas were developed and taken much further by other theologians and church activists, mostly Catholic but also some Protestants. Central to their critique was a rejection or amendment of the traditional view that the Church's primary concern was with individual sin, and an emphasis on the possibility of institutional and structural sin that was equally liable to God's judgement. In such circumstances the institutional Church did not just have a responsibility to condemn but also quite explicitly to take the side of the poor and the marginalised, even if on occasions this might necessitate supporting the use of violence against oppressors. Of course, in this context we cannot do the complexities of liberation theology full justice, but whilst critics clearly exaggerated the role of Marxism and the ambiguity about violence in order to undermine the wider critique, with hindsight it is clear that at least parts of the liberationist critique were inadequate. In particular it might be suggested that the excessive focus of the liberation theologians on socio-economic change (and occasional naivety about actually existing socialism) and, as we shall suggest later, their underestimation of the positive features of liberal democracy, all laid them open to criticism.[21]

Partly in response to developments in Latin American theology, similar critiques emerged in other parts of the globe. In Asia liberation theology influenced a younger generation of priests in the Philippines, and in South Korea the 'koinonia' movement developed a theology of suffering and sought to mobilise the resources of the people to transform society. In South Africa the 1985 Kairos Document, produced by a group of Christian theologians, challenged the way in which the apartheid state used theology in a distorted fashion to support the system of racial dominance and, by encouraging those churches which stressed individual repentance, promoted political quiescence. Instead the signatory churches called for a 'prophetic theology' that recognised that this was not simply a conflict between two equal sides but one between oppressors and oppressed in which the latter might have to rely on civil disobedience to attain justice.[22] In similar vein the writings of Alan Boesak were permeated with the idea of God as liberator, on faith as something that affects the individual in all aspects of life, and peace as not simply the absence of war but the 'active presence of justice'.[23] This concern with violence and peace was an intrinsic part of these new theological perspectives which on the one hand refused to rule out the right of the oppressed to use force in response to violence and on the other called on church and state leaders to adopt a less one-sided approach to peace.

Though holding little affinity with the radical liberationists, Cardinal Tarancón in Spain had earlier in his career offended the Franco regime by speaking up on behalf of the workers. By the late 1960s he had come to the conclusion that whilst the Church's early support for Franco was an understandable reaction to republican persecutions in the 1930s, this had led it to side all too easily with the victors in the civil war. Consequently in 1971 he persuaded a not entirely convinced Assembly of Bishops and Priests to issue a declaration which asked the nation's forgiveness 'because we were not able in due time to be true ministers of reconciliation in the heart of our people divided by a war among brothers'.[24] On other occasions this concern with peace drew churches into broader struggles for peace, as in East Germany during the 1970s and 1980s where religious activists often joined forces with more secular actors in arguing against the placing of nuclear weapons in Europe. Here too the link was made between peace, justice and human rights, and in making this connection religious bodies came into conflict with a state which depicted the West as the major threat to peace and rejected the idea that human rights were a problem in socialist society.[25] This concern with peace did not draw directly upon liberationist ideas, but it shared the view that religious organisations had to go beyond concern with individual salvation to engagement with the world.

For various reasons the liberationist perspective did not penetrate Europe in quite the same way, especially in Eastern Europe where the willingness of Latin Americans and others to draw on Marxist insights appeared problematic. Here there was far more scepticism about the possibilities of social transformation and, as we shall see below, more emphasis on the 'bourgeois civil rights' that tended to take second place to socio-economic rights in much of the 'third world' discourse. There was also considerable misunderstanding of what the 'liberationists' were after as can be seen in Polish priest Fr Franciszek Blachnicki's dismissal of their thought as an 'attempt to justify the use of violence in the struggle for social and political freedom by appealing to the Gospel'. Fr Blachnicki was founder of the Light-Life movement or Oasis movement, which organised summer camps for young Catholics in the 1970s and 1980s, much against the wishes of the state authorities. In an article published in 1984 he sought to develop a Polish 'theology of liberation' springing out of the specific Polish context. Built on the basic concept that faith cannot be other-worldly but requires a response in the here and now, Blachnicki saw the need for evangelisation to lead to liberation, that is to create people who would stand up for truth and state that they would rather obey God than man. If necessary this must mean a willingness to sacrifice oneself for the sake of truth.[26] What Fr Blachnicki perhaps failed to notice was that, with the exception of an absolute rejection of violence, his position was not that different from that of the liberationists in stressing the importance of a theology appropriate to the context, the need for theology to be prophetic in addressing injustice, and the importance of theology addressing the here and now as well as the other-worldly. And what is important at this stage is that in their various contexts all of the religious activists and institutions discussed here were united in condemning injustice and speaking up for justice, though they may have differed in how they understood what these concepts mean. Equally worth noting is that these arguments are essentially critical and do not offer solutions, and in particular they do not necessarily see liberal democracy as it had emerged in the USA and Europe as the most appropriate means of achieving justice.

In this they had much in common with liberation theology, though by the late 1980s its heyday had probably passed. With the election of Pope John Paul II in 1978 and following the Puebla conference of Latin American bishops in 1979, both the Vatican and local hierarchies became dominated by men suspicious of this particular perspective, though papal decrees continued to offer a critique of the consequences of unfettered capitalism and to condemn the human rights abuses that still characterised many Latin American regimes into the early 1980s. But as democratisation spread throughout the region during that decade, the radical perspective was increasingly challenged by realities on the ground as well as papal condemnations. Many of the original liberation theologians have developed a more sophisticated critique rooted in a nuanced view of the world and the possibilities of change, but their critique of social injustice and commitment to a theology rooted in popular suffering remains undiminished and they still, quite rightly, question the extent to which formal democratisation has enriched the life of the marginalised.

A voice for human rights

Whilst religious actors differed over concepts of justice, there emerged from the late 1960s onwards a fairly consistent critique of authoritarianism focusing on the abuse of human rights typical under such regimes, though it should be noted that thinkers such as Jacques Maritain had been developing Catholic thought on this subject long before Vatican II and had contributed to the discussion around the 1948 UN Declaration of Human Rights. For Catholic activists Vatican II's more explicit commitment of the Church to the idea that all persons, Catholic or otherwise, were possessed of human dignity that should be respected, played a key role. This was a perspective that tended to be shared in some other faith communities, though often less well articulated in a systematic theological sense. We shall say more later about the institutional structures developed by the churches to support human rights, and our focus here is more on the articulation of the human rights agenda. In many of the countries considered here, including a few of the communist countries, the churches remained the only institutions permitted a degree of autonomy from the State and, in those countries where regimes described their mission in religious terms, it was often hard for state authorities to handle criticism coming from religious institutions.

Numerous examples can be found of clerical leaders using their pulpits and public positions both to denounce human rights abuses and develop a more general defence of the whole concept of human dignity and human rights. In Spain during 1970 the bishops of the Granada region condemned the police shooting of demonstrators which left three dead,[27] while Fr Jose Maria Larrouri used his 1971 Good Friday sermon to condemn the torture and marks left on the bodies of prisoners which he had seen with his own eyes.[28] In the Basque territories Bishop Antonio Anoveros of Bilbao riled the Franco regime by speaking out strongly on the need for some degree of cultural autonomy to be given to the region and called for the release of non-violent political prisoners.[29]

Such public denunciations became even more common in Latin America from the late 1960s onwards, as both individual church leaders and several episcopal conferences issued frequent denunciations of human rights abuses. Of particular concern to many hierarchs was the fact that these regimes utilised the threat of subversion to justify brutal repression. In 1970 the Brazilian bishops' conference issued a document arguing that:

> The promotion of the individual should be sought by all levels of political and administrative organisations. This objective will not be attained when, to eliminate terrorist subversion, the concern for national security generates a climate of increasing insecurity. Terrorism by the repressive apparatus is not a legitimate response to terrorism by subversives.[30]

And in late 1973, on the anniversary of the United Nations Declaration on Human Rights, all the major Brazilian churches except the Pentecostals and some evangelical groups launched a nation-wide campaign for human rights.[31] Increasingly such campaigns moved beyond ritualised denunciations, as in November 1975 when the bishops of Sao Paulo issued a statement accusing the government of torturing and murdering political prisoners and proclaimed a day of fasting (reportedly joined by 2 million Catholics) to protest against ongoing abuses of human rights.[32] All of these developments in Brazil suggested that the Church had learned the lessons of Vatican II and that it was, in Casanova's words 'not defending the privileged rights of sacred persons but, rather, the sacred dignity of the human person'.[33]

Such initiatives and declarations could be cited from most of Latin America where repeatedly pastorals and speeches stressed the right of all to be treated humanely and justly and where, following the discovery of mass graves down a disused mine shaft in Chile, Cardinal Raul Silva Enriques could note that the Church 'raises its voice because human dignity had been violated in the most extreme way'.[34] Even in Argentina, where the attitude of the hierarchy towards the military regime was deeply ambiguous, the bishops in 1977 accompanied a routine condemnation of Marxist subversives with the statement that 'no theory of collective responsibility ... can be allowed to destroy the rights of persons'.[35] Here it tended to be individual bishops who adopted a more outspoken approach to human rights abuses, though sometimes this proved costly. Bishops Enrique Angelelli and Carlos Ponce de León died in mysterious car crashes after criticising the military, and a number of priests and nuns were simply 'disappeared'.[36] In Argentina, however, there were clergymen prepared to back the regime with Bishop Medina, vicar general of the armed forces, arguing in 1981 that 'sometimes physical repression is necessary, is mandatory, is legitimate' and Bishop Bonamin describing the war against subversion as a fight 'for the defence of morality, human dignity'.[37] Equally in many Latin American countries the rapidly expanding 'conservative' Protestant groups generally proved reluctant to speak out on human rights issues and on occasions, as in Chile, offered support to a military regime which came to view them in an increasingly favourable light as they fell out with their 'own' religious hierarchies. Here American televangelist Jimmy Swaggart praised General Pinochet for having destroyed the Left, and a Pentecostal Methodist leader described the military coup as an answer to prayer.[38]

Further proclamations in defence of human rights emanated from churchmen in various parts of the world, from South Korea, through Africa, to Eastern and Central Europe. In the Philippines Cardinal Sin at first was close to the

Marcos regime, but became increasingly critical of the ideology the president was promoting. In a lecture given in early 1984 he criticised the government's determination to 'view society as a single homogeneous structure with room for only one ideology, one power, one civic faith in one leader'. He went on to attack the regime's constant assaults on press freedom, arguing that a critical media was essential for curbing excessive government power, and concluded that 'the state exists to serve the common welfare in the areas of justice, peace, security and liberty'.[39] In Africa religious critiques focused on racial discrimination or on the self-aggrandisement at the expense of society typical of several African leaders. Though the Catholic Church was the dominant voice in many of these countries, others were active in defending human rights, including Anglican bishops in Kenya who called on believers to protest where 'God-given rights and liberties are violated' and argued that the Church had a special responsibility to 'give voice to the voiceless'.[40] The South African churches tended, because of their peculiar political context, to be at the forefront in developing a critical stance on human rights, as they vocally opposed the apartheid regime and argued, in Archbishop Tutu's words, that 'the white man will never be free until the black man is wholly free'.[41] Elsewhere in the continent this concern with human rights was a later development. Nonetheless in time church leaders who had traditionally supported governments or remained politically neutral began to speak out, as in Malawi where the 1992 Pastoral Letter of the Catholic Bishops criticised the autocratic style of rule exercised by Hastings Banda and condemned the lack of personal and political freedom in the country.[42]

Human rights also provided the focus for critiques of authoritarianism developed in the communist world, though in those countries where Orthodoxy and Islam were the traditionally dominant religions such discussions emanated from a few individuals rather than religious institutions as such. In the early stages of communist rule religious communities tended to focus on defending their own rights in the face of often brutal anti-religious campaigns, and many remained suspicious of secular oppositionists, fearing that they would be sucked into political conflicts that might damage the interests of the churches. For its part the secular intelligentsia in much of Central Europe initially remained sceptical about religious institutions that in the past had opposed pluralism. Gradually, however, relations between the various dissenting groups thawed, as in Czechoslovakia, Lithuania and, most importantly, Poland, the church proved increasingly vocal in defence of civil rights and willing to make common cause with other forces defending human rights. In Poland the campaigns for human rights were initially associated with the person of Cardinal Wyszyński (1901–81) who, from around 1970, increasingly went beyond defence of church interests to arguing that all had God-given rights which no political regime could legitimately transgress. In sermons during 1974 he called on the government to respect human rights and argued the need for a 'courageous defence of the right to free association as well as the rights to freedom of the press, expression of opinion and unrestrained scientific research'.[43] This position was reinforced after the events of 1976 which, as we shall see, led the Church to take an active role in defending the victims of abuses, and further still after October 1978 when Karol Wotyla ascended to the papacy. During his first visit to Poland in 1979 John Paul II repeatedly told people to learn to 'live in truth' and to 'think differently', and in subsequent years supported the Polish hierarchy in their calls for the observance of civil rights. Though Cardinal Glemp initially reacted cautiously towards the martial law regime, the Church remained an increasingly outspoken critic of official abuses throughout this period.

A voice for democracy?

Whilst religious organisations have often been outspoken in their criticisms of social injustice or human rights abuses committed by authoritarian regimes they have not always been as explicit in promoting democratisation as the answer. For the more radical liberationists social change tended to be seen as more important than institutional reform, and they remained suspicious of the major liberal democratic powers who promoted economic models that they argued were creating many of the problems facing the developing world. As Sigmund has noted, whilst writers such as Jose Comblin might recognise the importance of juridically guaranteed rights for the masses, many liberationists were almost dismissive of the notion of constitutional constraints on political leadership and tended to view them as secondary to the demands of social justice.[44] Voting was all very well but it did not put bread on the table. Nonetheless participation was a key theme of their discourse, and the documents of the Medellín conference of Latin American bishops argued that the political forms currently dominant in Latin America militated against the common good and called for 'the people of God' to 'inspire and press for a new order of justice that incorporates all persons in the decision-making of their own communities'.[45]

For liberationists the focus of participation was very much on the community, on building democracy from the bottom up as local groups challenged the power of oppressive employers, sought humane living conditions or challenged the brutalities of individual officials. Only on this basis could there be any guarantees against the inevitable corruption and clientelism characteristic of so much of Latin American politics. Many pinned their hope on the emerging *communidades eclesiales de base* (base communities, or CEBs) where church activists came together to study the scriptures and draw out messages that were relevant to people 'where they were' rather than relying on the grand theological constructs produced by church theologians isolated in universities or monasteries. As we shall see, the radical potential of these groups proved more limited, as pressures from the Vatican for de-politicisation and the 'demobilisation of society' associated with democratic consolidation often pushed such groups in a more 'spiritual' and less socially active direction. Nonetheless, it could be argued that in training a whole generation to link the theological and the political, and in spreading leadership beyond a clerical estate, these groups did in their own small way contribute towards democratisation.[46]

For the 'centrist' majorities in Catholic and other church hierarchies there was a growing recognition that 'procedural democracy', with its guarantees of rights and participation, was the best alternative to the various forms of authoritarianism on offer. As the centre of gravity in religious organisations shifted in this direction, they made their first significant, if sometimes unwitting, contribution to promoting democratic transformation by starting to undermine the legitimacy of authoritarian regimes. In Spain, from the early 1970s, Catholic organisations were increasingly prominent in promoting liberalisation and democratisation as the best way forward for the Spanish polity. During 1969 Bishop Florido of the Canary Islands insisted on the right to freedom of association and full participation in public life, whilst a joint assembly of bishops meeting in Madrid during September 1973 called on the government to permit citizens to participate in public administration.[47] When some governments started to flirt with elections, albeit closely controlled, church leaders were often the first to denounce abuses in the electoral process. In the Philippines it was the government's blatant abuses of the electoral process, along with the murder of Senator Aquino, that led Cardinal Sin to adopt a more critical stance towards the Marcos regime. One can see similar shifts in Poland, where a Catholic Church that had traditionally spoken in terms of defending the nation shifted towards 'a new language of universal rights', that – despite the Church's reluctance to demand the full institutionalisation of political rights during the martial law period – in effect helped to embed the later shift towards democratisation when communist rule collapsed at the end of the 1980s.[48]

* * * * *

This section has focused on what might be called the ideological relationship of the Christian churches with authoritarian regimes in the post-war era, as they shifted from a position that was quiescent if not supportive of authoritarianism, to a much more critical stance. This change was less notable amongst Protestant communities, with evangelicals and Pentecostals generally inclined to political passivity so long as they were permitted to preach and practise their faith. In a few cases, notably in the African continent, mainstream Protestant churches became involved in campaigns for human rights and democratisation – for example in South Africa, Malawi and Kenya – and in a few cases individual communities voiced active support for dictatorial regimes – as in Chile. At the forefront in most 'third wave' countries since the 1970s, however, was the Roman Catholic Church that, heavily influenced by teachings of the Second Vatican Council, promoted a broader understanding of social justice and human rights. Perhaps inevitably this new role posed dilemmas for a church, in so far as here we had a body that was internally hierarchical and sometimes authoritarian, seeking to encourage political regimes to open up the political world. Moreover, not all within the Church were convinced by the new direction and, as already suggested, Huntington's emphasis on the centrality of Vatican II fails to explain why some hierarchies responded and others did not. There are also questions about the extent of the religious commitment to democracy, as the dominant focus of most religious critiques was on what was wrong with the existing order, and on the need for social justice and a respect for human dignity. Though leading churchmen tended to speak in very general terms about the need for democracy or popular participation – and, in so far as democracy tends to guarantee human rights (if not always social justice), then democracy was the 'natural' solution to their society's ills – they were often wary of some of the likely consequences of majority rule. The key point of the section, however, is simply to note that alongside critiques of authoritarianism coming from academic analysts and opposition politicians, religious organisations were also able to make a contribution and one that was, in countries where religious leaders enjoyed an active or residual respect, often harder for authoritarian states to silence.

Creating space for civil society

Much of the literature on democratisation appearing during the 1980s and early 1990s fell into what might be called the 'transitological' camp, focusing heavily on the role of elites in negotiating change, organising 'pacts' and seeking to ensure that the removal of authoritarian regimes was not accompanied by instability.[49] Despite the media image of populations on the streets bringing down dictators, transitologists observed that in many democratisation processes the role of the masses appeared secondary. Yet even elite-led transitions required some support from below and Jean Grugel has argued that:

> Democracy requires that the subordinated groups have sufficient resources to play an important role within civil society and therefore also in relation to the state. Any explanation of democratisation, consequently, must pay attention to the concept of

civil society and to the struggles to extend rights and citizenship throughout society.[50]

For Grugel and others the emphasis was not just on the masses acting in rather inchoate fashion to overthrow an authoritarian regime, though this could be important, but on the emergence of a civil society that had the capacity to undermine such regimes and to provide the basis for the successful development of a balanced democratic system.

What we actually mean by civil society and its precise contribution to democratisation is the subject of a huge debate which we cannot explore here,[51] and for our purposes the concept is used rather conventionally to describe the realm of voluntary associations between the individual and the state – a free sphere in which individuals and groups can with some degree of openness debate matters of public concern and organise to advance their agendas. Whilst this realm may not always be used to promote values that are desirable from a liberal perspective, the assumption is that debate and action within this sphere are generally charac-terised by a degree of civility. There is a problem here, because not all would be happy to include religious groups within the realm of civil society. In the first place, their primary function is 'spiritual' and 'private' rather than public, as above all they seek to encourage their adherents in right belief, right ritual and right behaviour. Only when their 'interests' – whether material, institutional or value – are challenged do they tend to get engaged in the public sphere and then, because they make 'truth' claims that may deny rights to others, their actions can on occasion be seen as inherently 'uncivil'. In practice, however, they are not that different to other groups whose primary activities are not centred on influencing public policy, but who do sometimes find themselves acting in such ways. From De Tocqueville onwards, numerous writers have suggested that a strong civil society, in which the realm of voluntary organisations creates a free social space, provides the most appropriate bedrock for a truly democratic society. And when the 'third wave' of democratisation took off from the mid-1970s onwards several authors pointed to the role of 'alternative' politics and the creation of independent social groups in helping to undermine authoritarianism in some of these countries.[52]

In this section our concern is with the ways in which religious institutions have contributed towards the development and protection of civil society and thus, perhaps indirectly, have contributed towards the process of democratisation. In certain respects religious organisations have enjoyed a privileged position in many authoritarian systems, especially in those where the regime sees itself as committed to preserving 'Christian civilisation' against the forces of social disorder or the 'communist threat'. As such the rulers have to at least go through the motions of respect for religious institutions and, should the latter adopt a critical position, they have to deal with religious critics in ways that do not risk undermining their support within society. In communist systems the situation was more complex, because here the regimes were ostensibly anti-religious and committed to the long-term destruction of religious institutions. Yet once the Stalinist period was past, religious organisations were allowed to function – heavily controlled and subject to periodic waves of harassment in some of these countries – and often emerged as the only quasi-independent organisations within those societies. Moreover, when religious institutions gained some degree of space they also become attractive to those opposed to authoritarianism and could 'become important vehicles for the expression of popular discontent and for the elaboration of alternative survival strategies'.[53] Either separately or in tandem with other civil society groups, religious organisations have in some cases made a significant contribution to the development of civil society and, though their role has varied in scope and significance from country to country, during the 'third wave' we can identify religious organisations as involved in: the creation of alternative social organisations to those promoted by the state; the establishment of institutional structures to defend human rights; the organisation of demonstrations and protests; the utilisation of church rituals and symbols to articulate opposition; the use of religious mass media to offer alternative accounts of public affairs; the promotion of peaceful means of political change; the opening of physical space to non-religious actors; and the building of bridges to secular opposition figures. The rest of this chapter offers a few examples to illustrate some of these themes, before returning to some general questions about religion's contribution to the creation of civil society and the significance of this for transition processes during the 'third wave'.

In defence of human rights – the Vicaría de Solidaridad *in Chile*

We have already seen how Vatican II led to a major rethinking · of the Catholic position on political pluralism and religious liberty, and this effectively enabled the Church to buy into the international human rights discourse that emerged after 1945. Consequently the Catholic Church and some Protestant churches began to offer public criticism of the extensive abuse of human rights that characterised many authoritarian regimes. Such church-led campaigns could be found in most of South America, in Spain, in parts of Africa and Asia and in Central Europe, and in many cases church hierarchies went beyond critique to involvement in practical attempts to publicise and alleviate the miseries caused by arrest, torture, disappearances and murder. In some cases this was tied in with a wider assault on the nature of authoritarian regimes, but there was also some attempt to distance human rights activity from overt opposition. This was in part for tactical reasons, as the Church tried to persuade governments to change their practices with the argument that the observance of human dignity did not necessarily represent a challenge to the political order, and thus tried to separate human rights issues from questions of political change. It also stemmed from the traditional caution of most religious organisations who felt that political activity was not within their 'natural' remit, though in practice they often found that authoritarian leaders could not see the difference between opposition and the defence of human rights.

In South America perhaps the best-known example was provided by the Roman Catholic Vicariate of Solidarity (*Vicaría de Solidaridad*) in Chile. According to the 1990 Rettig Report, produced by the Chilean National Commission on Truth and Reconciliation, from very early on 'the only significant reaction to this pattern of human rights violations came from the churches, since they had the means and the willingness to act'.[54] Following the overthrow of Salvador Allende the Chilean church hierarchy had initially offered cautious support for the attempt to 'restore order', but called on the new rulers to respect their opponents and those fallen in battle, including Allende. At the same time they stressed the need to avoid bloodshed and violent repression and expressed reservations about the actions of the new regime. On 25 September 1973 Cardinal Silva visited the national stadium where the army was holding real and imagined subversives and Klaiber reports that he left in tears after 'finding himself in the presence of hundreds of prisoners who saw in him their one hope of leaving alive'.[55] In response he supported the creation of the Committee of Cooperation for Peace (COPACHI), an ecumenical venture involving Catholics, Protestants, Orthodox and Jews, a body which the Cardinal saw as necessary 'to help those who were in any economic or political need due to the recent political developments'.[56] This organisation provided aid to those dismissed from their work and sympathetic lawyers initiated legal action on behalf of more than 7,000 people arrested or 'disappeared' in 1973–74. Aguilar documents the gradual progression in the activity of the organisation as it moved from recording cases reported to the committee to taking direct action in the courts, for example in January 1974 filing writs to see those arrested, in an effort to determine whether they were still alive.[57] In addition COPACHI became involved in setting up community self-help projects, health clinics and soup kitchens for pre-school children, and in helping the persecuted leave the country. Though some bishops, including the future Cardinal Fresno, distanced themselves from Silva's critical position, the latter was increasingly seen by the regime as one of its major critics. His stance became even more critical after several physical attacks on clergy and lay activists – including the British doctor Sheila Cassidy who was tortured by the secret police. Increasingly irritated, General Pinochet singled out COPACHI as a body that was influenced by Marxist ideas and requested that the Cardinal dissolve it, which he did in December 1975.[58]

If the military regime thought this marked the ending of the Church's promotion of human rights it was very much mistaken, for on 1 January 1976 (one day after dissolving COPACHI) the Cardinal created the Vicariate of Solidarity as a formal part of Santiago's ecclesiastical structure. This organisation, provocatively located in Santiago's main plaza next to the cathedral, continued many of its predecessor's activities, but this time under direct church control. The government eventually came to accuse the Vicariate of being more communist than the communists, but throughout the Pinochet period this church body stuck to its task of defending those persecuted regardless of their beliefs, and of investigating the fate of those who had been 'disappeared'. In 1976 the Vicariate presented five bound volumes containing details of 900 people who had disappeared over the previous two years, but a promised meeting with Pinochet to discuss these failed to materialise. Though generally more cautious than COPACHI in publicising abuses within Chile, the Vicariate carefully documented hundreds of cases of unlawful arrest, torture and murder, and then sent them indirectly to the UN Human Rights Commission as a record of events within Chile. This issue of those who had disappeared became particularly pressing as a pastoral issue for the Church as those who had lost relatives sought comfort in the face of the lack of information or closure on the fate of their loved ones. Despite secret police pressures many fought a constant campaign to identify the fate of their relatives and then for the right to bury their remains when identified, and in this they were supported by the Vicariate.

Cardinal Silva declared 1978 a year of human rights in the Santiago diocese, and a series of conferences was held to discuss the Church's understanding of human rights and to discuss abuses taking place within Chile. This concern was reinforced towards the end of the year when the remains of about 15 people were found in a disused mine outside of Santiago and it quickly became clear that these were victims of extra-judicial killings. Once more the Vicariate took an active role in seeking a proper judicial investigation, but also in reminding the regime that failure to acknowledge these crimes would severely undermine any efforts at national reconciliation in the future.[59] Even though Silva's successor Cardinal Fresno adopted a more cautious position and steered the church away from confrontation with the regime, he maintained the position that brutality, torture and the abuse of human rights were unacceptable and was supported in this by Pope John Paul II during his visit to Chile in 1987. The Church's initiative in this area stimulated the activities of other groups at both central and local level, with local priests often playing a key role in documenting abuses outside of Santiago. All told it is estimated that around 700,000 people utilised the services of the Vicariate between 1975 and 1992 when its activities came to an end, and though the Church's political and social position became more conservative in the second half of the dictatorship, it remained committed to human rights activities and this proved its major contribution to the development of civil society.[60]

Whilst the Vicariate was one of the more institutionalised examples of human rights defence by a religious organisation, religious communities played a significant role through much of Latin America, Europe, Africa and Asia. In some case this may have involved local level grass-roots activities by individual priests, monks, nuns or laity groups, but in several states religious hierarchies gave their blessing and provided space and financial resources for both religious and secular human rights activities, or offered legal aid to those fighting their cause in the courts. As we shall see later, in Poland the Catholic Church supported the efforts of secular human rights groups to defend the victims of the 1976 shooting of striking workers, whilst during the state of emergency in South Africa during the late 1980s the South African Council of Churches established crisis centres that could dispense legal aid and financial support to the families of victims.[61] All of this suggested that the post-Vatican II commitment to promoting human dignity regardless of religious adherence had penetrated the wider church community, which proved capable of transforming it from rhetoric to practice.

Providing alternative information – religion and samizdat *in Eastern Europe*

In most authoritarian political systems the State seeks to control the flow of information reaching the public and to ensure that the messages the population receive help to legitimate and justify their right to rule, by focusing on the successes of the regime and discrediting alternative political visions. Nowhere did this go further than under the communist regimes which instituted a much more thorough-going pre-censorship of the media than was common under traditional authoritarianism, and spent large sums of money on preventing external media from reaching their countries. In response, pro-democratic forces can seek to undermine regimes through the provision of alternative sources of information, by trying to promote a more truthful version of what is going on in their countries – or on occasions an alternative mythology. The extent to which they are successful in creating an alternative reading of political developments has a direct bearing on both the richness of civil society – often said to be characterised by a plurality of social and political voices – and on the possibility of changing the public understanding of the nature of authoritarianism and the possible alternatives to such rule.

In the Soviet bloc the provision of alternative sources of information came to be associated with the Russian word *samizdat*, quite literally translated as 'self-publication'.[62] Emerging in the Soviet Union during the 1950s, the phenomenon of *samizdat* encompassed the production of typewritten manuscripts, initially of poetry and literature, produced by individuals without reference to the state publishing or censorship system. Over time the scope of self-published literature grew as historians provided alternative accounts of Soviet history, human rights activists argued for greater observance of the Soviet constitution, nationalists promoted their causes, and religious activists argued for religious freedom. In Skilling's words,

> In its simplest form it was a means of expressing one's thoughts and feelings openly and honestly, and of communicating these to others. It offered a way in which the individual could maintain his intellectual integrity and achieve a certain degree of freedom under repressive conditions ... *samizdat* served as a vehicle of expression which assured the continuity of national culture ... [helped] to protect and develop a second or independent culture ... served as a channel for the expression of political dissent and opposition and pointed a way for a possible transition to a freer and more humane society.[63]

Though the word came from Russian, the phenomenon spread to other parts of the communist world. Its extent and success varied considerably from country to country, depending upon both the efficiency of the regimes and the nature of the civil society. Perhaps not surprisingly it achieved its greatest influence in Poland and to some extent in Czechoslovakia, where large-scale publishing enterprises emerged that proved increasingly capable of producing larger numbers of banned periodicals, declarations and literary works. At one level, much of this material in and of itself did not directly challenge the regimes, for it encompassed novels, poetry, philosophical and religious discussions that ostensibly had no political import. Yet simply by living independently of the State, those involved carved out an area of personal and communal freedom that posed a challenge to official ideologies, and of course in many cases *samizdat* directly promoted alternative visions of the political order. Even more challenging from the official perspective was the fact that such material was not simply circulated in typescript within these countries, but was sent abroad where it was used to discredit the regimes but also on occasions professionally reproduced and returned to the country of origin in much larger quantities.

In several countries, including the USSR, Poland and Czechoslovakia, religious *samizdat* provided a substantial proportion of the emerging underground literature. In the Soviet Union dissenting Baptists led the way with detailed accounts of religious trials and appeals for religious freedom. From the early 1960s onwards *samizdat* materials from such groups kept a record of their situation as Khrushchev's anti-religious campaign led to the imprisonment of many who refused to ally with the officially recognised Baptist establishment. In subsequent years this record became increasingly detailed, with long verbatim records of trials, conversations with officials, accounts of the fate of young children taken from their parents, details of prison terms and details on several believers killed by the authorities.[64] All this set an example to other religious groups, as a small number of Orthodox priests and activists entered the *samizdat* arena in the late 1960s,[65] closely followed by the Catholics of Lithuania.

In this traditionally Catholic republic, religion provided the basis for an ongoing resistance to Soviet rule throughout the Brezhnev years, as religion reinforced the strong sense of national difference. After 1972 a focus for this documenting of abuses, protests and resistance was provided by the *samizdat* publication *The Chronicle of the Catholic Church of Lithuania*. Though primarily emphasising the travails of the church in the face of an atheist state, right up to the Gorbachev period it provided a major source of news on events within the republic, combining both reportage and opinion, publishing leaked government documents and accounts of religious and political trials, and seeking to ensure that the Vatican did not compromise with the Soviet authorities.[66] For example, Issue No. 66 dated 7 April 1985 included reports on the trial of Fr Jonas Matulionis – charged with organising religious processions that disrupted traffic and sentenced to three years in a labour camp – carried a letter from a priest about the KGB's attempts to recruit him, included various pieces of news from Lithuanian dioceses about petty harassment, reported on several new *samizdat* publications, and gave details on the treatment of Lithuianian religious and political prisoners. At the end it also included as a supplement the text of an unpublished 1974 regulation for local authorities on dealing with religious organisations, i.e. it described official ways of making their lives more difficult.[67] Though at one level simply descriptive, such publications in Lithuania and in other authoritarian contexts helped to circulate information about what was going on within society and to keep resistance alive.

*Creating different forms of social organisation –
base communities in Latin America*

In Brazil the Catholic hierarchy adopted an increasingly radical position as it became apparent that the military regime instituted in 1964 was unlikely to step down in the near future and that in the pursuit of order the military government was not going to be too fussy about the means used. As elsewhere, the Church was divided but, despite this, religious institutions increasingly played a key role in organising or supporting human rights movements, in providing physical spaces in which social movements could meet and organise, in making church radio stations available to publicise human rights abuses, and directly participating in protest activities whether in defence of specific individuals or communities or in demanding political liberalisation. At the same time individual hierarchs sought to empower civil society by encouraging alternative forms of social organisation that were less focused on opposition to the State – though they often were that – than on helping local communities seeking to control their own lives regardless of the actions of the State, and through this to demonstrate that the religious life was not purely 'other-worldly'.

Numerous accounts in the literature provide descriptions of the way in which such activity developed. Mainwaring recounts the story of Novo Iguaca, a large working-class suburb north of Rio de Janeiro where the Church was central to the emergence of social organisation. Here religious leaders moved beyond their traditional inclination to focus on negotiations with political elites to encouraging bottom-up social action. In 1960 Dom Adriano Hipolito became bishop and increasingly encouraged his clergy to develop closer ties to the people, through the development of Bible study groups, base groups and community groups whose primary concerns were religious but who were not afraid to draw out social and political implications from their studies and activities. Growing collaboration developed between the Catholic charity Caritas and secular doctors in creating clinics accessible to, and offering treatment affordable for, the masses. Local neighbourhood groups were allowed to meet in churches which sometimes provided financial support for their activities. Not all priests were happy with these developments, but Bishop Hipolito offered increasingly outspoken leadership and very publicly denounced the authorities for their unwillingness to tackle the death squads who took hundreds of lives in the region during the second half of the 1970s.[68]

For many church writers the emergence of the *communidades eclesiales de base* (CEBs or base communities) offered a new model of social development, rooted in the activities of local communities rather than the clientelist political organisations that tended to dominate when any degree of pluralism emerged in Brazilian society. In their original form these were primarily religious communities of local believers, who gathered to discuss the Bible but also to draw out lessons for their daily lives. Based at the local community level and not dominated by a church hierarchy, in theory these communities 'offered their members the possibility to grow, conduct dialogues and therefore become communities'.[69] Though these communities had emerged prior to Vatican II and Medellín, their activities were reinforced and in some cases radicalised by both the experience of repression and by the rise of liberation theology which informed the activities of many of those involved during the 1970s.

    Church intellectuals who saw 'participation as valuable in its own right' hoped that the CEBs would give people a sense of ownership in decisions that shaped social development and serve as a means of 'promoting social justice'.[70] For Christian Smith their primary roles were in creating 'open spaces' in civil society, fostering an attitude of 'engaged criticism', developing their members' 'organizational, communication and leadership skills' and thus contributing towards democratisation, and giving people a sense of responsibility for their own lives.[71] Training in leadership certainly appears to have been one of the more lasting legacies of these communities and there is some evidence that a number of political activists involved in the trade union movement and then the creation of the Workers Party had a background in the CEB movement.[72] Yet in practice the base communities were never able to fulfil the hopes of the intellectuals, with at their height no more than 4–5 million Brazilians involved – mostly from the respectable poor rather than the genuinely marginalised – and, following the achievement of democracy, many of those involved returned to purely 'spiritual' pursuits or saw members leaking to conventional politics, private pursuits or the charismatic/ Pentecostal movements.[73] In places where social conflict remained sharp, as in some of the shanty towns around large urban centres, and in land disputes in central Brazil, base communities continued to flourish, in many cases as purely religious communities but also in providing leadership (lay or clerical) in ongoing struggles for social justice. In the wider world they provided a model, whether for emulation or adaptation to local need, for those who sought to offer alternative or parallel models of social organisation to those provided by authoritarian states or the consequences of harsh neo-liberal policies. Though their ideological and theological perspectives were very different, the underlying rationale of those involved in the base communities was very similar to that of those promoting a 'parallel society' in Eastern Europe, for in both cases the aim was as much to give people a sense of autonomy and freedom as to oppose the State.

Symbolising resistance – sacred spaces, pilgrimages and funerals

In the struggle against authoritarian regimes religious communities often have far greater access than most other organisations to the symbolic arena, especially – but not only – where the dominant religious tradition has close ties to the historical evolution of the nation. In many countries they have places, myths and symbols associated with the community, places whose significance is or can be extended beyond the narrowly spiritual or ritual. Monasteries or temples may be associated with key historic events or the production of national languages; battlefields may be sacralised as places where martyrs met their end defending the nation; or pilgrimages to sacred places may be given political associations, especially where authoritarian governments are reluctant to prevent what at first glance are simply religious activities, even when those are sometimes transformed into overt demonstrations of protest or resistance.

In Spain during the late Franco years the Catholic Church often provided physical spaces where civil society movements, trade unions or even political parties could meet. One place in particular became a major symbol of resistance during these years, the Benedictine Abbey at Montserrat in Catalonia which served to promote democratic opposition in general and Catalan nationalism in particular. In 1963 the abbot of Montserrat, Aureli Escarré, gave an interview to *Le Monde* rebuking a 'regime which calls itself Christian and which, nevertheless, does not obey the basic principles of Christianity' in so far as it perpetuated the divisions of the civil war period, kept political prisoners and prohibited legitimate expressions of Catalan culture.[74] But it was less the overt opposition than the symbolism of Montserrat, with its very inaccessibility serving in part to encourage the perception of this as a place beyond the reach of Madrid. The Virgin of Montserrat is the patron saint of Catalonia and because the regime was reluctant to challenge Catholic symbolism, devotion to the Virgin and the monastery easily became associated with a resistance to Franco that combined political and national themes. At the same time monks from within the Montserrat community adopted a rather subversive role through their role as school teachers throughout the region, in their classes dropping the odd word of Catalan, or talking about the pre-Franco days. At one level this had more to do with promoting the idea of national autonomy rather than democracy, but it undoubtedly contributed to an opposistional mentality amongst a whole generation.[75]

In Poland pilgrimages to the Black Madonna at the Jasna Gora monastery at Częstochowa attracted tens if not hundreds of thousands and the monastery functioned like Montserrat as a symbol of resistance to alien rule, especially during the martial law period. The Virgin Mary had been declared Queen of Poland in the mid-seventeenth century in the context of the war against Sweden, and in subsequent centuries had come to be associated with defence of the nation against successive occupiers. According to some sources as many as two million came to the shrine during the 1970s, despite the attempt of the authorities to 'arrest' the Virgin, and when Pope John Paul II made his first visit in 1979 over three million people turned up to see 'their' Pope, to engage in religious devotion, and to make clear their opposition to the communist regime.[76] In neighbouring Lithuania pilgrimages and sites also provided the locus of opposition to the regime, most notably the Hill of Crosses near Siauliai which the Soviet authorities destroyed in 1961, 1973 and 1975, but which kept sprouting crosses as people found ways of evading the authorities to plant their crosses. Again, in neither case was this about promoting democratisation, but it was about promoting resistance to authoritarianism, and a desire for the personal and communal freedom that lies at the heart of the notion of democracy.[77]

Other religious rituals that often served as flash points for demonstrations against authoritarian regimes were the funerals of political and religious activists, especially those killed by government agents. In Poland the funeral of Fr Jerzy Popieluszko, brutally murdered by four secret policemen in 1984, was attended by around 600,000 people and turned into a major demonstration against the martial law government. In subsequent years his grave became a site of pilgrimage and a reminder to the authorities that dead priests could sometimes be as troublesome as live ones.[78] Similar events took place in South Africa where slow funeral processions gradually became more boisterous and culminated in sermons condemning the killers and the system that allow them to act with impunity. Quite often these ended with a march on symbols of authority such as police stations or local administrative offices and on occasions these ended with further tragedy as mourners and police clashed, leading in turn to further deaths and more funerals. Peter Walshe describes funerals and memorial meetings as providing a liturgical focus for resistance and notes that in 1985 30,000 attended the funeral of a murdered trade unionist to hear the local bishop speak of 'God's broken heart' in the face of such inhumanity.[79]

In all of these cases, religious institutions were able to provide a symbolic support for political resistance that was not always available to secular opposition groups, with the partial exception, perhaps, of those with a nationalist inspiration. In general they were often far more deeply rooted in local communities beyond the urban centres and had a tradition of providing services for people or nations at key points in their development. In particular they could offer physical symbols and rituals that offered a focus for resistance to the oppressors but also provided religious consolation in the face of oppression and gave some sense that the sacrifices were not in vain.

*   *   *   *   *

The importance of civil society has varied considerably during transition processes as has religion's contribution to the development of independent social spaces. In this chapter we have explored the role of religious organisations in developing a critique of authoritarian political orders and taking this beyond words to organisation in defending human rights, expanding the sphere of freedom of information, and creating alternative forms of social organisation. What has become clear is that during the 1970s and 1980s the Roman Catholic Church in Latin America, and parts of Central Europe and Asia, shifted from a position on public affairs that focused on defending its own interests to one that worked with some notion of a 'common good' rooted in the notion of individual human dignity and societal freedom. In so doing it helped to create a public sphere that was 'parallel' to or independent of the State, where people and groups could speak freely and live as if they were free. At the same time these activities helped to undermine the position of authoritarian regimes by demonstrating that there were other possibilities. Whilst these activities were not always directly concerned with democratisation, many of those involved hoped that the emergence of civil society would have the effect of democratising authoritarian regimes from below.

We will say more later about religious motivations and the factors explaining why some churches became more involved in such activities than others, but we can make a few brief preliminary comments here. Broadly speaking, the extent to which religious communities engaged in critique and civil society-building efforts seems to have depended upon three things. Firstly, the role of leadership and the willingness of religious hierarchs to engage with the political process directly or provide support for those within their churches willing to help build a freer society or defend the victims of authoritarianism. In Chile Cardinal Silva played a central role in creating a theological critique and practical response to human rights abuses, whereas in Argentina church leaders, with a few exceptions, stood to one side and relied on understated private communications rather than public protest or activity. Secondly, religious involvement in this area depends upon the 'resources' available to religious organisations that may strengthen their attempts to influence public affairs. Such 'resources' might be material, for example the possession of land or wealth; they might relate to institutional roles in the provision of education or welfare; they might be symbolic, stemming perhaps from the Church's position as defender of the nation. Finally, much also depended upon the nature of the regime and its willingness to allow religious institutions a role in public life. In Poland, religious activism stemmed from the positions adopted by religious leaderships and the national role of the Catholic Church, but was also made possible by the comparatively 'soft' nature of communist rule in Poland – in a more thoroughly repressive system even a Cardinal Wyszyński might have struggled to make an impression. Nonetheless, where the leadership was willing and the conditions allowed, religious institutions often made a significant contribution to the wider task of building a civil society that was capable of undermining authoritarian regimes and, some hoped, providing a basis for future democratisation.

Notes

1 S. Huntington, *The Third Wave: Democratization in the Late Twentieth Century* (Norman: University of Oklahoma Press, 1991), p. 45.

2 Ibid., p. 73.

3 Ibid, p. 75.

4 Ibid., pp. 73–4.

5 Ibid., pp. 76–85.

6 D. Philpott, 'The Catholic Wave', *Journal of Democracy*, 15:2 (2004), pp. 32–46; the other sources were cited in the introduction.

7 N. Cooper, 'The Church: from crusade to Christianity', in P. Preston (ed.), *Spain in Crisis* (London: Harvester Press, 1976), p. 49.

8 See A. Rhodes, *The Vatican in the Age of Dictators, 1922–45* (London: Hodder and Stoughton, 1973); for a very critical study of the role of Pius XII see J. Cornwall, *Hitler's Pope: The Secret History of Pius XII* (London: Penguin, 2000).

9 W. Callahan, 'The evangelisation of Franco's "New Spain"', in *Church History*, 56 (1987), pp. 491–6; J. Sanchez, *The Spanish Civil War as Religious Tragedy*, (Indiana: University of Notre Dame Press, 1987).

10 V. Perez-Diaz, *The Return of Civil Society* (London: Harvard University Press, 1993), pp. 125–40; Edouard de Blaye, *Franco and the Politics of the New Spain* (London: Penguin, 1976), pp. 409–13.

11 T. Bruneau, *The Political Transformation of the Brazilian Catholic Church* (Cambridge: Cambridge University Press, 1974), pp. 11–51.

12 S. Mainwaring, *The Catholic Church and Politics in Brazil, 1916–85* (Stanford: Stanford University Press, 1986), chapters 2–3.

13 Ibid., p. 83.

14 P. Snow and L. Manzetti, *Political Forces in Argentina* (Westport: Praeger, 1993), pp. 158–61.

15 J. Comblin, *The Church and the National Security State* (New York: Orbis, 1979), pp. 79–81.

16 D. Johnston, 'The churches and apartheid in South Africa', in D. Johnston and C. Sampson (ed.), *Religion, the Missing Dimension in Statecraft* (Oxford: Oxford University Press, 1994), pp. 177–207.

17 F. Lunnon, *Privilege, Persecution and Prophecy: The Catholic Church in Spain, 1875–1975* (Oxford: Clarendon Press, 1987), p. 245.

18 On this controversial bishop see Jose de Broucker, *Dom Helder Camara: The Violence of a Peacemaker* (New York: Orbis, 1970).

19 The statement issued by the bishops can be found at: http://personal .stthomas.edu/gwschlabach/docs/medellin.htm (accessed 10 March 2007).

20 G. Gutiérriz, *A Theology of Liberation:Liberation and Faith* (London: SCM, 1988).

21 Much of the literature on liberation theology is coloured by the author's position on the barricades, but a nuanced discussion which points to both positive and negative elements can be found in P. Sigmund, *Liberation Theology at the Crossroads: Democracy or Revolution* (New York, Oxford University Press, 1990).

22 *The Tablet*, 12 October 1985; Johnston, 'The churches and apartheid in

South Africa', pp. 193–4.

23 A. Boesak, *Black and Reformed : Apartheid, Liberation, and the Calvinist Tradition* (New York: Orbis, 1984).

24 Cooper, 'The Church: from crusade to Christianity', pp. 73–4.

25 R. Goeckel, *The Lutheran Church and the East German State: Political Conflict and Change under Ulbricht and Honecker* (Ithaca: Cornell University Press, 1990), pp. 255ff.

26 F. Blachnicki, 'A theology of liberation – in the spirit', *Religion in Communist Lands*, 12:2 (1984), pp. 157–67.

27 A. Brassloff, *Religion and Politics in Spain: The Spanish Church in Transition, 1962–96* (London: Macmillan, 1998), pp. 28–9.

28 De Blaye, *Franco and the Politics of the New Spain*, p. 416.

29 Cooper, 'The Church: from crusade to Christianity', pp. 76–8.

30 Mainwaring, *The Catholic Church and Politics in Brazil*, p. 132.

31 R. Della Cava, 'The "People's Church", the Vatican and *Aberatura*', in A. Stepan (ed.), *Democratizing Brazil: Problems of Transition and Consolidation* (Oxford: Oxford University Press, 1989), p. 147.

32 'Notes on church and state', *Journal of Church and State*, 18:1 (1976), p. 151.

33 J. Casanova, *Public Religions in the Modern World* (Chicago: Chicago University Press, 1994), p. 121.

34 *The Tablet*, 29 September 1979.

35 'Notes on church and state', *Journal of Church and State*, 19:3 (1977), pp. 609–10.

36 J. Klaiber, *The Church, Dictatorships and Democracy in Latin America* (New York: Orbis, 1998), pp. 81–2.

37 Snow and Manzetti, *Political Forces in Argentina*, pp. 158–61.

38 J. Klaiber, *The Church, Dictatorships and Democracy in Latin America* (New York: Orbis, 1998), pp. 52–3; I remember a conversation I had in the late 1970s with an evangelical missionary working in Brazil who described the criticisms of the military regimes as coming from communists and leftist Catholics, and seemed pleased that such regimes were restoring order. One would like to think that he was not aware of (or dismissed as propaganda) the well-documented abuse of human rights being instigated by such regimes.

39 *The Tablet*, 27 February 1984.

40 D. Throup, 'Render unto Caesar the things that are Caesar's: the politics of church–state conflict in Kenya, 1978–1990', in H. Hansen and M. Twaddle (ed.), *Religion and Politics in East Africa* (London: James Currey, 1995), p. 151.

41 Quoted in Johnston, 'The churches and apartheid in South Africa', p. 189.

42 K. Ross, 'Not catalyst but ferment: the distinctive contribution of the churches to political reform in Malawi, 1992–93', in P. Gifford (ed.), *The Christian Churches and the Democratisation of Africa* (Leiden: E. J. Brill, 1995), pp. 99–100; Throup, 'Render unto Caesar the things that are Caesar's', p. 151.

43 A. Bromke, 'A new juncture in Poland', *Problems of Communism*, No. 5 (1976), p. 11.

44 P. Sigmund, *Liberation Theology at the Crossroads: Democracy or Revolution?* (Oxford: Oxford University Press, 1990), p. 75.

45 A. Hennelly (ed.), *Liberation Theology: A Documentary History* (New York: Orbis, 1992), p. 93.

46 On the CEBs see Mainwaring, *The Catholic Church and Politics in Brazil* chapter 9; and essays by Smith, Adriance and Cavendish in W. Swatos (ed.), *Religion and Democracy in Latin America* (New Brunswick: Transaction Publishers, 1995).

47 Cooper, 'The Church: from crusade to Christianity'.

48 Casanova, *Public Religions in the Modern World*, pp. 100 and 107.

49 On these debates see J. Grugel, *Democratization: A Critical Introduction* (London: Palgrave, 2002), pp. 46–67; D. Potter *et al.* (ed.), *Democratization* (Cambridge: Polity Press, 1997), pp. 1–40.

50 Grugel, *Democratization*, p. 92.

51 For general discussions of the concept see: J. Hall (ed.), *Civil Society: Theory, History, Comparison* (Cambridge: Polity Press, 1995); J. Alexander (ed.), *Real Civil Societies: Dilemmas of Institutionalization* (London: Sage, 1998).

52 It might be worth noting here that several writers stress that the notion of a civil society is very much a Western construct that might not easily apply to other parts of the world. Hence Chris Hann's preference for a definition that was looser and referred to 'the moral community, to the problems of accountability, trust and co-operation that all groups face'. Quoted in D. Herbert, *Religion and Civil Society – Rethinking Public Religion in the Contemporary World* (Aldershot: Ashgate, 2003), p. 86.

53 N. Chazan *et al.*, *Politics and Society in Contemporary Africa* (Boulder: Lynne Reinner, 1999), p. 99.

54 Quoted in T. Quigley, 'The Chilean coup, the Church and the human rights movement', *America*, 11 February 2002, at http://web7. infotrac .galegroup.com/itw/infomark/624/3/60178090w7/purl=rc1_EAIM_0 (accessed 3 March 2005).

55 Klaiber, *The Church, Dictatorships and Democracy in Latin America*, pp. 50–1.

56 Quoted in M. Aguilar, *A Social History of the Catholic Church in Chile, Volume I: The First Period of the Pinochet Government, 1973–80* (Lewiston: The Edwin Mellen Press, 2004), p. 49.

57 Ibid., pp. 62–5.

58 Klaiber, *The Church, Dictatorships and Democracy in Latin America*, pp. 51–2.

59 Aguilar, *A Social History of the Catholic Church in Chile*, pp. 168–75.

60 E. Cleary, *The Struggle for Human Rights in Latin America* (Westport: Greenwood Press, 1997), p. 46.

61 P. Walshe, 'South Africa, prophetic Christianity and the liberation movement', *Journal of Modern African Studies*, 29. 1 (1991), pp. 43–8.

62 For an overview of the phenomenon see H. Gordon Skilling, *Samizdat and an Independent Society in Central and Eastern Europe* (London: Macmillan, 1989).

63 Ibid., p. 17.

64 See M. Bourdeaux, *Religious Ferment in Russia* (London: Macmillan, 1968).

65 M. Bourdeaux, *Patriarchs and Prophets* (London: Macmillan, 1970).

66 An overview of its activities can be found in V. Stanley Vardys, *The Catholic Church, Dissent and Nationality in Soviet Lithuania* (New York: East European Quarterly, 1978); an account relying on extensive extracts can be found in M. Bourdeaux, *Land of Crosses –The Struggle for Religious Freedom in Lithuania, 1939–78* (Devon: Augustine Publishing Co., 1979).

67 *Chronicle of the Catholic Church in Lithuania*, No. 66, 7 April 1985 (English translations of each edition of the *Chronicle* were published by Lithuanian Catholic Religious Aid in New York).

68 S. Mainwaring, *The Catholic Church and Politics in Brazil*, pp. 182ff.; M. Vasquez, *The Brazilian Popular Church and the Crisis of Modernity* (Cambridge: Cambridge University Press, 1997), p. 129.

69 T. Bruneau, 'Basic Christian communities in Latin America', in D. Levine (ed.), *Churches and Politics in Latin America* (London: Sage, 1979), p. 271.

70 Mainwaring, *The Catholic Church and Politics in Brazil*, p. 230.

71 C. Smith, 'The spirit and democracy: base communities, Protestantism, and democratization in Latin America', in Swatos, *Religion and Democracy in Latin America*, pp. 1–26.

72 Vasquez, *The Brazilian Popular Church and the Crisis of Modernity*, chapter 6.

73 Ibid., pp. 57–63; W. Hewitt, 'The changing of the guard: transformations in the politico-religious attitudes and behaviour of CENB members in Sao Paulo, 1984–93', *Journal of Church and State*, 38:1 (1996), pp. 115–36.

74 W. Callahan, *The Catholic Church in Spain, 1875–98* (Washington DC: Catholic University Press of America, 2000), p. 507. Though the Church defended the abbot, in 1965 the Vatican was persuaded to transfer him to another position.

75 H. Johnston, 'Towards an explanation of church opposition to authoritarian regimes: religio-oppositional sub-cultures in Poland and Catalonia', *Journal for the Scientific Study of Religion*, 28:4 (1989), pp. 499, 502–4.

76 Ibid., p. 499.

77 Bourdeaux, *Land of Crosses*, pp. 207–12.

78 T. Garton Ash, *The Polish Revolution* (London: Granta Books, 1991), p. 361.

79 Walshe, 'South Africa, prophetic Christianity and the liberation movement', p. 54; cf. http://cain.ulst.ac.uk/dd/report8/report8k.htm (accessed 20 June 2005).

4

The Catholic 'third wave': creating a new order

If the focus of the previous chapter was essentially negative, exploring ways in which religious organisations may have helped to undermine authoritarian regimes, the emphasis gradually shifts here to the issue of 'what happens next'. We shall examine in particular the role of religious leaders, who face the problem of combining prophetic denunciation of injustice with pragmatic concerns about keeping their often divided flock united and maintaining lines of communication with the political order. We then turn to some of the 'structural-situational' factors helping to determine religious influence, including the relationship of religious actors to other sectors of civil society and opposition, the special issues raised where religious and national identity are closely related, and the peculiarly Catholic dynamic arising from the fact that this is the oldest transnational organisation in the world. This takes us directly into the transition process, as some of these factors can help to determine the role played by religious actors in the final replacement of authoritarian regimes. This role may become central in times of transition, as authoritarian leaders seek to promote reform or at least ensure that the transition comes at minimal cost to their own position. At key moments religious leaders can provide the spark that brings down a regime, but they may also be involved in delicate negotiations that help to effect a peaceful transition. And in a couple of cases religious leaders have found themselves directly presiding over transitional constitutional orders. In the final empirical section we look at some of the challenges that have faced religious communities as they have to come to terms with new democratic political orders that may be accompanied by a decline in their own power and influence. The chapter concludes by returning to the issue of how we explain the predominantly Catholic contribution to the 'third wave' and why if, as Huntington and others suggest, Vatican II was crucial, individual national hierarchies varied considerably in their engagement with the democratisation process.

Charisma and caution: the dilemmas of religious leadership

Many studies of democratisation processes place a particular emphasis on the role of elites in bringing about change, focusing on their involvement in negotiating pacts aimed at bringing about an orderly transition and then in maintaining some form of consensus during the process to ensure the successful embedding of democratic structures and practices. In many of the countries whose experience we have discussed, a crucial factor in shaping religious responses to authoritarianism has been the role of leadership. Put simply, churches are most likely to promote democratisation in countries where national religious leaderships or a few key religious leaders choose to take a public stand on the issue of political change. The role that religious elites can play varies considerably depending upon context, upon their status within religious communities and ability to take their flocks with them, and on the respect accorded to religious leaders within the wider society. Ironically, it is less dependent upon whether religious organisations are themselves democratic, and the most pro-active leadership has generally been found in the more hierarchical churches where the role of leadership is important. Much also depends upon the attitude of the authoritarian regime, for in those systems ostensibly committed to 'strengthening Christian civilisation' it may be much harder to attack religious leaders, though in countries such as Chile and South Africa there was always the option of favouring one religious group over another. By way of contrast, communist authorities with their commitment to anti-religion could safely sideline or ignore leading clerics, except perhaps in Poland where the Catholic Church was able to retain its social authority. Alongside the context, it is worth noting that religious leadership could come in a variety of forms, with the charismatic and prophetic style tending to catch the headlines but sometimes the pragmatic or cautious proving just as successful. Speeches and pastoral messages may proclaim the need for religious and civil rights, but these same leaders – unless completely ostracised by the political order – often engage in regular contacts with regime spokesmen.

This section simply points to a number of relatively well-known individuals and outlines some of the ways in which they sought to promote political change. In many cases their initial concern was with defending the interests of the institutions, and most started their clerical lives with little interest or enthusiasm for politics and only gradually, and sometimes painfully, found themselves thrust into the political limelight. Amongst these was Archbishop Paulo Arns of São Paulo, a relatively conservative bishop radicalised by visiting a detention centre and discovering the pervasiveness of torture. In consequence, in late 1971 he helped to set up a Justice and Peace Commission that would investigate allegations of torture or abuse and seek legal redress for the victims.[1] At the same time he increasingly used the rhetoric of the liberationists in favouring the 'preferential option for the poor', making use of the diocesan radio to publicise mistreatment of the poor or the imprisoned, paying regular visits to prisons and mediating with officials. In 1973 he sold the large episcopal residence and use the profits to build community centres in peripheral areas, and distributed 150,000 copies of the UN Declaration on Human Rights.[2] During 1975 he acquired a national prominence after holding an ecumenical Mass for the Jewish journalist Vladimir Herzog who had died in police custody after writing material critical of the military regime.[3]

Perhaps the most instinctively cautious, but also the most stubborn, of these leaders was Poland's Cardinal Stefan Wyszyński whom secular dissident Adam Michnik praised for his 'often lonely but always unyielding defence … of freedom, tolerance and the rights of man'.[4] Appointed Archbishop of Warsaw in 1949, it was Wyszyński who had to lead the church into the new communist era at a time when nearly 300 priests were in prison. From 1953–56 he too was confined and his release was marked by public demonstrations which gave warning to the regime that it faced a very formidable opponent with strong public backing. In the first instance they tried to persuade him to set up a national church independent of the Vatican, but it soon became apparent that this was not the man to make such deals. For much of the 1950s and 1960s he saw his role primarily in terms of fighting for the institutional and spiritual rights of the Catholic Church in the new order. By the 1970s these were looking slightly more secure, at least relative to the position of co-believers in other communist lands, and by the early 1970s Wyszyński had come to see the need to go beyond institutional defence to a much broader concern with human rights. During this decade he started to speak more openly about human rights for all and in 1974 called for 'a courageous defence of the right to free association as well as rights to the freedom of the press, expression of opinion'.[5]

Following the repression of workers' demonstrations in 1976 the cardinal strongly backed those priests and religious activists who became involved in defending the victims of repression and their families, and also wider activities concerned with promoting human rights. Equally he welcomed the Solidarity movement and in February 1980 told a plenary council of the Polish bishops that:

> We must bring truth back into our society, not only into political organisations and the mass media, but also into our everyday life. It should be the fundamental duty of every Pole to witness openly to his convictions. We realise that this calls for tremendous civil courage and a strong will, but it is the only way to restore public confidence.[6]

Wyszyński's legitimacy and authority came from his firm and repeated association of the Church with the Polish nation, and in successive speeches he pointed to the historic role of his institution in defending national interests or in providing a voice for the people in the face of oppression. His concern throughout was with the interests of the Church but it was also fed by a strong conviction that to survive Poland had to be Catholic, and he said little about the type of regime he hoped to see emerge, beyond one that respected human dignity. He was a cautious and pragmatic individual, unbending on principle, but also concerned that radical elements within the Church and the secular opposition should not act in ways that jeopardised Polish freedom by provoking their more powerful Soviet neighbour.[7]

Cardinal Vincente Enrique y Tarancón of Madrid was in also in many respects a cautious leader, but one who emerged in a very different context. Whereas his Polish counterpart had to struggle against a regime hostile to religion, the Spanish Catholic Church in the post-civil war period was ostensibly a privileged institution and a central institutional pillar of the Francoist regime. In return for church support the government guaranteed the Catholic Church a near complete religious monopoly and provided financial backing for its welfare and educational activities. For all this, by the 1950s there were individual clerics beginning to find this relationship a constraint, as it had not contributed to a significant evangelisation of the population nor enabled the Church to serve the wider population. As a young clergyman Tarancón was very involved in social activism, castigating the authorities for their lack of concern for the poor during the 1950s and antagonising episcopal colleagues by his critique of Spain's formal religiosity which disguised the lack of real spiritual depth.[8] In 1971 Tarancón was elected president of the National Conference of Bishops, and under his leadership the Church openly committed itself to the campaign for liberalisation, in the process upsetting the Francoist establishment which saw a traditional ally deserting the regime. Taking up the archbishop's throne in Madrid in early 1972 he declared that 'during several centuries a symbiosis has developed in Spain between the Church and Politics. This long phase is now at an end, and will be replaced by a phase of independence of the Church in relation to the state'.[9] As a consequence of this changing position a growing number of religious activists found themselves joining the democratic opposition, participating in civil society activities, and criticising official policies on a variety of issues, and by the mid-1970s Tarancón had become one the of the most hated figures within the Francoist establishment, subject to abuse and even calls for his execution on one occasion. For all this he continued to lead from what some described as the 'radical centre' but, whereas the focus of Stefan Wyszyiński was primarily on national defence, Tarancón made clear his belief that democracy was the only political solution to Spain's needs, though after 1975 he was to express concern at some of its consequences.

Oscar Romero, Archbishop of San Salvador from 1977–80,

was an unlikely leader and an unlikely martyr. When he first became an auxiliary bishop in 1970 many had seen him as an essentially conservative figure who appeared more concerned with efficient administration than becoming a public figure. A man who took on board the teachings of Vatican II without following those of his contemporaries who gave it a more radical slant, Bishop Romero's transformation was rather like that of Cardinal Arns in being initiated by experience. In 1977 a radical priest known to him was murdered and the authorities proved reluctant to mount an enquiry. As he investigated this particular death Romero became more aware of the activities of the death squads in his country, which appeared committed to defending the interests of the powerful and wealthy by violent means. Opponents were dismissed as 'communists' who deserved no more consideration than vermin. In response Archbishop Romero called on soldiers not to obey their orders if it involved killing civilians, and sought to persuade the government to act more seriously in curbing the activities of what were effectively licensed killers. Increasingly he encouraged those within the Church who documented the abuse of rights and his regular Sunday sermons and radio broadcasts spoke out about the ongoing disappearance of men and women, most of whom were executed without reference to the judicial process. Following the murder of several priests and religious activists Romero became ever more outspoken, and in 1979 on a visit to Rome gave Pope John Paul II seven dossiers outlining the problems emerging in his country. Enjoying only limited support from some of his bishops, and under constant attack from regime spokesmen and the mass media, he was shot dead whilst celebrating Mass in March 1980.[10]

In Chile Cardinal Raúl Silva Henríquez was another unlikely regime critic, a man very much part of the Chilean social and political elite though one whose theological understanding was strongly influenced by the changes introduced at Vatican II. Very much in sympathy with the policies of the Christian Democrats, he also managed to maintain cordial relations with President Allende despite some tensions in Church–State relations. Following the military coup in 1973 a few bishops supported the takeover, but the Chilean Church's initial position was cautious, stressing the need for calm and order but also calling on the regime to respect the fallen. Yet, as we have already seen, Cardinal Silva very quickly became aware that order was being accompanied by significant human rights abuses and, as we saw in the last chapter, he helped to create a series of organisations that would seek to defend the rights of those arrested or victimised by the regime, as well as pursue the issue of torture, disappearances and extra-judicial killings.[11] This was not an instinctively confrontational individual or a radical liberation theologian – he had been very critical of the Christians for Socialism movement during the 1970s – but a moderate clergyman who could not keep silent in the face of injustice and who by speaking out gave the victims of the new order a sense that they did have a protector in the person of the Church.

What is clear from all these sketches is that inspirational leadership often came from very traditional religious leaders, people who were very much part of the mainstream of their religious organisations but who found themselves in leadership positions during unsettled times. In virtually every case their public prominence arose out of their perception of injustice, which in turn was shaped by their theological and, in the Polish case, national understandings. Most were often reluctant political actors, men who might have been happier pursuing the institutional and spiritual demands of the faith and the needs of their churches. At the same time all, with varying degrees of success, attempted to maintain some form of relationship with the state authorities, to act from within as well as without. More importantly, however, was their role in providing a voice for the voiceless, as in several cases without their leadership oppressive policies would have gone unopposed at home and unremarked abroad. In this sense they often acted in ways that served to undermine authoritarian regimes and then to promote the establishment of democracy.

Structural-situational factors

Working with society and nation

The potential influence of religious organisations was strengthened when religious leaders proved willing to engage with the public realm, but it was also made easier when certain 'situational' factors came into play, in particular when they possessed or were able to develop links to the wider society. In many of the cases we have discussed there was a growing willingness on the part of religious organisations to come to the defence of others unjustly persecuted and to develop relationships with non-religious critics of the regime. This might entail collaboration on specific tasks, the blessing of secular activities, or permitting religious space to be used for independent activities, even where some of these might not enjoy the approval of the churches or their members. In several Central European countries religious opening to the secular world was closely linked to nationalism, as the churches became the chief defenders of the national tradition in the face of external threats or foreign occupation.

Many of these trends were exemplified in the case of Poland. Whilst the Polish Catholic Church's primary concern in the initial years of communist rule was with ensuring its own survival, by the mid-1970s it had increasingly taken on a role as defender of both the individual and the nation. This was evident both in the rhetoric of leading bishops and in practical actions taken in response to the shooting of demonstrating workers in 1976. Prior to then the Church had often protested against repression, as in 1970–71, without actively taking up the cause of the workers. But in 1976 the Church gave its active support to the Workers' Defence Committee, a group set up to provide legal support for those arrested, and financial support for the families of those imprisoned, and delegated Fr Jan Zieja to sit on its executive body.[12] The other role the Church increasingly adopted from the 1970s onwards was that of defender of the nation in the face of external dominance but in ways that did not threaten to bring down the full might of Soviet power. Taras notes that:

> In Poland Catholicism … fostered internal critique not only because it was well established in Polish culture, but also because it did not legitimate any radical opposition to the Soviet backed regime. Catholics sought for a definition of a realist policy, i.e. a policy that would not jeopardise the existence of nation and state. The policy of forcing evolutionary change by increasing social pressures owes a great deal to the involvement of Catholicism in politics.[13]

And as he suggests, this growing involvement in politics rarely took the form of direct confrontation with the authorities but rather a gradual carving out of a social space independent of the State in which society could begin to breathe. In so doing the Church contributed towards the development of civil society, in Herbert's words by (a) providing institutional space, (b) providing a symbolic resource or fund of collective memories which were mobilised against the official ideology, (c) functioning as an institutional and ideological connection with an international order, and (d) functioning as an intellectual force from which opposition thinking and identities could be self-consciously constructed.[14]

During the pre-Solidarity period, following the linking up of Church, workers and intellectuals after the 1976 events, the church authorities made space available for those organising non-sanctioned activities, as in the early summer of 1977 when a hunger strike was held at St Martin's church in Warsaw to put pressure on the authorities to release those arrested in 1976 as well as those arrested for trying to help them. As one striker put it, the church was a place of safety but more importantly a place where people do not lie.[15] Churches were also used to hold exhibitions, conduct group meetings and to host the seminars of the 'flying university' which sought to provide access to bodies of knowledge or critical perspectives not made available in official educational institutions. All of this was reinforced by the election of Karol Wotyła to the papal throne in October 1978 which emboldened the Church and made it much harder for the regime to tackle church opposition. Though the primary causes of the worker unrest emerging in 1980 may have been economic, the Pope's first visit to his homeland in 1979 was described by some as equivalent to a 'psychological earthquake', because he said in public what many had said in private for so long, and broke the cycle of fear and rekindled national consciousness and pride.[16]

During the Solidarity period religious symbols decorated virtually every workers' demonstration and workplace Masses became commonplace. After General Jaruzelski imposed martial law, and after an initially ambiguous reaction from Cardinal Glemp, the Church returned to its role of protecting civil society. Secular dissident Jan Lipski noted that:

> Today in Poland only the Church lives an authentically free life under the tolerance of the authorities. December 1981 further strengthened the influence and authority of the Church, along with its real potential for focusing social energies ... The Church often donates its organisational, housing and other facilities for social, educational and cultural work.[17]

In similar vein Adam Michnik noted church pulpits as 'the only place where language has not been defiled – true words are spoken about the national condition'.[18] Once again individual parish priests played an active role in seeking to defend the accused, meet the pastoral needs of the detained and the material needs of their families, and opened church buildings for acts of defiance. On occasions the hierarchy was wary of more outspoken activities and initially sought to curb the more radical critique offered by priests such as Jerzy Popiełuszko who held regular Masses for the nation and offered forthright criticisms of the martial law regime. Yet despite its avoidance of an overtly critical position during the first years of martial law, and despite the formal denunciations coming from Rome, Catholic charities backed by the episcopate provided over 150,000 tons of food aid in 1981–85 and continued to take up individual cases of injustice. All of these activities were aimed not just at defending religious interests or even the general defence of human rights, but at helping Polish society to breathe more freely. Equally, the ability of the Catholic Church to play the 'defender of the nation' role was aided by the fact that the 'occupying' power was perceived to be of a different religious tradition – whether that be perceived as Orthodox or communist.

Mobilising international resources

Whilst the key role of religious organisations lay in the leadership and support for change they provided at the domestic level, the degree of their influence was also affected by international factors and, in particular, their ability to call upon transnational support for their activities in critiquing authoritarianism or promoting democratisation. Clearly the Roman Catholic Church, as an institution with an extensive experience and tradition of global activity, was at an advantage here, though other religious communities were on occasions able to draw on international support for their activities. This was perhaps most notable in the campaign against apartheid where religious activists successfully took their case to inter-church bodies such as the World Council of Churches (WCC), which comprised a variety of Protestant and Orthodox churches. From the late 1960s onwards the WCC played an active role in developing various programmes to combat racism that were aimed specifically at the South African regime, and in 1970 it took the controversial decision to provide humanitarian aid for liberation movements. Not all of the Council's constituents accepted this proposal, especially when it became apparent that at least some of the funding might leak to military activity. There was also a certain suspicion generated by the speed with which the WCC proved willing to condemn South Africa or Israel, compared to its ambiguous role in dealing with communist regimes. For all this the WCC persisted in seeking ways to end apartheid and mobilised church opinion in favour of the campaign for majority rule. In pursuit of these causes it was joined by various other Protestant groups, including the World Alliance of Reformed Churches which in 1982 condemned apartheid as heresy and in the early 1990s supported Malawi's Presbyterian Church leaders in their campaign for human rights in Malawi.[19] Other Protestant groups were more wary of political involvement, with most evangelical groups adopting a more quietist approach. In the USA, however, the Christian Right was actively involved in supporting the Contra campaign in Nicaragua, whilst the Central American director of Campus Crusade for Christ stressed that the 'struggle in which we are engaged not only in Central America, but in the whole world, is an ideological one' aimed at undermining communism through discrediting liberation theology and liberal pastors.[20] In so far as engaging with this 'greater task' meant co-operating with authoritarian regimes and ignoring human rights abuses, such activities made little direct contribution to democratisation.

In the case of the Roman Catholic Church we have already noted the centrality of the Second Vatican Council to the changing theological and political perspectives of national hierarchies, but it also backed this up with support at the international level.[21] This is not the place to explore the diplomatic structures of the Roman Catholic Church, beyond simply noting a few key structural features that may affect its ability to influence processes of democratisation. In particular it should be stressed that it is the Holy See, based in the Vatican City State, which is the body that carries out diplomatic activity and within the Holy See the departmental titles of the bodies which have engaged in this activity have changed over time. Most important for our purposes is the role of papal legates or nuncios who are formally enjoined to ensure unity between Rome and local churches, and who play a key role both in representing the international Church to nation-states but who are also are consulted in the process of appointing local bishops. And these choices can help to shape the very nature of the hierarchy and in turn influence their attitude to political life.[22]

The stance of the Holy See can be crucial in determining whether national hierarchies will gain international support when they make interventions in the public sphere. After Vatican II local bishops and priests who spoke out on behalf of human rights would, at least in theory, have the support of the international Church, and this in turn made it far harder for authoritarian governments simply to dismiss them as 'communist sympathisers' or as 'naive'. The stance adopted by the Vatican could often send a clear signal of where its sympathies lay, as happened in Spain during the 1960s when Pope Paul VI urged the Spanish bishops to greater boldness in promoting social justice and human rights. This led to tensions with General Franco who saw himself as the defender of Catholic Spain, and had practical consequences when he refused to appoint Vatican-approved bishops to vacant dioceses.[23] In similar vein, following the 1973 military coup in Chile the Pope publicly expressed his concern at the reported human rights abuses in that country, a stance that was supported by American bishops and several Protestant churches.[24]

At the institutional level the Vatican could bring various pressures to bear, although sometimes these could be double-edged. For example, in many Latin American countries a key role was played by foreign priests and religious, whether from Europe or America. Such individuals, often influenced by their European theological education and their work in the toughest parishes, often found themselves at odds with the authorities when they sought to look after the interests of their parishioners. In some countries these priests were essential to the pastoral needs of the local churches, but at the same time they were very vulnerable. On the one hand, if they were assaulted or killed it provoked outrage in the home country, but on the other, as foreigners they could more easily be characterised as troublemakers and expelled from the country, thus leaving parishes without any pastoral care. Visiting religious delegations were harder to deal with, because they were rarely convinced by government prepared meetings, and sought to engage directly with human rights activists or victims. On their return home they often published critical reports that served to undermine the position of these regimes abroad. In countries where the authoritarian regime claimed to be Catholic, simply refusing access to such groups was rarely an option. More problematic was controlling financial support given to human rights or pro-democracy groups by the churches, as many religious charities saw this as part of their natural work. For example, the Chilean churches received substantial financial support during the 1970s, with US Catholic organisations raising $34 million and the European churches raising $32 million, some of which went to the Vicariate of Solidarity, much to the annoyance of General Pinochet.[25]

Brian Smith points out that in the Chilean case there was extensive international Catholic involvement after 1973 as:

> Vatican and international Episcopal statements all provided strong legitimation for involvement in the promotion of human rights by national churches. Moral and political support has been given by these international Church groups to the Chilean Church's particular efforts in this area. At the regional level of Latin America itself the Latin American Episcopal Conference has focused attention on the dangers of the national security state and has emphasised the Church's responsibility to oppose it. What has been even more important has been the significant increase of financial assistance since the coup from international ecclesiastical and secular sources.[26]

Other sources have similarly noted the extensive involvement of German Catholic organisations in supporting welfare and human rights projects in Latin America, with over DM130m going to Brazil and Chile in the period 1962–77.[27]

Finally, in several of the democratising countries a key role was played by the papal nuncio, who represents the papacy in all those countries with which the Vatican has a formal relationship. Much depended upon the character of the individual occupying this position, and their stance on political involvement. For example, in Portugal the nuncio adopted a conservative position and the Church was at the margins of the process of political change, whereas in Spain the more activist role of Archbishop Tarancón was reinforced by the support of the nuncio. Here, where General Franco had the right to block diocesan Episcopal appointments, the nuncio Cardinal Dadaglio supported Tarancón in appointing a whole series of auxiliary bishops who were supportive of political change and had more open attitudes on issues such as religious liberty and human rights.[28] We might also note the case of Chile where, as we shall see, the papal nuncio made his residence available for a series of discussions amongst various opposition groups, and also for talks between them and government representatives. Yet we should also note that in some areas the Vatican's representative sought to restrain political activity, as in the Philippines where even in early 1986 the nuncio sought to prevent the Church raising questions about the recent presidential elections.[29] So the international Church's stance was by no means always on the side of democratisation, but by and large after Vatican II the institution's centre of gravity shifted and this led it as a general rule to support local activity aimed at promoting human dignity or social justice.

This role was both reinforced and qualified with the election in October 1978 of Pope John Paul II, a man with personal experience of authoritarian government, albeit of a peculiar sort, and with strong views on how best to handle such regimes. This did not necessarily entail outright confrontation on all fronts, but did mean the maintenance of a firm position in defence of core values and to some extent of core institutional interests. In so far as the question of human rights was concerned the new Catholic leader was an unashamed proponent of Vatican II teachings, though he was equally concerned to promote traditional Catholic teachings on sexuality, reproduction and leadership roles within the Church. In consequence some have argued that that whilst his commitment to human rights could not be questioned, his commitment to democracy was always secondary and dependent upon the moral choices that would be made by democratic governments. In Hehir's words his style was good at pushing for change but for some he came across as 'too sure, too impatient, and immune to compromise on forging a civil consensus' in divided, post-transitional societies.[30] Yet it has also been noted that on economic issues he could also promote a critical agenda that was sceptical about unfettered capitalism and the pursuit of individual gain, and that in the last period of his office Pope John Paul II was an active opponent of warfare as the solution to international conflict.

For our purposes, however, it is his contribution to the overthrow of authoritarian regimes that is of primary interest. In the context of Latin America one might argue that his role was largely secondary to that of local religious organisations, supportive rather than determinative. Here he made clear his suspicion of radical theologians who focused on social justice or advocated alliance with revolutionary groups. Yes, the Church should be involved in dealing with social problems, but not to the extent of neglecting its core spiritual tasks – a distinction he believed that many liberation theologians failed to see. Despite these reservations he rarely lost an opportunity to admonish Latin American leaders about their human rights records, though he was always sensitive to local circumstances. For example, his arrival in Chile in April 1987 followed an attempt on Pinochet's life and a growing polarisation within society, and the church hierarchy sought to ensure that the visit would not be politicised by state or opposition. Nonetheless, though rejecting violence Pope John Paul II used the visit to call for reconciliation, forgiveness of one's enemies and the restoration of democratic institutions. For some his willingness to meet with Pinochet was regrettable, but his own position was that reconciliation required all sides talking to each other.[31]

If the positions he adopted in Latin America often seemed traditional in countries with considerable experience of social action, in the communist world he appeared a dangerous radical. The Kremlin was clearly uneasy with his selection and the Central Committee archives in Moscow include a series of files containing reports from security operatives throughout the Soviet bloc assessing his likely impact upon both Catholic and wider populations, as well as recommending measures to neutralise his influence.[32] Yet clearly the immediate impact of his election on Poland and several of the traditionally Catholic countries was considerable, and we have already noted elsewhere the impact of his first visit to Poland in 1979 which gave many people the courage to join the Solidarity movement which emerged in the following year. His calls for people to live truthful lives fell on receptive ears during those crucial years and provided the social bedrock for the later changes that would be made possible by the emergence of a reforming leader in Moscow.

Negotiating transition

The popular image of religious leaders during times of change focuses primarily on their prophetic role, denouncing injustice, protecting the victims of human rights abuses and propounding their message to the world's media. Yet in practice their role was often much wider, rooted in their position as part of the traditional social establishment or as legitimate representatives of substantial faith or even national communities. While they may have confronted government leaders, most of the figures we have mentioned sought to keep open channels of communication with authoritarian regimes, whether with the leaders of those polities or with those seen as 'moderates' within them. At the same time they often offered their services to mediate between different groups in the opposition in an effort to ensure the creation of a unified 'shadow government'. For their part government leaders, realising the need for social support or moderate change, will want to keep contact with groups that are generally not considered 'extremist'. In consequence religious leaders have sometimes been able to play a role in bringing government and opposition together (Chile), in moderating transition talks (Poland), in monitoring the process of change (Chile, Poland, Zambia) or even in presiding over transitional government arrangements (Benin).

The Philippines presents a special case in some respects, in so far as at a crisis point in the conflict between the Marcos regime and the opposition, Cardinal Sin, the leader of the Catholic Church, acted decisively to obstruct the regime and thus effectively ensured its downfall. Originally the cardinal had been a supporter of Ferdinand Marcos and had tried to influence the regime from within, but gradually, under the impact of changes within Catholic thinking as well as under pressure from within his own Church, his position had changed considerably. When President Marcos first declared martial law in September 1972 several churchmen within the Catholic Church and the mainstream Protestant churches condemned it as immoral, though the evangelicals tended to support the president right up until 1986. But with growing attacks on church institutions as well as high levels of corruption, Cardinal Sin and his colleagues increasingly distanced themselves from the regime from the late 1970s onwards.[33] The breaking point came in 1983 following the assassination of Senator Aquino which provoked mass protests and reportedly led some two million people to follow his funeral procession. Cardinal Sin pointedly refused to join the government commission of enquiry and made clear who he thought was responsible for the murder. A key role during all these events was played by the Catholic radio station *Veritas* which offered critical coverage from the time of Aquino's murder onwards and clearly enjoyed the support of the Catholic hierarchy in the positions it adopted.[34]

During the course of 1984 the cardinal threw his weight behind the National Movement for Free Elections, which was increasingly supported by other sectors in society, including the business classes. When it became clear that the parliamentary election had been stolen by Marcos, the Catholic Bishops' Conference declared that 'a government that assumes or retains power through fraudulent means has no moral basis', and they went on to declare that the only remaining means of resistance was through a 'non-violent struggle for justice'.[35] Supremely over-confident, Marcos called a presidential election in 1986 but, just as he claimed victory, key elements in the army abandoned him and, on 22 February, prepared to stage a coup whilst calling on Cardinal Sin for support. Over the following hours Radio *Veritas* stayed on the air, calling on people to gather at EDSA square where they were led in prayers by bishops and where the media captured dramatic shots of nuns confronting tanks.[36] In such a situation, unable to rely on his soldiers to preserve his position, Marcos had little alternative but to flee the country and allow the emergence of a new democratic order, albeit one whose development was to continue to prove problematic. He was certainly not brought down by the Catholic Church, but equally the Cardinal's decisiveness at a key moment brought hundreds of thousands onto the streets and effectively destroyed the old regime.

In Chile we have already noted the role of Cardinal Silva in promoting the defence of human rights, but we should also note that throughout the 1970s he also sought to deal with the government, frequently attempting to meet with General Pinochet to discuss specific cases or attempting to persuade the legal system to investigate abuses. Cardinal Silva was replaced in 1983 by Cardinal Fresno, a man who had initially welcomed the military coup and who appeared less likely to challenge the regime, though he made clear his continuing support for the Vicariate of Solidarity. Under Fresno's leadership and with the support of the papal nuncio who made his residence available for talks, the Church's first major intervention came in the mid-1980s as it sought to persuade the various opposition parties to work together. In 1983 the Church encouraged talks between the Interior Minister and the newly formed Democratic Alliance, and then publicly blamed the government when those talks broke down. In practice the talks faltered because, whatever the desires of some government representatives, General Pinochet was unwilling to curtail the activities of the security services. Further meetings took place at a Jesuit retreat house outside Santiago and eventually this issued in a 'National Accord for the Transition to Full Democracy' which was supported by most opposition leaders and signed by 11 leaders representing around 80% of the electorate.[37] This called for the direct election of the President and Congress, eschewed retribution on the military and called for a return of exiles and a free press. Cardinal Fresno agreed to present this proposal to Pinochet on 24 December 1985, but in the event was given 20 minutes and not permitted to discuss the Accord. Leaving aside General Pinochet's reluctance to leave power, part of the problem stemmed from the fact that for all the Church's aspirations to serve as a neutral mediator, repeated security attacks on its personnel and institutions meant that inevitably it found itself associated with the very changes that the regime leaders opposed.[38]

The situation was complicated by an attempt on Pinochet's life in September 1986, which led the Church to issue a forthright critique of attempts to resolve political differences through violence and to order priests to steer clear of overt political involvement. Nonetheless, discussions continued, reinforced by John Paul II's visit to Chile in April 1987 when he called on all to engage in dialogue and stressed the right of all 'to freely and actively participate in the establishment of the legal foundations of the political community and in the administration of public affairs, and in the determination of areas of action and boundaries of the different institutions, and in the election of public officials'.[39] Though many of the newer, more 'conservative' bishops remained wary of political involvement, from June 1987 the Church started to encourage voter registration for the forthcoming plebiscite on the political future of the country, and in 1988 brokered a social compact between unions and employers. In the run-up to the plebiscite many bishops allowed church property to be used for voter registration campaigns. Officially, the Church remained neutral, merely insisting that everyone who cared about Chile's future should vote, but in practice it tended to be seen as backing the 'no' campaign that would have ended General Pinochet's term of office. Moreover, though Cardinal Fresno insisted that churches only be used for voter registration, in practice many parishes priests and religious activists made it clear that they opposed Pinochet's attempt to remain in power via the plebiscite.[40] As a consequence of the no vote Pinochet was persuaded by his military colleagues to accept the people's verdict and in 1989 the first free elections in nearly two decades were held in Chile. Again the Church as an institution formally remained neutral, though its preference for the Christian Democrats was known to most. For our purposes, however, the key thing to note is the way in which the Catholic Church acted to facilitate the transition process. It sought to create unity within the opposition, it kept channels of communication open to more moderate elements within the regime, it tried to connect opposition and government, and, once a political process emerged, it involved itself in voter registration and education to ensure a relatively high turnout. In and of itself the Church was not central to the process, but nonetheless it did play a facilitating role that contributed towards democratisation.

The Polish Catholic Church played a very similar role in the period from the declaration of martial law in 1981 until the ending of communist rule in 1989, though its early response to martial law suggested a certain ambiguity. Broadcasting to the nation on 13 December 1981 Cardinal Glemp appeared to justify martial law as the 'lesser evil', and said that 'assuming the correctness of such reasoning the man in the street will subordinate himself to the new situation'. The key now, he said, was to preserve human life and avoid bloodshed, to avoid a war of Pole against Pole. This stance, shaped by a perspective that confronting the communist authorities would prove disastrous or draw in Russian troops, met with bitter criticism from many within Solidarity's ranks and from some amongst his own colleagues,[41] and very quickly the Church sought to make amends by providing support for the families of those detained under martial law. Though Cardinal Glemp remained wary of radical priests who offered full-blooded critiques of the regime, throughout the early 1980s the Church's Charity Commission provided tons of food and medical supplies to those most in need. At the same time it maintained contacts with the regime, and some noted that institutionally the Church did rather well out of the martial law period as more churches gained permission to open, perhaps in an effort to keep the Church 'onside' and provide a safety valve for popular dissatisfaction.

By the summer of 1988 Poland faced a new wave of strike activity, precipitated by more radical elements within Solidarity and perhaps encouraged by developments in the USSR where Gorbachev's programme was just beginning to take a more radical turn. On several occasions religious leaders played a key role in resolving potentially explosive situations, as in May 1988 when Bishop Tadeusz Goclowksi of Gdansk helped to resolve a shipyard strike before the police could use force to disperse striking workers.[42] During the mid-1980s there had been a series of talks between Archbishop Dabrowski and government leaders, and these resumed in August 1988 when Interior Minister General Kiszczak and other government officials met with Lech Walesa in the presence of the archbishop. Further meetings were held in Gdansk during subsequent months and these led in early 1989 to the Round Table talks between 29 government and 26 opposition delegates, with three observers from the church who did not participate directly in negotiations but did, according to participants, incline to the opposition side.[43]

In many African countries religious organisations, both Catholic and Protestant, offered a critical perspective on authoritarianism, but in several cases they went beyond simply confronting those regimes guilty of human rights abuses. This went furthest in Benin, where Mgr Isidore de Souze, Archbishop of Cotonou presided over the national conference designed to negotiate change and on several occasions managed to prevent a complete rupture between the negotiating parties. Though presided over by a Roman Catholic, there was some attempt to make the proceedings inclusive and the conference was opened with prayers from Muslims, Catholics, Protestants and *vodun* priests appealing to the spirit of their ancestors. As a result of the conference a transition process was set in motion, with the archbishop presiding over the High Council of the Republic which was effectively the legislative arm of the transitional government.[44] According to Paul Gifford senior Catholic leaders were also involved in transitional processes in the Congo, Togo, Gabon and Zaire in the early 1990s,[45] though Jeffrey Haynes has suggested this was as much a product of their role in the local political establishments as any commitment to democratisation and that therefore the importance of this should not be over-stated.[46] Elsewhere in Africa the churches (Catholic and Anglican) were to be found involved in conflict resolution in Mozambique, whilst in Zambia they played a particularly important role in monitoring transitional elections in 1991. Several months before the elections were due they came together to form the Christian Churches Monitoring Group which made a significant contribution to the process of election monitoring. In this capacity they trained a huge army of volunteers to run election booths and set out to provide voter education, including information on the mechanics of voting as well as setting out the peoples' rights to attend rallies or support parties.[47] Whilst the significance of these activities varied considerably from country to country, all point to the fact that in many democratising situations religious communities often made a vital contribution to the transition process.

Religion and democratic consolidation

Political scientists analysing the 'third wave' of democratisation have often distinguished between two stages in the process of transformation, those of 'transition' and 'consolidation' – though the relationship between them is far more complex than this linear, almost mechanical, distinction would suggest. During a transition the old authoritarian regime is displaced and there emerges agreement amongst key political actors over the procedures which will produce an elected government with the authority to develop policies of its own. Democratic consolidation has been defined in a variety of ways. Guiseppe di Palma emphasised the creation of a situation where democracy is 'the only game in town', and one accepted by all the major political and societal actors.[48] Juan Linz and Alfred Stepan elaborated further in stressing that a democracy can be considered consolidated when both key elites and the mass of the population accept that political conflicts will be regulated within a framework of specified laws, procedures and institutions that apply to all.[49] Most authors have also deemed it essential that the mass of the population come to accept the legitimacy, if not always the efficacy, of the new system and develop value orientations that are accepting of diversity and difference.[50]

Much of the writing on religion and democratisation has focused on the early parts of this transition stage, exploring the ways in which religion has contributed towards the downfall of authoritarian regimes. Less attention has been paid to the role of religion and religious communities in the consolidation of democratic political orders, and the concern of this section is with how religious communities contribute towards or hinder the process of embedding democratic polities. In doing so we make no special claims for the central significance of religious actors, for even in those countries where religious institutions have played a crucial role in bringing down an authoritarian regime, their salience has generally declined during the process of transition. We are simply interested in looking at the role of one set of elites or actors in supporting or hindering the process of democratic consolidation.

Religious institutions and democracy as 'the only game in town'

Religious institutions may have contributed to the downfall of the old authoritarian regimes, but with democratisation their role is fundamentally changed. Under the libertarian and pluralist pressures of a democratic transition any doubts about democracy suppressed during the struggle for liberty are allowed to surface. At the same time the political role of religious institutions is reduced, for they are no longer a primary focus of opposition to the existing order. Other avenues of articulation and mobilisation become available for would-be political actors, and church leaders often feel that political changes give them the opportunity to steer their organisations back to more traditional or 'spiritual' activities. Nonetheless, the ways in which religious institutions handle these changes can impact upon the success of the democratisation process. In particular, the activities of religious institutions, and their willingness to play by democratic rules, can strengthen or weaken the notion of democracy as 'the only game in town'.

At the rhetorical level religious establishments have frequently made clear their preference for democratic solutions and offered a public commitment to the new order. In the Catholic countries this in part reflected the wider church's post-Vatican II commitment to democracy as the best available political option, as well as the fact that in countries such as Spain, Poland and parts of Latin America the churches played a part in bringing about the transition. Despite this rhetorical support not every religious leader has been enthusiastic about all aspects of the transition process. Encouraging a wider commitment to democracy as 'the only game in town' was not helped when individual church leaders became associated with groups or movements hostile to democracy. In Spain some priests and bishops remained supportive of the 'bunker' throughout the late 1970s; in Latin America former military chaplains and a few bishops became associated with anti-democratic movements. In part their post-transition concerns stemmed from what were perceived as the moral and spiritual threats posed by the new pluralism which we discuss below. But there were other concerns. In Portugal during the revolutionary upheavals of 1974–76 the resolutely anti-communist Archbishop of Braga took a dim view of a political system which allowed Marxist parties to flourish.[51] There were occasionally other hints that the church might be wavering in its support for democracy, as in Spain following Tejero Molina's seizure of the Cortes in 1981 when there were accusations that the Spanish hierarchy had been slow to denounce the coup attempt.[52]

Beyond verbal offers of support, ongoing religious commitment to democratisation might be measured against the willingness of religious elites to stick with democratic rules of the game in pursuing their own institutional interests or promoting causes dear to their hearts. In many cases churches quickly adapted to the new lobbying possibilities provided by the democratic order. During the 1980s the Spanish Church 'played by the rules' in mobilising public support in defence of church-based educational institutions, encouraging Catholic politicians to speak out in the Cortes and bringing 250,000 people onto the streets shortly before a parliamentary vote.[53] More problematic may have been the attempt by religious elites to shape political behaviour, though again it might be argued that the church has as much right as any institution to seek influence over voting patterns. In April 1976 the Portugese hierarchy called upon voters not to support parties 'opposed to the Christian conception of man and society',[54] and during the Spanish elections of 1977 a number of bishops sought to dissuade their flocks from voting socialist or communist.[55] Nearly twenty years later the Polish Catholic leadership issued a similar appeal, in August 1995, urging Catholics not to support presidential candidates 'who participated in the exercise of power at the highest party and government levels under totalitarian rule' and to back political aspirants 'who defend ethical and evangelical values'. Yet many polls in the latter country revealed considerable scepticism about clerical involvement in politics, and in practice nine million Poles ignored this injunction not to vote for the former communists.[56]

As a general rule, religious institutions in newly democratising countries have held back from overt political involvement. In particular they have feared that encouraging certain patterns of voting behaviour or promoting religious parties might serve to divide both the church and the wider society at a time of rapid change. In a number of countries there have been attempts to create religious-based parties but these have generally met with limited success, except in countries such as Chile where there are long Christian Democratic traditions. In the post-communist world religious based parties have generally attracted derisory votes,[57] and even in Poland, which might be thought to offer more fertile ground, attempts to create parties of a Christian Democratic type have proved problematic. Various efforts encouraged by some church leaders have come adrift upon the ambitions of potential leaders with the result that by the mid-1990s no party could offer adequate representation of the views of the sizeable religious constituency in Poland.[58] Though in each case specific factors can be cited for the failure of such parties, it may simply reflect the declining significance of religious cleavages in modern Europe which have reduced the possibility of creating distinctive political parties on the basis of such constituencies.

Perhaps the greatest tensions have arisen over what the churches in general, and the Catholic Church in particular, perceive of as moral issues, areas where it is felt that majority decision-making is inappropriate. In 1990 Poland's Cardinal Glemp expressed unease over a conception of democracy rooted in the belief that every issue could be resolved by the vote of a majority, and in discussing social and political pluralism suggested that 'a crowd of individuals and egoists cannot form a society'.[59]

This attitude has led to repeated conflicts over issues relating to marriage and divorce, pornography, sexuality and abortion. In Argentina divorce legislation proposed in 1986 was denounced by one Catholic paper as the thin end of the wedge, as likely to lead to the legalisation of abortion, drugs, euthanasia and homosexuality, and moves were made by some bishops to deny Communion to deputies favouring divorce reform.[60] Similar intemperance was also evident in Chile where the naming of pro-abortion deputies by church newspapers was criticised by some Christian Democratic deputies as an inappropriate means of promoting a legitimate cause.[61] Such arguments and debates also occurred in Spain and, most heatedly, in Poland where in 1991–93 the church backed legislation that effectively rendered abortion illegal in the vast majority of cases. For the Catholic Church under John Paul II this was simply an issue on which there could be no compromise and which could not simply be resolved by the will of the majority.

A final area one might explore is how religion copes with the new democratic rules of the game related to the pursuit of privilege.[62] To what extent do religious institutions seek the maintenance or establishment of a position of privilege within the new political order, and how do they set about this? Such attempts may, as in Spain, stem from a reluctance to let go of the Church's recent role as effectively a part of the state apparatus. It may, as in Poland, originate in a belief that in a country where most are Catholic and where the Church played such a key role in the resistance, it could not simply be treated as just another pressure group. Or it might stem, as in Poland and (as we shall see) in Russia, from a strong conception of the Church as a major shaper and protector of the national tradition. Such perceptions may lead religious leaders to seek privileged access to policy-makers, relying on informal contacts in the corridors of power rather than on public debate and policy-making. In a number of countries church leaders have intervened during constitutional debates in an effort to ensure some guarantee of their position. During debates over the new Spanish constitution in the late 1970s, the Catholic Church reacted angrily to a draft document which failed to mention their place in national life. Eventually church leaders had to be satisfied with a clause that proclaimed the State's willingness to 'take into account the religious beliefs of the Spanish people and to maintain appropriate relations of co-operation with the Catholic Church and other denominations'. Even then some bishops remained unhappy with the effective recognition of state neutrality and urged their flocks to vote against the constitution.[63] Even fiercer public arguments emerged during Poland's protracted process of constitution-making as the Church fought for an explicitly Christian preamble and guarantees of the protection of life from the moment of conception to be inserted into the constitution. In the face of such a stance even moderate Catholics, such as former Prime Minister Tadeusz Mazowiecki, expressed unease at the Church's failure to recognise that not all Poles were believers.[64]

In most of the 'third wave' countries the dominant religious institutions have made public their commitment to democratic politics and acceptance of democratic norms. At the same time individual religious leaders and, on occasions, religious establishments have made clear their reservations about some democratic assumptions or about some of the consequences of political and social pluralism. In the vast majority of cases their response to negative phenomena has been promoted within the framework of democratic rules and procedures. Thus whatever one thinks of particular platforms articulated by religious leaders, there is no democratic reason why they should not pursue these through the normal channels of persuasion, lobbying of governments and parties, or by seeking to persuade the public of the rightness of their cause. Where difficulties may arise for newly democratic states is when churches or religious leaders claim that certain areas of public life are 'reserved' or beyond the domain of the secular state. Clearly one would not expect democratic majorities to define doctrines or resolve theological conflicts, but the issue becomes problematic when 'moral' issues are at stake and when the Church's teaching may be at odds with the wishes of the majority. Whilst one could not expect religious elites to compromise on such issues, as Fleet and Smith observe in their study of Chile and Peru, if the Church could claim reserved areas in which they have the right to over-rule the majority, why should not other institutions such as the military or the secret police do likewise?[65]

Religious institutions and the promotion/obstruction of democratic values and attitudes

In analysing any religious contribution to democratic consolidation one needs to explore the ways in which religious elites and organisations promote democratic values and attitudes. This might involve exploring their contribution to processes of reconciliation in divided societies and encouraging the peaceful resolution of conflicts, or their response to pluralism in general – that is, whether they are supportive of diversity and encourage tolerance – and to religious pluralism in particular. Under this category one might also discuss the churches' vision of democracy. As we have already seen, many churchmen are unhappy with a system that allows all issues to be decided by reference to the will of the majority, but do they offer alternatives? To what extent do they support a more participatory vision that goes beyond the 'low intensity democracy' that has emerged in much of the developing world since the late 1970s? Alternatively, do religious responses give validity to older patterns of behaviour that encourage the maintenance of hierarchical attitudes or reinforce clientelistic political styles? And in the case of the Roman Catholic Church one might ask how the contradictory messages emanating from the Vatican over recent years – both 'conservative' and 'radical' in their implications – impact upon local churches and in turn upon their ability to affect the promotion or hindrance of democratic values.

One area where one might expect religious bodies to play a role is in helping democratising societies to come to terms with the past. In most of the 'third wave' countries there have been intense debates over how to handle the legacy of the old regime, over the possibilities of retaining elements of inherited institutions and personnel, and over ways to deal with those guilty of gross abuses of human rights.

In some countries the emphasis has been on wiping the slate clean and starting afresh; in others agonising debates have taken place over culpability and over how far the prosecution of those responsible for human rights abuses should go. All too often the church has proved divided, its stance in part determined by its position during the authoritarian period. In Argentina, critics have charged that most bishops kept quiet at the time of repression and 'disappearances', and this led to ambiguous responses when efforts were later made to try members of the junta. Whilst the Bishop of Quilmes saw the trials as essential in bringing about reconciliation in Argentine society, the Archbishop of La Plate saw the trials as the revenge of criminals and subversives.[66] This ambiguity was in turn reinforced by John Paul II during his visit to Argentina in 1987 when he thundered against abortion and divorce but failed to mention the 'dirty war', instead calling for an end to the pursuit of guilty officers in the name of reconciliation.[67]

In Chile the Catholic Church repeatedly called for justice, especially in the early 1990s following the discovery of several mass graves, but has been reluctant to provoke the military too far. Nonetheless it maintains the belief that for any full reconciliation time is not enough and has argued that whether or not there is any formal reparation or retribution, it would be helpful if the families of the disappeared could at least know the fate of relatives and friends.[68] Here, as in other countries, religious organisations have often provided vital evidence to Truth and Reconciliation Commissions. The Chilean Catholic Church's *Vicaria de la Solidaridad* provided considerable documentation on human rights abuses, though was denied a formal role in the proceedings because of conservative perceptions of the organisation as infiltrated by leftist elements.[69] Even better publicised has been the work of the South African Truth and Reconciliation Commission, chaired for a while by Archbishop Desmond Tutu. The fourth volume of their report published in 1998 focused on the role of different institutions within the apartheid system and devoted a chapter to the role of faith communities. This emphasised both the sins of commission, whereby religious communities reinforced injustice, and sins of omission, whereby they failed to react to such abuses.[70] In most of these cases the churches have sought to emphasise that the process of democratisation has a moral component, and that building a new order requires reconciliation and a degree of repentance for past abuses.

In all of these activities the often well-publicised behaviour of religious elites sends messages to the wider public about the legitimacy or otherwise of democratic procedures and patterns of behaviour. As we shall see, this may have little import in countries that are more secularised, but in conditions where religious institutions at least initially enjoy considerable respect it may have some impact upon the development of a democratic consciousness. One way in which religious institutions can contribute towards the development of democratic attitudes is in their response to pluralism. This is not to say that they should accept all the consequences of pluralism, but rather that their response should be fashioned in such a way as to encourage the growth of tolerance and acceptance of diversity even when the social consequences of the new order are viewed with suspicion. At the societal level the most obvious problems stem from the perceived growth in 'immorality' that accompanies democratisation. With censorship restrained or removed, state control over people's private lives no longer acceptable, and various interests groups able to promote their own vision of the good life, the ideals promoted by religious bodies often come under threat. In most of the newly democratising countries this has proved problematic, for in most of the old authoritarian regimes traditional moral values favoured by the Church were often reinforced by the State. In consequence, and as we have already seen, the emergence of legislation on divorce or abortion, the coming into the open of pornography or homosexuality, and the new consumerist mentality have all proved hard to cope with. This was particularly so in Catholic countries such as Spain where the Church claimed to respect the new plurality 'yet not infrequently spoke as if it held the monopoly of ethics for the whole'.[71]

Even more important in terms of the message sent to the wider population may be the question of how the churches respond to religious pluralism. It is all very well to accept social pluralism, but the real test of whether an institution accepts and promotes diversity comes when its own interests are more directly threatened. One of the by-products of democratisation is the emergence of a free market in religious ideas, and in many of the countries dealt with here there has been considerable resistance from Catholic hierarchies to the spread of Protestant groups and new religious movements. In both the Iberian peninsula and Latin America the process of democratisation has been accompanied by the growth of Protestant influence which has challenged the cultural dominance of the Catholic Church. During 1992 the Chilean bishops attacked the aggressive proselytising activities of groups such as the Mormons, and suggesting that many evangelical groups were dividing communities and encouraging disrespect for Catholic symbols.[72] Elsewhere in Latin America both Catholic traditionalists and liberation theologians have proved suspicious of a conservative Protestantism that challenges hierarchy or promotes political passivity.

Much of what we have said so far has focused on religious reservations about aspects of democratic politics and the impact these might have upon public attitudes. Yet it should also be noted that in some of the 'third wave' countries, elements within religious bodies have tended to a position of critical support for democracy, aware of its failings and perhaps favouring a more expansive vision of democracy that extends power beyond the new elites and encompasses a vision of social change. Whereas the new political elites have been content with an 'electoralist' vision, church leaders have expressed reservations about the benefits this brings to the mass of the population. The Roman Catholic Church under John Paul II often managed to combine a moral and theological conservatism with a radical critique of the excesses of free market capitalism. And in so doing it raised difficult questions about what it means to have the vote when so large a proportion of the populations of Latin America and elsewhere are socially and politically marginalised.[73]

More radical still was the participatory vision associated with the 'popular church' of Latin America during the 1970s and early 1980s. Here there emerged a certain antipathy to the bargaining and compromises characteristic of liberal democratic polities. Instead activists argued that people should be encouraged to solve their own problems through grass-roots efforts, that might entail the meeting of economic needs, defence of community rights, support for the victims of the dictatorship or the promotion of a sense of community. All of these activities would be supported by the local churches and pastors, and would find spiritual expression in the life of the 'base communities' which, despite the popular image, often focused as much on purely 'religious' as 'political' activity.[74] With the downfall of dictatorship radical activists saw these communities, especially in Brazil where they were most significant, as providing the means whereby the new democracies could avoid some of the weaknesses of the old. Thus base communities were seen as organisations which created 'open spaces' in civil society and developed political and leadership skills amongst their members. It was also hoped that they might serve to 'deepen' the democratic experience, encouraging 'real' participation by the people, maintaining some degree of popular mobilisation, and promoting notions of accountability and respect for civil rights. Simultaneously they were seen as offering a challenge to the dominant culture of 'monistic corporatism' and hierarchy.[75]

Yet in practice the impact of these visions remained marginal, even in Brazil where they had been strongest. On the one hand the evolution of liberal democratic politics was accompanied by a demobilisation and to some extent a marginalisation of social movements and radical activists. Moreover, despite the proliferation of such communities in Brazil, those involved still made up a tiny minority of the population. And within the international Church, the whole atmosphere changed as Pope John Paul II oversaw the appointment of more conservative bishops suspicious of the liberationist and participatory vision of many social movement activists.[76] Under the new dispensation the Catholic Church in particular often offered a rhetorical critique of the failings of democracy and the market from Latin America to Eastern Europe, but often preferred to rely on contacts with other elites and traditional levers of influence to seek change from above. Individual pastors and priests might affect the lives of individual communities, but the overall contribution of religious bodies in general to changing public attitudes and reinforcing democratic mentalities appears to have been marginal in most cases.

The limits of religious contributions to democratic consolidation

Broadly speaking the potential for religious institutions to impact upon the process of consolidation during recent transition processes has been limited by two factors. On the one hand there is their declining social reach and influence when it comes to the political choices made by the democratic citizen. Even in countries where religion retains a strong public influence there are limitations on the ability of religious institutions to impact upon political attitudes. Numerous surveys reveal considerable divergences between religious teachings and the behaviour of believers, notably on matters of sexuality, whilst in Poland and elsewhere many citizens remain sceptical of clerical attempts to influence their political choices. Equally, across Eastern Europe the evidence suggests only a limited relationship between religious beliefs and adherence to particular political ideologies or parties.[77]

In the Catholic countries the situation has been more complex with some of the conflicts that have arisen stemming from a misunderstanding on the part of the Church of its actual influence. In both the Iberian peninsula, Latin America and Central-Eastern Europe a strong cultural Catholicism has not always been accompanied by the same levels of theological commitment. In Spain during the late 1970s the Vatican often did not understand why Archbishop Tarancón failed to push religious agendas more vigorously, attributing this to unwanted liberalism when it owed more to realistic perceptions of how far the public would follow the Church. Surveys in the early 1980s showed that whilst 78% of Spaniards described themselves as Catholic only 14.4% of the population were willing to follow church advice on political matters and 70% favoured a free choice on abortion. In similar vein, surveys in many Latin American countries showed high rates of Catholic support for the liberalisation of divorce laws.[78] Equally, political elites, who formally show considerable respect for religious leaders, have not always taken kindly to interventions by their clerical counterparts. In Brazil, for example, the attempts of the hierarchy to protect the Amazon Indians from the assaults of commercial interests or expose corruption in high places have met with vigorous rebuttals, whilst attempts to involve international agencies have met with charges of unpatriotic behaviour.[79]

The second factor limiting religious influence stems from the probably inevitable tension that must exist between the claims of the 'two cities'. Adam Przeworski has defined democracy as 'organised uncertainty', that is, as a political system in which outcomes are not predetermined and indeed are perhaps less important that the procedures by which they are arrived at. In a democracy the various actors compete for votes and even within the assembly have constantly to bargain and compromise, a process that often leads to outcomes that could not have been foreseen.[80] In such a context there is little room for absolute truth and, should the people so desire, they can in principle vote for whatever they like. For this reason there must inevitably be tensions between majoritarian political systems and religious institutions which proclaim eternal verities. These are perhaps further exacerbated when the largest religious denominations, both Catholic and Orthodox, are themselves hierarchical and authoritarian internally. In such circumstances their proclamation of democratic values and support for participatory politics will always be treated with suspicion by many.

Understanding the Catholic wave

There remains the question of why the Catholic Church shifted from being a central opponent to becoming a key supporter of democratisation, and earlier we pointed to several explanatory models. One focuses on what I have called *altruism*, on the centrality of theological change in the Roman Catholic Church which led it to revise its attitude to the temporal order. Jeffrrey Haynes was more sceptical, arguing that underlying religious support for democratisation lay the desire of religious organisations to preserve their *hegemony*, whilst Anthony Gill suggested that the preservation of *market share* lay at the heart of the Catholic change of heart and argues that this approach also helps to explain why some national hierarchies did support democratisation whilst others opposed it.

Our concern here has been two-fold. We have focused on why the Christian churches, led to a large extent by the Roman Catholic Church, shifted from overt support for authoritarianism or political quietism to a position supportive of democratic change; and then asked why this change was not evident in every Christian country. Essentially what we described as the altruistic explanation developed by Samuel Huntington appears to answer the first of these questions, but is less successful in dealing with the issue of variation. There are, of course, problems with the focus on Vatican II as pivotal for, as Gill rightly points out, individual priests, bishops and even national hierarchies had begun to act on behalf of the marginalised long before the 1960s. Equally, theologians such as John Courtney Murray had begun to explore the importance of human rights within the Catholic tradition. Yet Vatican II does mark a sea change in Catholic thinking that stretched beyond the confines of a single branch of the Christian Church. It fundamentally shifted the 'centre of gravity' within the Catholic Church in terms of its understanding of the relationship between the sacred and temporal orders. The 'official' Catholic position on human rights, religious freedom, political engagement and democracy post-1965 were very different than hitherto, and this provided support for a more critical stance towards authoritarian governments by local hierarchies – though, as was initially apparent in Spain and elsewhere, it did not guarantee changing attitudes. Vatican II was also important for some Protestant churches in that it fed into their thinking about politics and created the possibility of co-operation on questions of human rights and social justice.

Where John Paul II fits in this picture is harder to say. Clearly the election of a Pope with experience of a particular type of authoritarianism and also one who was willing to openly challenge regimes on questions of human rights reinforced the Catholic commitment to human rights and gave it a powerful voice. As Weigel suggests, he played a particularly important role in giving the populations of Central Europe a greater confidence in facing up to the compromises demanded by their regimes. Yet in seeking to redress the balance and quite rightly to emphasise the 'spiritual' dimension of the changes in the communist world, Weigel surely overstates the role of religion. In particular he neglects the fact that without Gorbachev it is unlikely that sufficient space would have opened up *when it did*, within which independent society could re-emerge, and equally he perhaps over-states the importance of Poland to the whole process. Clearly John Paul II did play a major role, but he was able to do so in part because of developments in the wider world and also because of the changes stemming from Vatican II which influenced his thinking (in both positive and negative directions), made the Church responsive to his words, and made it harder for authoritarian regimes to resist church criticisms.

So we can accept that Vatican II did play a major role, as suggested by Huntington, in shifting the Catholic Church's internal 'centre of gravity', in pushing the churches into taking a more pro-active role in support of democratic values, and in influencing the political stance of other religious communities. In turn this new stance gradually fed into changes taking place within local political cultures, as the churches acted in a more pluralistic and less hierarchical fashion, but also pragmatically as they helped to tip the balance of social forces in a more pro-democratic direction. Yet as Gill points out, this focus on theological and organisational change does not in itself explain why some religious hierarchies became active supporters of change and others resisted it or continued to provide legitimacy to authoritarian regimes.

In many respects the hegemony argument faces the same

problems in that it offers a general explanation but arguably does not account sufficiently for variation in religious behaviour. Clearly in traditionally Christian countries the churches have enjoyed a hegemonic position, with religious leaders part of the social and often political elite, and acting in ways that are supportive of the status quo. In Africa and elsewhere it may be that they did buy into the 'big man' syndrome, and enjoyed considerable material rewards as a result of their position. Haynes documents the ways in which Zaire's President Mobutu suborned the Catholic hierarchy through material inducements and offering formal respect, and suggests that the Church's leadership had almost to be forced into pro-democratic action by younger priests and nuns committed to change.[81] Gifford also provides further support in noting the case of Liberia where President Tolbert was president of the Baptist Union and his vice-president a bishop in the Methodist Church. Yet he also notes that here the Catholic Church had never been part of the social elite, which was often deeply anti-Catholic, and here it was the Catholic Archbishop of Monrovia who played the key role in speaking out against corruption and human rights abuses.[82]

The problem with hegemony-oriented explanations is that they are good at explaining why, historically speaking, traditionally dominant churches might have supported existing regimes, but they are not entirely satisfactory in explaining why some church leaders opted for change and others did not. Part of the problem is that Haynes only sketches out the argument, leaving it undeveloped in terms of both theoretical exposition and empirical detail, leaving him open to the charges of Gifford that this approach is too general and too subject to exceptions to have much explanatory power. If we extend it beyond Africa to Latin America, we find that in most of the region the Catholic Church was initially privileged by military regimes, yet in some cases they turned against them and in others they did not. In the communist countries the churches were very much outside the official regimes, though one might argue *pace* Ramet that once the temporary aberration of the communist order had passed the churches (Catholic and Orthodox) sought to recreate a past order – both real and imagined – where religious institutions enjoyed respect, influence and privilege (hegemony). We should, however, be wary of Ramet's suggestion that the

Polish Catholic Church had a conscious 'game plan' to restore its influence, though of course hegemony arguments do not necessarily require that political choices by religious leaders are based on a conscious or explicitly worked out agenda for achieving status or privilege. This also reminds us that it tends to be in the 'consolidation' phase of a transition processs that a focus on the pursuit of hegemony seems more useful, as in Brazil where several commentators have noted the tendency of the bishops to return to bargaining in the corridors of power, rather than relying on popular movements, once democracy was restored. One way out of this to suggest that the reason specific religious leaders decided to opt for democracy was tied into their calculations about how best to preserve their hegemonic position. It is not clear, however, where this differs from saying that the pro-democratic turn, and the often inconsistent position on this of churches and religious leaders, was simply a matter of the contingencies of time and place.

At first sight rational choice approaches appear to offer a better explanation of why some religious elites favoured democratisation whilst others maintained their traditional commitment to authoritarian political orders. As Gill notes the countries where the churches were most prominent in their opposition to authoritarianism (Brazil and Chile) were the very places where Protestant, especially Pentecostal, competition was particularly strong, whilst in Argentina Pentecostalism did not really begin to take hold until the latter part of the twentieth century. However, these were also the two Latin American countries with perhaps the strongest traditions of Catholic social activism, though prior to the 1970s this had often been deeply paternalistic in Brazil (much in line with the tradition of Leo XIII's *Rerum Novarum*) and closely linked to the governing Christian Democrats in Chile. In addition Chile had a much longer experience of stable democratic governance than most Latin American countries and this had largely been accepted by religious leaders with close ties to the governing elites. Hence, when Vatican II shifted the ideological and theological centre of gravity within the Church it was hardly surprising that these hierarchies were amongst the first to shift in a more pro-democratic direction. Various critics of Gill have also pointed to examples that seem to contradict the thesis – in Guatemala the episcopacy largely supported the regime despite Protestant growth – or to the excessive focus on decision-making by religious elites, even though there is little concrete evidence of changing political positions stemming from concern over religious competition. And again, the role of contingency and experience seems to have played a key role in effecting changing attitudes amongst individual religious leaders – both Cardinal Silva in Chile and Archbishop Arns in Brazil were partly galvanised into social action after they came across the victims of torture and abuse.[83]

There is also the question of whether the approach works very well when extended beyond Latin America. In communist Eastern Europe, for example, the Polish Catholic Church enjoyed a near religious monopoly (and considerably greater toleration than its neighbouring hierarchies), whilst its Hungarian counterpart existed in a more pluralistic religious context, and yet religious opposition to the regime was greater in the former than the latter. Obviously, the Polish hierarchy enjoyed far greater resources and had more support within society, but this takes us beyond a simple explanation in terms of competition alone and returns us, as with Chile and Brazil, to the centrality of history and context. Whilst the market analysis may apply better to the consolidation phase of transition, as monopoly religious suppliers seek to restrict entry into the market by lobbying governments for legislative and administrative support of their position, it is not entirely clear that, on its own, it provides an over-arching explanation of why some religious institution supported democratisation and others did not.

A fourth approach has been offered by Daniel Philpott, who stresses the complexity of the Catholic contribution to democratisation, emphasising the Church's gradual rapprochement with democracy culminating in Vatican II. His argument, in stressing complexity and contingency, also tends to be wary of macro-explanations, though he does isolate several factors that are likely to increase the effectiveness of religious organisations in promoting democracy. These include differentiation of the Church from the State, a tradition of religious autonomy from political power, strong transnational ties, links to other civil society groups and connections to national identity.[84]

Where does this leave us? It seems that over-arching theoretical explanations purporting to explain everything rarely do so and that, as Philpott suggests, much often depends upon contingencies of time and place. Certainly hegemonic theory and rational choice theory do not claim to explain what might be called 'micro-decision making', i.e. why one bishop intervenes on behalf of an imprisoned individual or decides to set up a human rights committee or authorises his priests to make connections with secular opponents of authoritarian regimes. They perhaps offer slightly more insight into why national hierarchies adopted a primarily supporting or constraining position with regard to political change, though as we have suggested this is not entirely convincing when we take the discussion beyond a few cases. Once again, then, we return to the ideological or theological explanation, because arguably without the changes introduced at Vatican II and paralleled by new ideas about politics emerging within Protestantism *the possibility of making these choices would not have existed or would have been less evident*. Without Vatican II the hegemonic 'common sense' in most cases would be to strengthen the connection with the ruling elites, an alliance that could be utilised to preserve the dominant religious community's market share by keeping out competitors. Theological change was crucial because *it opened up other choices or possibilities* for church leaders seeking to defend their spiritual and institutional interests. This is not to deny self-seeking, rational, hegemonic aspirations on the part of many religious leaders, but to suggest that the new theological imperatives helped to push a sufficient number of them into positions supportive of democratisation in many countries.

Notes

1 S. Mainwaring, *The Catholic Church and Politics in Brazil, 1916–85* (Stanford: Stanford University Press, 1986) pp. 105–6.

2 W. Hewitt, *Base Christian Communities and Social Change in Brazil* (Lincoln and London: University of Nebraska Press, 1991), pp. 31–4.

3 'Notes on church and state', *Journal of Church and State*, 18:1 (1976), pp. 150–1.

4 A. Michnik, *The Church and the Left* (Chicago: Chicago University Press, 1993).

5 A. Bromke, 'A new juncture in Poland', *Problems of Communism*, No. 5 (1976), p. 11.

6 'Developments in the Catholic Church in Poland before the Second Papal Visit', *Religion in Communist Lands*, 11:3 (1983), pp. 239–40.

7 J. Casanova, *Public Religions in the Modern World* (London: University of Chicago Press, 1994), pp. 94–103.

8 F. Lunnon, *Privilege, Persecution and Prophecy: The Catholic Church in Spain, 1875–1975* (Oxford: Clarendon Press, 1987), p. 245.

9 Edouard de Blaye, *Franco and the Politics of the New Spain* (London: Penguin, 1976), p. 415.

10 J. Klaiber, *The Church, Dictatorships, and Democracy in Latin America* (New York: Orbis Books, 1998), pp. 173–5.

11 Ibid. , pp. 50–6.

12 J. Rupnik, 'Dissent in Poland, 1968–78: the end of revisionism and the rebirth of civil society', in R. Tokes (ed.), *Opposition in Eastern Europe* (London: Macmillan, 1979), pp. 60–112.

13 R. Taras, *Consolidating Democracy in Poland* (Boulder: Westview Press, 1995), p. 99.

14 D. Herbert, *Religion and Civil Society: Rethinking Public Religion in the Contemporary World* (Aldershot: Ashgate, 2003), pp. 197–212.

15 P. Jeglinski and A. Tomsky, '*Spotkania*: Journal of the Catholic Opposition in Poland', *Religion in Communist Lands*, 7:1 (1979), pp. 23–8.

16 T. Garton Ash, *The Polish Revolution* (London: Granta Books, 1991), pp. 25–6.

17 J. Lipski, *History of the Workers' Defence Committee in Poland, 1976–1981* (London: University of California Press, 1985), p. 464.

18 A. Michnik, *Letters from Prison and Other Essays* (London: University of California Press, 1985), pp. 34ff.

19 D. Johnston, 'The churches and apartheid in South Africa', in D. Johnston and C. Sampson (ed.), *Religion, the Missing Dimension in Statecraft* (Oxford: Oxford University Press, 1994); K. Ross, 'Not catalyst but ferment: the distinctive contribution of the churches to political reform in Malawi, 1992–93', in P. Gifford (ed.), *The Christian Churches and the Democratisation of Africa* (Leiden: E. J. Brill, 1995), pp. 101–2.

20 P. Deiros, 'Protestant fundamentalism in Latin America', in M. Marty and R. Scott Appleby (ed.), *Fundamentalisms Observed* (Chicago: Chicago University Press, 1991), p. 163.

21 For a general survey of Vatican diplomacy in recent years see M. Walsh, 'Catholicism and international relations: papal interventionism', in J. Esposito and M. Watson (ed.), *Religion and Global Order* (Cardiff: University of Wales Press, 2000), pp. 100–18, and also J. Casanova, 'Globalizing Catholicism and the return to a "universal" Church', in S. Rudolph and J. Piscatori (ed.), *Transnational Religion and Fading States* (Boulder: Westview Press, 1997), pp. 121–43.

22 This paragraph draws heavily on Walsh, 'Catholicism and international relations: papal interventionism'.

23 A. Brassloff, *Religion and Politics in Spain: The Spanish Church in Transition, 1962–96* (London: Macmillan, 1998), pp. 29–30; C. Powell, 'International aspects of democratization: the case of Spain', in L.

Whitehead (ed.), *The International Dimensions of Democratization: Europe and the Americas* (Oxford: Oxford University Press, 2001), pp. 307–8.

24 B. Smith, *The Church and Politics in Chile* (Princeton: Princeton University Press, 1992), p. 323.

25 E. Cleary, *The Struggle for Human Rights in Latin America* (Westport: Greenwood Press, 1997), p. 132.

26 Quoted in A. Angell, 'International support for the Chilean opposition, 1973–89: political parties and the role of exiles', in Whitehead, *The International Dimensions of Democratization*, p. 187.

27 A. Hurrell, 'The international dimensions of democratization in Latin America: the case of Brazil', in Whitehead, *The International Dimensions of Democratization*, p. 154.

28 R. Graham, *Spain: Change of a Nation* (London: Joseph, 1984), pp. 210–27.

29 F. Bautista, *Cardinal Sin and the Miracle of Asia* (Manila: Vera Reyes, 1987), pp. 174–5.

30 J. B. Hehir, 'Catholicism and democracy: conflict, change and collaboration', in John Witte (ed.), *Christianity and Democracy in Global Context* (Boulder: Westview, 1993), p. 30.

31 M. Fleet and B. Smith, *The Catholic Church and Democracy in Chile and Peru* (Notre Dame: Notre Dame University Press, 1997), pp. 131–3.

32 Full archive references to these archives can be found in J. Anderson, *Religion, State and Politics in the Soviet Union and the Successor States* (Cambridge: Cambridge University Press, 1994), pp. 104–5.

33 C. Neal Tate, 'The revival of church and state in the Philippines: churches and religion in the people power revolution and after', in E. Sahliyeh (ed.), *Religious Resurgence and Politics in the Contemporary World* (Albany: SUNY Press, 1990), pp. 145–6.

34 Bautista, *Cardinal Sin and the Miracle of Asia*, pp. 124ff.

35 D. Wurfel, 'Transition to political democracy in the Philippines: 1978–88', in D. Ethier (ed.), *Democratic Transition and Consolidation in Southern Europe, Latin America and Southeast Asia* (London: Macmillan, 1990), p. 90.

36 Tate, 'The revival of church and state in the Philippines'; Bautista, *Cardinal Sin and the Miracle of Asia*, pp. 188ff.

37 C. Meacham, 'Changing of the guard: new relations between church and state in Chile', *Journal of Church and State*, 29:3 (1987), pp. 411–33; Fleet and Smith, *The Catholic Church and Democracy in Chile and Peru*, pp. 120–2.

38 Ibid., p. 121.

39 H. Stewart-Gambino, 'Redefining the changes and politics in Chile', in E. Cleary and H. Stewart-Gambino (ed.), *Conflict and Co-operation: The Latin American Church in a Changing Environment* (Boulder: Lynne Reinner, 1992), p. 31.

40 Fleet and Smith, *The Catholic Church and Democracy in Chile and Peru*, p. 122ff.

41 T. Garton Ash, *The Polish Revolution*, pp. 280–1.

42 *Keston News Service (KNS)*, 26 May 1988.

43 W. Osiatynski, *The Round Table Negotiations in Poland* (Working Paper No. 1 of the Centre for the Study of Constitutionalism in Eastern Europe).

44 R. Joseph, 'The Christian churches and democracy in contemporary Africa', in J. Witte (ed.), *Christianity and Democracy in Global Context* (Boulder: Westview Press, 1993), pp. 241–2; B. Magnusson, 'Testing democracy in Benin', in R. Joseph (ed.), *State, Conflict and Democracy in Africa* (Boulder: Lynne Reinner, 1999), pp. 220–2.

45 P. Gifford, *African Christianity: Its Public Role* (London: Hurst, 1998), p. 24.

46 J. Haynes, *Religion and Politics in Africa* (London: Zed Books, 1996), p. 109.

47 Gifford, *African Christianity: Its Public Role*, pp. 196–7.

48 Guiseppe di Palma, *To Craft Democracies* (Berkeley: University of California Press, 1990).

49 J. Linz and A. Stepan, *Problems of Democratic Transition and Consolidation* (Baltimore: Johns Hopkins University Press, 1996), p. 5.

50 A. Leftwich, 'From democratization to democratic consolidation', in D. Potter *et al.* (ed.), *Democratization* (Cambridge: Polity Press, 1997), pp. 524–32; for more nuanced approaches to the concept of consolidation see W. Merkel, 'The consolidation of post-autocratic democracies: a multi-level analysis', *Democratization*, 5:3 (1998), pp. 33–67, and A. Schedler, 'How should we study democratic consolidation?', *Democratization*, 5:4 (1998), pp. 1–19.

51 R. A. Robinson, *Contemporary Portugal: A History* (London: Allen and Unwin, 1979), p. 238; D. Porch, *The Portugese Armed Forces Movement and the Revolution* (London: Croom Helm, 1977), pp. 199–200.

52 Brassloff, *Religion and Politics in Spain*, pp. 107–8.

53 W. J. Callahan, 'Church and state in Spain, 1976–91', *Journal of Church and State*, 34:3 (1992), pp. 503–19.

54 Robinson, *Contemporary Portugal*, p. 238.

55 Brasloff, *Religion and Politics in Spain*, p. 93.

56 *Open Media Research Institute (OMRI) 168*, 29 August 1995; J. Luxmoore, 'Eastern Europe 1995: a review of religious life in Bulgaria, Romania, Hungary, Slovakia, the Czech Republic and Poland', *Religion, State and Society* 24:4 (1996), p. 358; J. Karpinski, 'Poles divided over church's renewed political role', *Transition* 5:4 (1996), pp. 11–13.

57 For a useful analysis of the failure of Russian Christian Democracy see R. Sakwa, 'Christian Democracy and civil society in Russia', *Religion, State and Society*, 22:3 (1994), pp. 273–304.

58 On the problems of party formation in Poland see F. Millard, 'The shaping of the Polish party system, 1989–93', *East European Politics and Society*, 8:3 (1994), pp. 467–94; W. Wesolowski, 'The formation of political parties in post-communist Poland', in G. Pridham and P. Lewis (ed.), *Stabilising Fragile Democracies: Comparing New Party Systems in Southern and Eastern Europe* (London: Routledge, 1996), pp. 229–53.

59 *Keston News Service (KNS) 352*, 14 June 1990, p. 17; since then various Polish church leaders have stressed the importance of human law corresponding to natural law. See S. Ramet, *Nihil Obstat: Religion, Politics and Social Change in East-Central Europe and Russia* (Durham: Duke University Press, 1998), p. 336.

60 E. Mignone, 'The Catholic Church and the Argentine democratic transition', in J. Epstein, *The New Argentine Democracy* (London: Greenwood Press, 1992), p. 164; P. Snow and L. Manzetti (ed.), *Political Forces in Argentina*, 3rd edition (Westport: Greenwood Press, 1993), p. 162.

61 C. Meacham, 'The role of the Chilean Catholic Church in the new Chilean democracy', *Journal of Church and State*, 36:2 (1994), pp. 277–99; see also L. Haas, 'The Catholic Church in Chile: new political alliances', in C. Smith and J. Prokopy (ed.), *Latin American Religion in Motion* (New York: Routledge, 1999), pp. 43–66.

62 For a general discussion of the pursuit of 'privilege' or 'recognition' see J. Anderson, *Religious Liberty in Transitional Societies: The Politics of Religion* (Cambridge: Cambridge University Press, 2003).

63 Paul Heywood, *The Government and Politics of Spain* (London: Palgrave, 1995), pp. 49–51.

64 Cf. *The European*, 22 February 1991; Karpinski, 'Poles divided over church's renewed political role', p. 13; J. Karpinski, 'The constitutional mosaic', *Transition*, 11 August 1995, p. 9.

65 Fleet and Smith, *The Catholic Church and Democracy in Chile and Peru*, p. 179.

66 Mignone, 'The Catholic Church and the Argentine democratic transition', p. 161.

67 P. Hebblethwaite, 'John Paul II', in A. Hastings (ed.), *Modern Catholicism: Vatican II and After* (Oxford: Oxford University Press, 1991), pp. 453–4.

68 Fleet and Smith, *The Catholic Church and Democracy in Chile and Peru*, pp. 163–9.

69 See N. Kritz (ed.), *Transitional Justice*, Volume 1 (Washington DC: United States Institute of Peace, 1995), pp. 453–510.

70 A summary of the text can be found on the Commission's website at www. truth.org.za/final/4chap3.htm (accessed 1 June 2003); see also www.doj.gov.za/trc/index.html.

71 Brassloff, *Religion and Politics in Spain*, p. 86.

72 Fleet and Smith, *The Catholic Church and Democracy in Chile and Peru*, pp. 176–9.

73 Meacham, 'The role of the Chilean Catholic Church in the new Chilean democracy'; cf. E. Cleary, 'The Brazilian Catholic Church and church–state relations: nation building', *Journal of Church and State*, 39:2 (1997), pp. 253–71.

74 For a general discussion of the 'Popular Church' see S. Mainwaring and A. Wilde (ed.), *The Progressive Church in Latin America* (Indiana: University of Notre Dame Press, 1989).

75 Cf. R. Ireland, *Kingdoms Come: Religion and Politics in Brazil* (Pittsburgh: University of Pittsburgh Press, 1991); W. E. Hewitt, *Base Christian Communities and Social Change in Brazil* (London: University of Nebraska Press, 1992); W. Swatos (ed.), *Religion and Democracy in Latin America* (London: Transaction Publishers, 1995).

76 See some of the essays in Cleary and Stewart-Gambino, *Conflict and Co-operation*.

77 See Stephen White *et al.*, *Religion and Political Action in Postcommunist Europe* (Strathclyde: Studies in Public Policy, 307, 1998).

78 Brasslof, *Religion and Politics in Spain*, p. 117; Mignone, 'The Catholic Church and the Argentine democratic transition', p. 163.

79 T. Bruneau and W. Hewitt, 'Catholicism and political action in Brazil: limitations and prospects', in Cleary and Stewart-Gambino, *Conflict and Co-operation*, p. 52.

80 A. Przeworski, *Democracy and the Market: Political and Economic Reforms in Eastern Europe and Latin America* (Cambridge: Cambridge University Press, 1991), pp. 10–14; Przeworski adapted this comment from Adolfo Suarez's address to the Spanish constituent assembly where he announced that henceforth 'the future is not written, because only the people can write it'.

81 Haynes, *Religion and Politics in Africa*, p. 110–12.

82 Gifford, *African Christianity*, p. 48.

83 See the extended discussion of Gill's book and rational choice theory applied to religion at www.providence.edu/las/discussion.htm (accessed 1 September 2006).

84 D. Philpott, 'The Catholic Wave', *Journal of Democracy*, 15:2 (2004), pp. 32–46.

5

The Orthodox hesitation: Church, State and nation

As in previous chapters, the first aim of this examination of Eastern Orthodoxy is to tell the story of its engagement with democracy, and then to try and explain what I will describe as the Orthodox 'hesitation' about democracy. In most studies of democratisation the relatively poorly known Eastern tradition receives little attention, the default assumption being that Orthodoxy has made little contribution to the removal of authoritarian regimes and that if anything it is more likely to serve as an obstacle to democratisation. More recently, however, scholars such as Alfred Stepan and Elizabeth Prodromou have suggested that there are both pragmatic and theological factors encouraging a stronger Orthodox engagement with democracy – perhaps recast and without some of the accompanying liberal assumptions – in the future.

Analysing the Orthodox engagement with democracy and democratisation is far more problematic than with Western Christianity, for a number of reasons, and most sources have focused on the reasons underlying the tendency of the Orthodox churches to support whatever regime was in power. Some pointed to the absence of a developed tradition of social and political theology comparable to that of both Protestant and Catholic traditions, and in particular a lack of substantial discussion of democracy as a political system. For some the absence of an international religious centre and the linkage of the autocephalous churches to individual states in an age of nationalism served to reduce the political autonomy of religious organisations and communities, tying them in to close links with states that granted the national churches privileges or protected them from competition. Others noted the historical experience of Byzantium, Ottoman rule, and state dominance in Russia and the USSR which rendered the Church defensive, concerned above all with survival rather than theological and social thought. In addition, in those countries where Orthodoxy has been the dominant tradition, there has been limited experience of democratic governance until very recently.

In his book on the 'third wave', Samuel Huntington had very little to say about Orthodoxy, beyond the vague suggestion that it might contribute towards the emergence of democracy in the post-communist states.[1] In the original 'clash of civilizations' article, however, he began to develop the argument that Orthodoxy could prove problematic for democracy because of its socio-political location:

> the most significant dividing line in Europe, as William Wallace has suggested, may well be the eastern boundary of Western Christianity in the year 1500 ... The peoples to the north and west of this line are Protestant or Catholic; they shared the common experiences of European history – feudalism, the Renaissance, the Reformation, the Enlightenment, the French Revolution, the Industrial Revolution: they are generally economically better off than the peoples to the east; and they may now look forward to increasing involvement in a common European economy and to the consolidation of democratic political systems. The peoples to the east and south of this line are Orthodox and Muslim: they historically belonged to the Ottoman or Tsarist empires and were only lightly touched by the shaping events in the rest of Europe; they are generally less advanced economically; they seem much less likely to develop stable democratic political systems.[2]

In the later book-length version he seems to go further in suggesting that to become democratic, countries such as Russia essentially had to become Western – by accepting the rule of law, social pluralism, individualism, separation of Church and State etc. – and claimed that 'if Russia becomes Western, Orthodox civilization ceases to exist'.[3] To those who might point to the case of Greece, where democracy and Orthodoxy had co-existed for several decades, Huntington suggested that Greece 'is not part of Western civilization, but it was the home of Classical civilization which was an important source of Western civilization' and that it was 'an anomaly, the Orthodox outsider in Western organizations'.[4]

Huntington was here reiterating his earlier suggestion that of all the religious traditions, only those associated with

Western Christianity had made a significant contribution to democratisation and that, in certain respects, Orthodoxy was amongst those traditions that might serve to inhibit democratic development. In terms of making any significant contribution to the democratic wave of the 1980s and 1990s this was certainly correct for, as we shall see, its involvement as an institution was at best marginal and at worst obstructive. Yet in so far as he was suggesting that Orthodoxy offered some form of permanent obstacle to democratisation his argument was problematic. A particularly coherent reply was offered by Alfred Stepan, who suggested that like all religious traditions Orthodoxy was multi-vocal and contained within it resources for those supportive of democracy as well as those opposed to it. Whilst accepting that Orthodoxy was unlikely to prove a strong, pro-active ally for democracy he remained sceptical about it as presenting a strong obstacle to democracy in those countries where it was dominant. In particular, Stepan suggested that the much-maligned tradition of political quietism and subordination to whatever regime was in power might, ironically, contribute in situations where political elites were promoting democratic change, for here the national churches would tend to follow the lead of the dominant politicians. He notes the case of Greece, where since the overthrow of the military the Orthodox Church has not fundamentally challenged the democratic order, though he perhaps understates the extent to which it feels uneasy with aspects of the democratic settlement.[5]

In these two chapters we explore some of these issues, focusing first of all on the engagement of the Orthodox tradition with democratic ideas and looking at its very limited contribution to democratisation in recent decades. Whilst accepting that this is very much a product of historical circumstance and that there is no inherent incompatibility between Eastern Orthodoxy and democracy, the experience of the last two decades suggest that there are some points of tension that should not be glossed over and that what I have called the tradition's current 'centre of gravity' may not be overly conducive to supporting democratisation. In particular there are issues relating to the relationship of the Church to the State, to the nation, and to the individual which are capable of resolution but which can also push national

Orthodox churches into supporting an excessively close relationship with the State that may serve to restrict the rights of others – and thus negate one feature of democracy as commonly understood – and into an excessively close relationship with nationalist movements of a chauvinist, exclusivist or even violent nature.

Some of these issues are yet to be resolved within Eastern Orthodox thinking and in the states where Orthodoxy is the dominant religious tradition, though there is a counter-argument emerging from within the Orthodox community. This is explored in Chapter 6 where we note the suggestion that it is less democracy that the tradition has a problem with, than the liberal assumptions that underlie its Western manifestations, with their assumption that there is only one appropriate model of Church–State relations and their prioritisation of the rights of the individual over any sense of obligation to the wider interests of the community. Whilst such arguments can serve to mask self-interest and offer an excuse for restricting minority rights in the name of cultural distinctiveness, there is a debate here that mirrors discussion within other parts of the world about the appropriate role of religion in the public sphere. We point to some of the questions raised by Orthodox spokespersons, examine how countries with traditionally dominant Orthodox traditions handle issues of sexual and religious difference, and then take a very brief look at how the minority Orthodox communities in the USA have reconciled faithfulness to tradition with the pluralism of North American society. We also point to some of the ways in which Orthodoxy might contribute to the building of a civil society that would prove supportive of democratisation, although some Orthodox commentators have argued that the Western-based concept of civil society as a sphere between State and individual is perhaps inappropriate in the 'Eastern' context. Many of these arguments have some validity, but the suspicion in much of the former communist countries is that the problems with democracy – however defined – are not just about ontological differences, but also about how religious elites seek to defend and justify both privilege for themselves and restrictions on others.

Orthodoxy and democracy

We have already suggested that in the post-communist world democratic governance initially struggled to take root in those countries with an Orthodox tradition, and it has been argued that there might be elements within the Orthodox tradition that help to inhibit the progress towards full democratisation. It is not so much that religious traditions are determinative, but rather that they feed into 'political cultures' in ways that can either restrict or promote democratic development, and in the Orthodox case it might appear as if the former is more common. Part of the problem in elaborating an Orthodox perspective on democracy is the relative paucity of political thinking within the tradition, in comparison to the Catholic and Protestant traditions with their highly developed engagement with social and political ideas. Theoretical engagement has also been stymied by the fact that until very recently Orthodoxy has been dominant in countries where democracy was not on the political agenda, whether as ideal or threat, and therefore responding to the challenges it poses had not been necessary – though the sizeable Orthodox communities in America and elsewhere have had to address this issue.

Orthodox theorising about politics and democracy

There is an Orthodox story about 'what went wrong' with the religion–politics relationship, which suggests that once upon a time there was a golden age of 'symphonia' where Church and State worked harmoniously to look after the spiritual and material interests of their communities. Only after the fall of Byzantium and the shift of Orthodoxy's centre to Russia did things begin to go wrong, as a combination of Tatar–Muscovite practices and the Lutheran-inspired subordination of Church to State finalised by Peter the Great turned the Orthodox Church into a department of state. This model was later followed in the Balkans as national churches previously subordinated to the Ottomans now became instruments, more or less willingly, of the new national states.[6] Though this tale has a mythological quality, it is not without some basis in reality. The traditional Byzantine perspective did depict a clear 'distinction between the imperial authority (*imperium*) and the priesthood (*sacerdotium*), the former being concerned with human affairs and the latter with things divine'.[7] This shared authority, sometimes referred to as *symphonia*, in principle offered a clear division of labour, though in practice over the centuries each side sought to assert its supremacy, and it all too easily tended to slip into a Caesaropapist reality (or what in the Russian context I have called an 'assymetric symphonia')[8] where the Church became an instrument of state.[9]

According to Papanikolaou:

> Although distinctive institutions, the roles of the emperor and the bishop were understood and justified within the same Christian framework. The Byzantine theocracy called for the emperor and the bishop to cooperate for the sake of the unity of the Christian empire, the image of the heavenly kingdom, and the unity of the faith ... The theology of culture implied in the Byzantine theocracy is one that does not value multiculturalism ... The principle of cultural unity within the empire was Orthodox Christianity, with its system of beliefs, institutions, practices, literature, and art. The emperors saw themselves as enforcers of both civil and religious laws.[10]

In consequence there was no distinction between religious and political obligation, with separation from the Church effectively meaning separation from the political community, with at times serious consequences. In Gvosdev's words, 'uniformity of faith was seen as both desirable and necessary for the cohesion and maintenance of the commonwealth'.[11] Of course, this parallel identification was common throughout the Christian world at the time, and the notion of tolerating difference was weakly enshrined in most political orders. Yet, whilst it has more or less disappeared from Western Christian thought it is, as we shall see later, a position that some Orthodox leaders would still maintain. To this one might add the argument that dominated by a theology geared more towards liturgy than social practice, and towards heaven rather than earth, the Orthodox Church has tended intellectually (if not always in practice) to treat the social order with a degree of disdain – the troubles of this time are as nothing when compared to the centuries in which the Church thinks. Consequently Orthodox churches have been able to live with a variety of political regimes, from the Ottoman Empire – where they generally sought to adapt, despite occasional forays into supporting nationalist movements in the nineteenth century – to the communist regimes of the twentieth century.

Post-Byzantium the Ottoman *millet* system (which effectively allowed minority religious communities to govern themselves, within certain limits) turned Orthodox religious leaders into representatives of the Orthodox community but also reinforced their dependency upon state authority, albeit now a Muslim one. The rise of nationalism in the nineteenth century created new problems for the Orthodox churches but brought them no nearer to engaging with democratic ideas. Many church leaders were initially wary of Greek aspirations for independence, though once this was achieved in 1830 the new Greek state set about establishing an autocephalous hierarchy independent of the Patriarch in Istanbul. In the new political order the Church was formally established as the state church, though even before independence was achieved the Provisional Constitution of 1823 defined a Greek as someone who believed in Jesus Christ, who lived in the area and expressed a desire to be a Greek national – thus early on establishing the link between religious and national identity. Under the auspices of the Catholic Otto of Bavaria an ecclesiastical structure was created that left the Church very much subordinate to the State. The details of subsequent developments can be found elsewhere,[12] but the key point to note was that from the time of independence up until 1974 the Greek Church's leadership found itself in a privileged and constrained position, supported by successive, mostly authoritarian, governments but equally subject to the political whims of those in power. Much the same could be said of other national churches in the Balkans, accepted as key national institutions and institutional pillars of the political order but often finding their freedom of action restricted by those same orders. In Romania the 1866 constitution described the Orthodox Church as the 'dominant religion',[13] whilst in Bulgaria its role was even recognised by the communists whose 1949 law on religion described the Orthodox Church as 'the traditional religious denomination of the Bulgarian nation'.[14]

In Tsarist Russia, Peter the Great's reforms at the beginning of the eighteenth century had already helped to turn the Church into an instrument of state. By the second half of the nineteenth century it was seen by many as an essentially

reactionary force, an image not helped by the State's requirement that priests reported what they heard in the
confessional to the police, by the Church's continued support
for the persecution of religious minorities, or by the scandals
associated with Rasputin. In the Russian case the Orthodox
Church on the eve of the revolution still lacked many of the
'potentialities' enjoyed by the Western churches – despite a
reform movement that emerged at the turn of the century.
Social theology was weakly developed and, as Richard Sakwa
has pointed out, the core notion of 'sobornost', with its
implicit rejection of the distinction between separate spheres
of state and society worked against the creation of a liberal
democratic ideology.[15] Moreover, even the Slavophiles, who
often argued against coercion in religion, still suggested that
the non-Orthodox could not enjoy the same political rights
as Orthodox citizens.[16] The Church also lacked the wide
array of clerical and lay institutions and associations that
underlay the creation of Christian social movements in
Western Europe at the end of the nineteenth century. In
1917, as today, the Russian Orthodox Church had a mass
nominal following, but was largely cut off from the broad
current of social change and found it hard to mobilise its
adherents. Then, as later, the Church's reputation had been
weakened by past compromises with the state order. There is,
of course, a danger of over-stating this inheritance and ignoring the movements for reform that were evolving within
Russian church circles at the turn of the century. In the years
around the 1905 revolution there was an attempt to establish
a church council (*sobor*) that would move the Church away
from its Petrine dependence upon the State and create an
independent institution capable of working with the State
but also of promoting moderate reform within the wider
society.[17] A full Russian Church *Sobor* was eventually held in
1918, which led to the recreation of the Patriarchate and
proposed a partial democratisation of church government,
but any contribution it might have made to reform was effectively ended by the Bolshevik revolution, the consequences of
which were disastrous for the Orthodox community and the
impact of which was to promote a highly defensive attitude
within Orthodox institutional structures that survived
beyond the collapse of communism.

During the communist period the Orthodox churches

were forced by circumstances to fall back on liturgical celebration and the struggle for survival in the face of hostile regimes. Despite some involvement with the ecumenical movement the East European Orthodox churches had limited opportunities to develop a social theology and there was no equivalent of Vatican II to galvanise the Church into rethinking its relationship with the world in the modern era. The 1918 Russian Church Council might have served that purpose but this possibility was aborted by the Bolshevik revolution. Thus the religious component of Russian political culture experienced little change, and was perhaps reinforced by the hierarchic, authoritarian and collectivist nature of communist rule that in turn developed quasi-religious rituals for its own mobilising and legitimising ends. At the same time Soviet rule removed religious influence from the political sphere and cowed the Church, which turned increasingly inward in an effort to preserve a limited institutional base.[18]

These historical experiences have impacted to varying degrees on all the Orthodox churches of Europe. The situation has been further complicated by the fact that the schism between the Eastern and Western churches contributed to an anti-Westernism that has reinforced suspicion of pluralist visions of politics as somehow alien, a product of Western Christianity and perhaps not best suited to the Orthodox world. For Papanikolaou:

> The present-day Orthodox churches are the inheritors of the Byzantine theological legacy. The Orthodox Church's encounter with modern democracy raises the broader question of how a religious tradition, whose own theologies of state and culture were shaped within the context of an empire in which it was the state sponsored religion and, hence, the primary principle of cultural unity, is able to accept democratic forms of government and a multicultural society. The Orthodox Church was unprepared to face issues of democracy and human rights because its own theologies of state and culture were formed within a context in which democracy had no meaning. The question is whether there are resources within its theological tradition that would allow it to give unequivocal support to democracy.[19]

To this question several scholars have responded positively. Vladimir Wozniuk has noted the ways in which the pre-revolutionary Russian thinker Vladimir Soloviev developed an early defence of human rights in general and freedom of conscience in particular, evident in his suggestion to Tsar Nicholas II that restricting the rights of religious minorities undermined the mission of the Orthodox Church.[20] David Koyzis has suggested that whilst traditionally the Orthodox emphasis has been on the sovereignty of God and the depiction of the earthly kingdom as a pale reflection of divine monarchy, a more Trinitarian emphasis would make space for the role of participation in both heaven and on earth and for a more transformative vision of politics.[21] In similar vein Elizabeth Prodromou has pointed to the centrality of human freedom in Orthodox thought and the Trinitarian emphasis on diversity within unity as underlying an Orthodox vision of democracy.[22] What the implications of these arguments might be for practical politics is less clear, and it remains the case that until very recently such discussion as there has been about democracy has remained characterised by a degree of hesitancy.

Orthodoxy and the 'third wave'

These understandings and experiences alike may help to explain why the Orthodox churches made no significant contribution to democracy's 'third wave'. In Greece only Bishop Panteleimon of Salonika offered any opposition to the military junta, and this had little to do with any democratic commitment on his part.[23] Perhaps less surprisingly, the Orthodox churches in the Soviet bloc located, in all but the Yugoslav case, in the more repressive of the communist states, offered no serious resistance to the regimes in power. In terms of the contributions isolated in earlier chapters with regard to Western Christianity, they enunciated no clear critique of authoritarianism, made limited contributions to the development or protection of civil society, and played no role in negotiating transition processes. Of course there were exceptions, individual bishops, priests and laypeople who stood up to the state authorities, defended human rights and contributed to debates over political futures, but in no cases could we say that these played a significant role in bringing about political change.

In the Soviet Union Orthodox activism was sparked by Nikita Khrushchev's renewed assault on the churches in 1958–64, and perhaps strengthened by awareness of the activities of groups such as the Baptists in campaigning vigorously to defend their faith communities. As in Poland, the primary concern was with defending religious freedom and the right to believe, with a few individual Orthodox bishops quietly working to limit the damage caused by anti-religious campaigns and to revitalise parish life, often while simultaneously offering public support for the regime. In 1965 Orthodox dissent went public, as Archbishop Yermogen of Kaluga called for the repeal of certain church regulations effectively supporting state control of the Church, and Frs Gleb Yakunin and Nikolai Eshliman offered a very public critique of official policies and church compliance. Over the next few years they were joined by a handful of priests and lay activists, with some support from public intellectuals who dressed their support in terms of campaigns on behalf of national culture, but the institutional Church remained silent, especially when religious dissenters began to link up with other human rights activists during the 1970s.[24] Similar situations prevailed in Bulgaria and Romania, where if anything the Orthodox churches were even more quiescent. In both countries a few individual priests and laymen occasionally launched protests on behalf of the Church or human rights more generally, but these individuals made virtually no contribution to the overthrow of the communist governments. Unlike Poland, such individuals enjoyed no support from their own religious hierarchy and little overt support within the wider Orthodox community, and were subject to more thoroughgoing repression than their Catholic counterparts. Additionally they suffered from being members of autonomous national churches that lacked the transnational organisational structures and networks that helped to sustain Catholic resistance to authoritarianism. When change did start to affect the predominantly Orthodox countries during the late 1980s a few individuals became involved in committees and organisations focusing on promoting political change, but in virtually every case their role was marginal.

It was only during the process of democratic consolidation that the issue of Orthodoxy's relationship to democracy became a subject of debate, as in the post-communist world it was often the countries with a dominant Orthodox tradition that struggled most to consolidate democratic orders. This was not inevitable, as was evident from the Greek case where the Church had managed to adapt (if not without occasional ambivalence) to the realities of a democratic order following the fall of the colonels' regime in 1974. Yet in the post-Soviet world, religious hierarchies conditioned by their communist era experiences did struggle to come to terms with a more pluralistic environment and focusing on this period enables us to isolate some of the tensions that may remain in the Orthodox–democracy relationship. In particular these churches are having to rethink their understanding of the relationship between the Church and the State, the nation and the individual citizen in the political realm. And as they face up to these dilemmas, many within those churches and countries are asking whether the nature of the relationships in the 'Western Christian world' are the only ones compatible with democratic politics or even whether democracy is the most appropriate form of government.

The twin temptations

Church and State

Alfred Stepan has stressed that the most appropriate relationship for religion and democracy is rooted in what he calls 'the twin tolerations', the first of which requires that in a democracy political institutions should be able to generate policies that are not subject to veto from 'constitutionally privileged' religious institutions. At the same time democracies should permit freedom of worship and ensure that religious institutions and individuals are free to promote their values in society so long as the advancement of these values does not impinge on the liberties of others or violate the law.[25] In evaluating religious support for democracy and democratisation this would mean exploring how they handle the question of relations with the State and in particular the question of whether they play by the 'rules of the game' in seeking to pursue their goals. It should be stressed here that the argument is not about the precise formal relationship of Church and State in a democratic setting, for different structural arrangements can have very different outcomes – separation in the USA does not exclude a significant religious input into the political sphere, whilst establishment in the UK does not entail a fundamental restriction of religious liberty. Rather the concern is with whether the Church–State relationship sought by traditionally dominant churches endows them with an advantage that is incompatible with democratic assumptions. Of course, defining what is legitimate or illegitimate may be problematic, for some might argue that where a religious tradition is sociologically dominant it is not inappropriate to give it due recognition. Against that, we would suggest that in a democratic order an 'illegitimate advantage' would be one that constitutionally and legally gave rights to one religious institution that were not given to others; that perhaps gave them financial support, institutional access, educational rights or a degree of access to policy-makers that was denied to other groups; that gave them effective veto rights in certain policy areas; that supported the campaigns of traditionally dominant religions to restrict the rights of other religious communities (covered in the next chapter); and that permitted them to intervene in electoral politics in ways prohibited to other religious communities.[26] Yet having stated this rather simple position, we have to acknowledge that reality is far more complex, for many countries give rights to traditionally dominant churches in ways that in the early twenty-first century do not fundamentally undermine democratic governance.

In exploring the Church–State relationship, it should be remembered that with the exception of Greece, all of the major Orthodox churches had just resurfaced from lengthy periods of subordination to anti-religious governments, although on occasions they had still been treated as somewhat more than first among equals. Yet each could look back to earlier periods in their history when they had enjoyed very close ties to the State and political authority and, following transition, the question arose as to whether they should seek to recreate these old ties. For the Greek Church the situation was a little different, in that it had since independence effectively operated as a part of the state structure and that following the removal of the military it had retained its position as the 'prevailing religion' of the Greek state.

The Greek case also differs from that of the other Orthodox countries in that the authoritarian regime overthrown in 1974 claimed to be restoring and protecting Greece's Christian civilisation and it did not touch the effective establishment of the Church. Though some on the

Left hoped that the overthrow of the military junta would be followed by a separation of Church and State, there has been no significant support for this in Greek society. The constitution adopted in 1975 started with an invocation of the Trinity and went on the describe Orthodoxy as the 'prevailing religion in Greece', though many Orthodox spokesmen deny that this amounts to establishment, let alone privilege. In practice, however, the Constitution supported the Church, committed the State to an understanding that the only doctrine and scriptural texts permissible were those sanctioned by the Greek hierarchy, and to the development of the 'national and religious consciousness' of the citizen. At the same time the document defended freedom of conscience and allowed freedom to 'all known religions'. Yet as we shall see later, the constitution was reinforced by a series of 'para-constitutional' regulations, many left over from the pre-war Metaxas dictatorship which to varying degrees undermined this proclamation of religious liberty. Critics have also noted that church salaries and the maintenance of church properties continue to be paid for by the State, and that religious (Orthodox) education is obligatory in schools. Though in theory members of other religious traditions can avoid this, in some areas there is considerable social pressure to participate. This formal privileging is defended with reference to the sociological reality that most Greeks are Orthodox.[27] It is also clear that in Greece the Orthodox hierarchy has gradually come to terms with the nature of democracy and has become a skilled player of the democratic game, utilising the media, encouraging protest, and organising public pressure in pursuit of its goals. Yet it remains hostile to any formal separation of Church and State, arguing that this is not necessary on democratic grounds and that it would contradict the special relationship of religion and ethnicity in Greece.

In Bulgaria and Romania post-communist constitutions have offered little formal recognition to the Orthodox churches, though in both, as in Greece, the churches have enjoyed a pre-eminence of status that means that they tend to be seen as established churches. Black-robed clerics are present at all major state occasions, as well as key local ones, and leading bishops are often involved in ceremonies such as the swearing in of new presidents – in 1996 Emil

Constantinescu became the first post-communist president to take his oath on the Bible.[28] In Bulgaria the constitution refers to Orthodoxy as 'the traditional religion' of the country and there have been subsequent, unsuccessful, attempts to strengthen the legal status of the Orthodox Church by requiring the State to pay special attention to the needs of the national church.[29] The Romanian Constitution of 1991 is even less explicit, making no mention of the Orthodox Church, though in 1994 the Church proclaimed itself the 'national church' and in 1999 sought to amend the law on religion to gain this same status. At the same time several hierarchs sought to gain political representation for the Church, by suggesting that every member of the Synod should sit in the Senate.[30]

In both countries additional state support has also been evident in official backing given to Orthodoxy being taught in schools and the provision of chaplains for military units and prisons. In Bulgaria the weakness of a church divided internally in consequence of past compromises with the old regime limited the claims it could realistically make on the State. Nonetheless, by 1997 it had succeeded in getting religious education introduced into schools, though it was often hard to find qualified teachers and there was some concern over the situation of children from religious minorities and over the quality of the supporting textbooks. The extent to which such education penetrated the country was far from clear, and in 2000 attempts were made to create some form of equality in predominantly Muslim areas where elective classes in Islam were introduced in elementary schools in over 20 cities, but in general the assumption remained that what was taught in most of the country had a predominantly Orthodox flavour.[31] Similar debates took place in Romania, where very early on the Orthodox Church sought to promote compulsory religious education throughout the school curriculum. Here the 1995 law on education made religious teaching compulsory at primary school level and optional at the secondary level, but in consequence a significant proportion of young people simply opted out. Without an adequate supply of religion teachers, this meant that Orthodox priests provided most of the education and its content was often outdated, negative about other religious groups, and critical of contemporary scientific knowledge.[32]

Russia presents a more complex picture, for here the Church managed, with the support of leading politicians, to draw a veil over past compromises, and society seemed less concerned. Surveys throughout the 1990s and beyond demonstrated a considerable degree of trust in the Orthodox Church, whilst political leaders paid at least lip service to the importance of Orthodoxy to both national identity and moral values, often in the hope that it would reinforce their own legitimacy.[33] Constitutionally Church and State remained separate, and Orthodox spokesmen repeatedly stressed their desire to avoid returning to the gilded cage relationship they had with Tsarism.[34] Yet whilst the *Bases of the Social Concept of the Russian Orthodox Church* adopted by the Moscow Patriarchate in 2000[35] formally recognised that the old notion of *symphonia* was not compatible with modern notions of the State, the behaviour and comments of the church hierarchy often suggest that this remained the preferred model. For Zoe Knox:

> *Symphonia* is not possible in a modern democratic state for two principal reasons: it makes one confession the sole repository of faith and it elevates the temporal leader to the position of God's representative on earth. It does not co-exist with other social organisations in the 'sphere of associations' or take its place among other religious bodies in the pluralist religious sphere. Instead, one church is situated in the political sphere, influencing state policies, while the state is guided by its custody of that church.[36]

In an ideal world it might see this not in terms of subordination but as a partnership in which the Church offers a sort of moral guardianship over the State or acts as a 'pastoral counsellor' to state officials.[37] Whilst officially condemning overt religious involvement in politics, the *Social Concept* rejected the idea that the Orthodox Church should not influence public life. Indeed, its delineation of where the Church should be involved and where it should not was heavily weighted in favour of the former, with a list of sixteen areas of Church–State co-operation (as opposed to three areas where it was inappropriate). In several areas, such as patriotic education, chaplaincies and the fights against 'pseudo-religious structures' it effectively claimed a privileged position for Orthodoxy, for the assumption is that the Orthodox will dominate in such activity.

According to the *Social Concept* the Church 'has the right to expect that the state, in building its relations with religious bodies, will take into account the number of their followers and the place they occupy in forming the historical, cultural and spiritual image of the people and their civic stand' and 'one cannot altogether exclude the possibility of such a … spiritual revival of society as to make natural a religiously higher form of government'. In other words, the Church accepts its current constrained position within a quasi-democratic political order, but suggests that should there be a serious turning to Orthodoxy by the population its preference would be for other forms of government where it occupies a more significant role in decision-making. And in this major statement of its current political and social thought it makes clear its preference for Old Testament-style judgeship that represented a form of theocratic rule, or for monarchy. In this conception democracy is definitely a second best that to some extent panders to the need of a modern humanity insufficiently in touch with its spiritual dimension.[38]

Church and nation

There is a view which suggests that many of the problems the Orthodox churches have with pluralism are rooted in a theological and cultural emphasis on the centrality of the community over the individual. We shall return to this in our later discussion of liberalism, but the essence of the argument is that faith is not a product of individual choice but of sharing collective worship and living in community. At one level this might be seen at the level of the parish where all contribute and participate in social and religious life, but it is also tied to larger communities and, in the modern era, to ethnic communities. In the case of the Eastern Orthodox churches, this is especially important because they have at least since the Ottoman period tended to be identified with specific ethnic groups and, ecclesiastically speaking, have no over-arching authority comparable to the Vatican in the Roman Catholic tradition. Whilst this linkage may have been useful in preserving religious and national identities in times of occupation and dominance by other powers, it has also rendered the churches more susceptible to control by political rulers, whether nationalist or communist. More importantly for our purposes is the argument that this strong connection to the nation may undermine the commitment of a democratic state to inclusiveness and reinforce the arguments of those who want to restrict participation to members of the dominant nationality. In the worst case scenario, it might be used to justify restriction of minority rights and even physical repression of those belonging to other ethno-confessional communities.

We can certainly see this in Greece, where there has historically been little distinction between being Greek and being Orthodox. The first constitutional text of 1822 classifies as Greeks 'all natives who believe in Christ', and this assumption underlay much constitutional thinking throughout the nineteenth century. Chrysoloras comments:

> Orthodoxy in Greece is mostly experienced as a 'way of life' rather than as an attachment to metaphysical beliefs ... The Church has been responding to these strong feelings of affiliation for the Greek public by acting as a political and cultural agent, which mainly aims to counter the effects of the 'westernisation' of Greece by articulating a nationalist discourse, while at the same time protecting and promoting its political privileges. It regards itself as the guardian of the 'Greek identity' and continuously interferes in Greek political affairs.[39]

This association has continued into modern times, and the 1975 constitution opens with an invocation of the Trinity and a statement about the proper definition of Orthodox doctrines. The language about the intimate connection of nation and faith springs in part from historical experience, from the time when the Ottomans recognised communities as faith based *millets* but also from the absence of a strong supra-national element in Orthodoxy that might transcend national particularities. At the same time it helped to define 'the other' or 'the threat', which in turn justified what George Mavrogordatas has called the 'endangered nation syndrome' that has been used by the Church in defence of establishment and legal privilege.[40] For all this, there remain ambiguities about who is the leading partner in the relationship, with Petrou and Tsironis suggesting that it may not be Orthodoxy that has determined the national identity of modern Greeks, so much as the 'national state ... that imposed ethnocentricity on the Orthodox Church in Greece'.[41]

The continued salience of these issues can perhaps best be illustrated by the debate over identity cards in the late 1990s and the beginning of the new century, when the dynamic Archbishop of Athens Christodoulos led a very noisy campaign against the removal of the religious question from Greek identity cards. In essence his concern was not primarily religious but national, and he sold himself as a defender of the nation's identity against the forces of globalisation, denationalisation and multiculturalism.[42] According to Molokotas-Liederman, both sides in this argument accepted that Orthodoxy was a part of the national heritage, but those who favoured retaining the religious question:

> conceive faith as a determining factor of individual and collective identity. In their view, Orthodoxy is not only a religious tradition, but also a whole culture and way of life; Orthodoxy becomes synonymous not only with Hellenism and the cultural and historical identity of Greece, but also with Greek nationality ... In their view, the elimination of religion from identity cards constitutes an attempt to discredit the religious identity of the country and disconnect Greek people from Orthodoxy in an overall attempt to transform Greece into a non-religious or secular country.

Those opposing them, on the other hand, 'reject the exclusivity of Orthodoxy in defining Greekness' and because Orthodoxy is a majority religion see no need to mention it on official documents.[43]

Chrysoloras offers an interesting analysis of the rhetoric and writings of the leading Orthodox spokesman in this debate, Archbishop Christodoulos of Athens, who even before his appointment was speaking of the need to protect Greece's distinctly Orthodox identity. He argues that the discourse of Christodoulos has as its first rhetorical strategy the:

> construction of a logic of equivalence ... In this case the Archbishop refers to the 'people' as a unified and undivided entity. He then constructs a set of ideological and political frontiers between the people and its enemies ... 'The history and the will of the people are above the constitution and the laws' ... Another emblematic example of populist practice is Christodoulos' tactic of presenting himself as a direct and unmediated representative of the people, one who rejects the modern unpopular bureaucratic procedures, and his words appeal to the nation as a whole, independently of party attachments.[44]

Arguably, Chrysoloras paints too one-sided a picture, but there is an element of truth in his suggestion that the rhetoric of the Archbishop and other leading churchmen at the time of the identity card debate did create the impression that a true Greek had to be Orthodox – and by implication, those who were not Orthodox were in some sense not really Greek.[45]

This emphasis on distinctiveness, on linking religion with ethnicity, and the tendency to focus on 'others' or 'enemies' can also be found emanating from the post-communist Russian Orthodox Church. A particular cause of irritation was the perceived influx of foreign missionaries during the 1990s who saw themselves bringing faith and civilisation to countries about which they knew very little, and the fact that missionaries were often targeting members of the Orthodox community rather than those without faith. Strongly connected to this were arguments about Russia as essentially Orthodox and thus not a legitimate place for other religious communities to work, except amongst their own co-ethnics – Lutherans were welcome to minister to ethnic Germans, and Catholics to Poles, but they should leave Russians well alone. Metropolitan Kirill of Smolensk suggested that so-called mission was actually 'spiritual colonialism' and undermined the basic principle which 'stipulates that the church in a given place shall be fully responsible for the people before God' though, as Phillip Walters suggests, even with this principle it is not clear in all areas of Russia why only the Russian Orthodox Church should have that responsibility,[46] nor what this meant for Orthodox communities in non-Orthodox countries.

This underlying concept of one church for one nation was also clear in some of the debates surrounding discussion of the 1997 law on religious freedom when one group of nationalist writers argued that religious pluralism had the potential 'to destroy traditional spiritual-moral values' and that a more restrictive law was required to protect 'the spiritual-cultural distinctiveness and national state interests of Russia'.[47] Writing one year later, Sergei Dunaev commented that the law's approval marked Russia's declaration of 'sovereignty in matters of religious distinctiveness'.[48]

This view was reinforced in the *Social Concept* approved by the Russian Orthodox Church in 2000, which stated the importance of ethnic harmony and condemned chauvinism. Nonetheless, it reminded its readers that 'the universal nature of the Church, however, does not mean that Christians should have no right to national identity and national self-expression', and argued that 'when a nation, civil or ethnic, represents fully or predominantly a mono-confessional Orthodox community, it can in a certain sense be regarded as the one community of faith – an Orthodox nation'. Avoiding chauvinism, the Orthodox Christian should nevertheless manifest a patriotism of the sort that 'is manifested when he defends the fatherland against an enemy, works for the good of the motherland, cares for the good order of ... life through, among other things, participation in the affairs of government. The Christian is called to preserve and develop national culture and peoples' self-awareness'.[49] Yet the implication of the text is clear – Russia is Orthodox, with the consequence that those who are not Orthodox are in some sense not real Russians. Of course, the Orthodox community is itself pluralistic and there are a range of views on these issues, but in so far as the *Social Concept* represents the official position of the Russian Orthodox Church one could argue that its impact upon the community of faithful is to root the Church's centre of gravity on public affairs in a defensive position that is sceptical of aspects of inclusive democratic governance – as opposed to the Vatican II declarations which shifted the Roman Catholic Church's centre in a more pluralistic direction.

Most problematic for the evolution of a more pluralistic politics has been the contribution of religion to ethnic conflicts and violence in the former Yugoslavia, though it should be emphasised that religion in general, and Orthodoxy in particular, was not the cause of conflict. Most sources agree that religion was something that was manipulated by former communists, turned nationalists, to build unity within their own communities as well as to legitimate actions against others,[50] though it is recognised that in the absence of other clear distinctions religion often did serve to divide the various communities. Moreover, one should not neglect the role that religion has played historically in creating and maintaining cultures and a sense of belonging to a shared community – as well as in defining those who do not belong. In the Serbian case the Orthodox Church played a key role during the Ottoman occupation as 'guardian of the Serbian people's national culture and traditions. The Church fostered education and cultivated resentment of the Islamic conqueror'.[51] Then as the Serbian state achieved independence, nationalists emphasised the role of Orthodoxy in defining the nation, with nineteenth-century linguistic reformer Vuk Karadžić going so far as to suggest that Jesus and the apostles were Serbs.[52] Despite this association with nationalism and growing privileges within Serbia from the turn of the century, and evidence of some political influence during the inter-war years, the events of 1939–45 allowed the re-appearance of the victim mentality, with the Church depicting itself as an 'embattled warrior for Christ'.[53] The war proved disastrous for the Orthodox Church as hundreds of clergy were killed and churches destroyed by Croat forces, and these very real crimes (often reciprocated at the time and sometimes exaggerated later) reinforced communal hatred that could be called upon again after communist control had loosened.

The collapse of communism and the appearance of Slobodan Milošević as Serbian leader created a new situation for the Church. Its primary concerns were with restoring its fortunes after a lengthy period subordinate to an anti-religious regime and it had very little interest in whether the new order was more or less democratic. A new programme of church construction began, religious access to the media and publishing opportunities increased, and clergymen enjoyed a new status in a more nationalistically inclined Serbia.[54] Simultaneously, and despite a sometimes ambiguous relationship with the country's new leaders, the Church found it easy to buy into some of the new regime's nationalistic rhetoric and conspiracy theory-dominated thinking. As Ramet notes, 'a clear relationship can be detected between the conspiratorial mood that seized the Serbian Church as it worried about a worldwide Vatican-Islamic plot against Serbdom and the Milošević regime's claims that a Vatican-German-Croat-Muslim conspiracy existed against the Serbian nation'.[55]

Once overt conflict began, Orthodox churchmen played a key role in dragging up often distorted memories of past oppression by Catholics and Muslims – 'this was not the first time for the Serbian people in their history to have experienced crucifixion'[56] – in blessing religiously ignorant soldiers, and denying that Serbs were committing atrocities against other groups within the region. During the successive wars of the 1990s religious symbols were utilised by field commanders, priests were attached to armed units, religious sites were increasingly targeted by the armies of all sides, and a sense of belonging to a threatened community was exacerbated by appeals to religious difference and past rivalries and atrocities. Sabrina Ramet, summing up the Church's role in the conflict, has argued that:

> The Serbian leadership and the Serbian church hierarchy have each promoted the notion that Serbdom means Orthodoxy, albeit for distinctly different reasons. For the leaders, this manipulation serves to create a point of cultural unity, to build a bridge to nationalism as an alternate source of legitimacy ... For the Serbian Church hierarchy, this manipulation served the obvious objective of placing the Serbian Church at the ideological centre of creating an artificial (i.e. nonspiritual) attraction to the Church.[57]

For our purposes, what is more important is that by buying into this nationalist vision the Church reinforced non-inclusive visions of the future. By focusing on the nation and stressing the distinction between 'them' and 'us', it neglected to articulate a positive vision of what sort of society it wanted to see develop after communism. And once a relative peace came at the beginning of the new century, it again focused its energies on preserving its own dominance and in finding new 'others' to demonise – whether religious or sexual minorities. In so doing effectively it acted as one of those forces in society seeking to restrict the realm of freedom that is generally associated with democratic governance.

★ ★ ★ ★ ★

In this chapter we have started to address the issue of Eastern Orthodoxy's 'centre of gravity' in an attempt to determine the nature of the Orthodox engagement with the democratic project in those countries where it is traditionally dominant. We have suggested that in part the tradition as a whole has been pushed into a position that is hesitant about the virtue of democracy because of its historical experience, in particular the very limited experience of living under, and therefore engaging with, the realities of democratic governance. Most of these churches were under communist rule until 1989/91 and they have often struggled to define their role in the new political orders emerging since then. When they emerged from authoritarian rule they not only had little experience of democratic governance, but the tradition as a whole lacked well-developed intellectual and theological resources upon which church leaders and activists could draw to think about how best to engage with the new political orders. Though some Orthodox scholars still insisted that the traditions of *symphonia* could be drawn on and applied to contemporary conditions, in reality this was of very limited practical utility in meeting the real challenges of contemporary pluralist politics.

In consequence, as we have seen, the traditionally dominant Orthodox churches tended to look to the past, focusing at the institutional level on developing close ties with the State – whilst denying any intent of returning to the pre-revolutionary relationship –and arguing that this was perfectly legitimate in countries where the majority of the population identified, however loosely, with the Orthodox tradition. What was at issue was not religious establishment, which in itself is not incompatible with democracy – though increasingly hard to justify in modern Europe – but the question of whether religious institutions pursued this close relationship with power for the purpose of acquiring special privileges within the new political orders. At the risk of generalisation, our all too brief survey suggests that Orthodox churches have to some degree sought special rights in terms of access to education, some degree of state funding, and provision of religious support in prisons, hospitals and army units. As we shall see in the next chapter, in all of the countries concerned they have sought to prevent other religious communities from achieving the same degree of access, and have sometimes attempted to restrict their right to 'free exercise', though the extent to which they have been successful should not be exaggerated. They also tend to have more access to policy-makers than other religious groups, though again the extent to which this represents more than symbolic power varies according to country, region and context. What is important for our purposes is less the success they enjoy, than the fact that in all of these countries the focus of religious hierarchies has tended to be more on acquiring influence with the State rather than developing their role in civil society – though some within the churches have been active here. In this sense they rejected Casanova's argument that in democratic societies the most appropriate sphere of action for religious bodies is in the realm of civil society.[58]

Perhaps even more problematic have been the continuing efforts of many within these churches to identify a special connection between themselves and the national community, by suggesting that in some sense religious and political belonging are identical. As we shall see in our discussion of the debates over religious pluralism, there have occasionally been hints that somehow the non-Orthodox are not really part of the community, whether it be Russian, Greek or Serbian, whilst it is hard to see how the tone of some of the arguments for privileging the Orthodox does not lead minorities to feel excluded from the public realm. This official church attitude in turn reinforces intolerance of difference within society, in so far as church publications and spokespersons tend to lump all non-Orthodox groups into the category of 'sects' or 'cults'. In the extreme case of the former Yugoslavia, this focus on 'them' and 'us' has served to reinforce difference, to demonise others, and permit a dehumanisation that opens the door to violence and ethnic cleansing. Of course in the Balkans it is not just the Orthodox that have been guilty of this, but arguably the Serbian religious leadership has utilised rhetoric that has fed into conflict and failed to be sufficiently forthright in challenging the violence encouraged by power-holders.

We shall return to some of these issues at the end of the next chapter, but our primary point here is to suggest that in their engagement with democracy and democratisation the Orthodox churches have been hampered by the more limited range of theological and intellectual resources dealing with socio-political issues, and by a tradition that still tends to believe that a very close relationship with state and nation is the most appropriate form of political engagement. None of this is meant to suggest that Orthodoxy is inherently anti-democratic, or to suggest that there are no resources capable of supporting democratisation within the tradition, or to deny that there are those within all of these churches who have for a variety of reasons sought to push the churches into adopting a more pro-democratic stance. Rather, it reinforces my wider argument that at particular points in history the over-arching 'centre of gravity' within religious communities tends to act more in one direction than another, and that in the Orthodox case this has tended in recent decades to operate in ways that encourage what I have called a 'hesitation' about democracy rather than an Orthodox opposition to or embracing of democracy. We shall develop this argument further in the next chapter, whilst also pointing to further reasons that may underlie this hesitation but also noting several trends within Orthodoxy that may eventually help to push the churches, perhaps screaming and kicking on occasions, into developing a positive attitude towards democracy.

Notes

1 S. Huntington, *The Third Wave: Democratization in the Late Twentieth Century* (Norman: University of Oklahoma Press, 1991), p. 289.

2 S. Huntington, 'The clash of civilizations?', *Foreign Affairs*, 77 (Summer 1993), p. 30.

3 S. Huntington, *The Clash of Civilizations and the Remaking of World Order* (New York: Simon and Schuster, 1996), p. 139.

4 Ibid., pp. 162–3.

5 A. Stepan, 'The world's religious systems and democracy: crafting the "twin tolerations"', in *Arguing Comparative Politics* (Oxford: Oxford University Press, 2001), pp. 147–50.

6 There are hints of this argument even in a book as generally sophisticated as that of N. Gvosdev, *An Examination of Church–State Relations in the Byzantine and Russian Empires with an Emphasis on Ideology and Models of Interaction* (Lewiston: Edwin Mellen Press, 2001), pp. 178–91.

7 F. Cross and E. Livingstone (ed.), *The Oxford Dictionary of the Christian Church* (New York: Oxford University Press, 1985), p. 771, quoted in S. Harakas, *Living the Faith: The Praxis of Eastern Orthodox Ethics* (Minneapolis: Light and Life Publishing, 1993), p. 259.

8 J. Anderson, 'Putin and the Russian Orthodox Church: assymetric symphonia', *Journal of International Affairs*, 61:1 (2007), pp. 185–201.

9 See F. Dvornik, *Early Christian and Byzantine Political Philosophy: Origins and Background*, Volume 2 (Washington: Harvard University, 1966), pp. 724–850.

10 A. Papanikolaou, 'Bzyantium, Orthodoxy and democracy', *Journal of the American Academy of Religion*, 71:1 (2003), pp. 82–3.

11 Gvosdev, *An Examination of Church–State Relations in the Byzantine and Russian Empires*, p. 57.

12 C. Frazee, 'Church and state in Greece', in T. Koumoulidis (ed.), *Greece in Transition: Essays in Modern Greek History, 1821–1974* (London: Zeno Publishers, 1977), pp. 128–44.

13 T. Gallagher, *Theft of a Nation: Romania since Communism* (London: Hurst, 2005), p. 24.

14 J. Anderson, *Religious Liberty in Transitional Societies: The Politics of Religion* (Cambridge: Cambridge University Press, 2003), pp. 94–5.

15 R. Sakwa, 'Christian democracy and civil society in Russia', *Religion, State and Society*, 22:3 (1994), pp. 273–304.

16 Gvosdev, *An Examination of Church–State Relations in the Byzantine and Russian Empires*, p. 56.

17 J. Cunningham, *A Vanquished Hope: The Movement for Church Renewal in Russia, 1905–1906* (New York: St Vladimir's Seminar Press, 1983).

18 For a general survey of the Orthodox Church's dealing with the State in the late Soviet and early post-communist period see J. Anderson, *Religion, State and Politics in the Soviet Union and the Successor States* (Cambridge: Cambridge University Press, 1994).

19 Papanikolaou, 'Bzyantium, Orthodoxy and democracy', p. 77.

20 V. Wozniuk, 'Vladimir S. Soloviev and the politics of human rights', *Journal of Church and State*, 41:1 (1999), pp. 33–50.

21 D. Koyzis, 'Imaging God and his kingdom: Eastern Orthodoxy's iconic political ethic', *Review of Politics*, 55:2 (1993), pp. 267–89.

22 E. Prodromou, 'The ambivalent Orthodox', *Journal of Democracy*, 15:2 (2004), pp. 62–75.

23 On the Church's response to military rule see P. Scwab and C. Frangos (ed.), *Greece under the Junta* (New York: Facts on File, 1970), pp. 29–30; Frazee, 'Church and state in Greece', pp. 149–51.

24 Anderson, *Religion, State and Politics in the Soviet Union and the Successor States*, pp. 82–5; cf. P. Valliere, 'Russian Orthodoxy and human rights', in I. Bloom, J. P. Martin and W. Proudfoot (ed.), *Religious Diversity and Human Rights* (New York: Columbia University Press, 1996), pp. 278–312.

25 Stepan, 'The world's religious systems and democracy: crafting the "twin tolerations"', pp. 216–17.

26 Even this latter concept is problematic, because in many countries the practising religious constituency is very different from that section of the population which describes itself as Orthodox, Catholic or Protestant. In Russian perhaps 70% of the population considers itself Orthodox and the hierarchy claims special privileges on this basis, but perhaps 5% of the population attend church on a regular basis.

27 For a more extended discussion see Anderson, *Religious Liberty in Transitional Societies*, pp. 47–51.

28 L. Stan and L. Turcescu, 'The Romanian Orthodox Church and post-communist democratisation', *Europe-Asia Studies*, 52:8 (2000), p. 1473.

29 Anderson, *Religious Liberty in Transitional Societies*, pp. 97–8.

30 Stan and Turcescu, 'The Romanian Orthodox Church and post-communist democratisation', pp. 1475–7.

31 *Tolerance* (Sofia), January 1998, p. 2.

32 Stan and Turcescu, 'The Romanian Orthodox Church and post-communist democratisation', pp. 1477–9.

33 Anderson, *Religious Liberty in Transitional Societies*, pp. 94–8 and 120–6.

34 See the comments of Metropolitan Kirill of Smolensk quoted in V. Fedorov, 'Barriers to ecumenism: an Orthodox view from Russia', *Religion, State and Society*, 26:2 (1998), p. 143.

35 This was perhaps the first time any national Orthodox Church had adopted an explicit document setting out its social thinking. English and Russian texts can be found at the Moscow Patriarchate's website: www .mospat. ru/index. php?mid=90 (accessed 5 April 2007).

36 Zoe Knox, 'The symphonic ideal: the Moscow Patriarchate's post-Soviet leadership', *Europe-Asia Studies*, 55:4 (2003), p. 577.

37 D. Davis, 'Editorial: The Russian Orthodox Church and the future of Russia', *Journal of Church and State*, 44:3 (2002), pp. 653–70.

38 www.mospat.ru/index.php?mid=90.

39 N. Chrysoloras, 'Why Orthodoxy? Religion and nationalism in Greek political culture', Paper given at first LSE Symposium on Modern Greece, p. 3; a version of this paper was later published in *Studies in Ethnicity and Nationalism* 4:1 (2004), pp. 40–61.

40 G. Mavrogordatas, 'Orthodoxy and nationalism in the Greek case', in J. Madeley and Z. Enyedi (ed.), *Church and State in Contemporary Europe: The Chimera of Neutrality* (London: Frank Cass, 2003), pp. 117–36.

41 I. Petrou and C. Tsironis, 'Orthodoxy and cultural identity in modern Greece', in J. Sutton and W. van den Bercken (ed.), *Orthodox Christianity and Contemporary Europe* (Leuven: Peeters, 2003), p. 506.

42 Anderson, *Religious Liberty in Transitional Societies*, p. 183.

43 L. Molokotos-Liederman, 'The Greek ID card controversy: a case study of religion and national identity in a changing European Union', *Journal of Contemporary Religion*, 22:1 (2007), pp. 187–203.

44 Chrysoloras, 'Why Orthodoxy?', pp. 10–13.

45 In several interviews with non-Orthodox believers in Athens in the summer of 2000 this sense of being somehow painted out of 'Greekness' was recognised, though it was also stressed by some evangelicals that the general atmosphere was less oppressive than in the past and that perhaps membership of the EU was helping to change the attitudinal as well as the legal context.

46 P. Walters, 'Russian Orthodoxy and pluralism in Russian society today', in Sutton and van den Bercken, *Orthodox Christianity and Contemporary Europe*, p. 403.

47 *Rus Pravoslavnaya*, 23 January 1997. PS (I use PS when I refer to the Russian Religious News service translations provided by Paul Steeves and that can be found at: www.stetson.edu/~psteeves/relnews).

48 *Nezavisimaya gazeta*, 15 July 1998.

49 www.mospat.ru/index.php?mid=90.

50 For various views on the role of religion see M. Sells, *The Bridge Betrayed: Religion and Genocide in Bosnia* (Berkeley: University of California Press, 1996); P. Mojzes (ed.), *Religion and the War in Bosnia* (Atlanta: Scholars Press, 1998). See the debate on this moderated by M. Velikonja, 'The role of religions and religious communities in the war in the ex-Yugoslavia, 1991–1999', at www.georgefox.edu/academics /undergrad/departments/soc-swk/ree/2003/velikonja03.html (accessed 25 March 2006).

51 S. Ramet, *Nihil Obstat: Religion, Politics and Social Change in East-Central-Europe and Russia* (Durham: Duke University Press, 1998), p. 151.

52 Ibid., p. 152.

53 S. Ramet, *Balkan Babel: The Disintegration of Yugoslavia from the Death of Tito to the Fall of Milošević* 4th edition (Boulder: Westview, 2004), pp. 101–2.

54 Our concern here is only with the Orthodox and we will not comment on the role of other religious communities.

55 Ramet, *Nihil Obstat*, p. 172.

56 Quoted in Ramet, *Nihil Obstat*, p. 174.

57 Ibid., p. 175.

58 J. Casanova, *Public Religions in the Modern World* (Chicago: Chicago University Press, 1994).

6

The Orthodox hesitation: the 'liberal-democracy' paradox

What has become increasingly clear since the collapse of communism is the fact that much of the Eastern Orthodox 'hesitation' about democracy stems from the linkage between democracy and 'liberalism'. Though in principle willing to accept any form of government, many Orthodox leaders and commentators have begun to argue that democracy has to be adapted to local circumstances, that it should not require that they uncritically accept the liberal assumptions that have come to dominate Western democracies and, in a few cases, that perhaps democracy is not appropriate to their societies. In response liberal critics such as Sabrina Ramet have suggested that you cannot have democracy without accepting its six fundamental principles, i.e. 'the rule of law, individual rights, tolerance, the harm principle, equality, and the neutrality of state in matters of religion'.[1] If this bald statement is too simplistic, in so far as it fails to recognise the importance of cultural context and the fact that understandings of rights and tolerance will always be contested, the Orthodox critique of liberalism can all too often appear as little more than a conservative attempt to preserve hegemony within rapidly changing societies.

In this chapter we explore further the Orthodox hesitation about democracy, starting with a brief unpacking of the reservations about the ways in which an unqualified, individual-focused liberalism and unrestricted pluralism are sometimes marketed as an essential part of the democratic package. We then turn to see how traditionally dominant churches have handled two developments in their societies following the collapse of authoritarianism – the acceptance of a wider range of sexual difference, with the focus here on homosexuality, and the growth of religious free markets. The latter subject is particularly interesting because the ability to accept pluralism in 'one's own backyard' is often a particularly good test of democratic commitment. In the third section we look for more positive ways in which Orthodoxy may be able to contribute to democratisation, looking at its role in civil society-building in Russia and the experience of minority Orthodox communities in the USA. Our conclusion draws together the evidence presented in these two chapters, looks at whether the explanatory models developed earlier are useful in analysing the Orthodox experience, and reiterates our view that whilst Orthodoxy is multi-vocal its current 'centre of gravity', characterised by hesitation, does remain problematic in many respects and that therefore it is unlikely to make a major contribution to reinforcing democratisation in the immediate future.

Liberalism – the besetting sin of democracy

When commentators suggest that Eastern Orthodoxy exhibits ambiguity towards democracy, one response from within the tradition is to suggest that the real problem is not with democracy per se but with the liberal ethos that has emerged out of the Western Christian tradition. Thomas Hopko, writing as a US citizen of Orthodox faith, puts it thus:

> As the grandson of Carpatho-Russian immigrants to the United States, I cannot imagine my life in any other society except with gratitude for my personal destiny ... As an Orthodox Christian ... I cannot imagine a way of life more insidious to Christian Orthodoxy and more potentially dangerous to human being and life.[2]

Pluralism is viewed positively because it brings freedom of worship, particularly important for churches that have experienced communism; it brings competition – which Hopko can accept, though many of his co-religionists in the Orthodox world cannot – but it also brings a new set of values and attitudes that chip away at attempts to speak in terms of absolute religious truths and to preserve faith (and sometimes ethnic) communities.

This dilemma has perhaps been best expressed by

Elizabeth Prodromou who recognises that the Orthodox churches have often been ambivalent about aspects of the pluralism that characterises democratic regimes. In trying to resolve this problem she separates out pluralism from democracy, the former characterised by an emphasis on competition and difference which can sometimes create self-destructive elements within mature and new democracies alike.[3] Following Alfred Stepan she would want to stress that Orthodoxy, like other religious traditions, is multi-vocal and to argue that there are theological resources within the tradition that can make a distinctive contribution to both the understanding and practice of democracy. For example, she suggests that Orthodoxy's understanding of human freedom and agency, and its view of humans as made in the image and likeness of God but still flawed, can contribute to the self-limiting of individual desires that has to be part of the democratic process. Prodromou also suggests that the Trinitarian emphasis promotes the notion of pluralism in unity, and that the Church, though claiming to be universal, can live with a plurality of orders and jurisdictions. Nonetheless, ambivalence remains, as many see 'competition and difference as problematic phenomena that must be managed according to national particularities rooted in historical experience and contemporary confining conditions'.[4] For Prodromou there remain questions about how closely pluralism and democracy should be tied, about the roles that history and tradition play in the reception of democracy, and how pluralism should be managed in societies undergoing rapid social change. She goes on to argue that an 'aggressive-seeming' focus on religious liberty issues and insistence that traditionally Orthodox countries follow Western patterns of development might be replaced with a focus on encouraging notions of citizenship that would aid democracy-building in ways consonant with historical and local concerns.[5]

Prodromou is right in many respects, in particular in suggesting that Western religious liberty campaigns can be seen as somehow anti-Orthodox, yet she fails to elaborate what her emphasis on nationally sympathetic democracy-building actually means. The same applies to many Orthodox spokespersons in the former communist bloc who reject secularism as a necessary condition of modernity, who wish to build their own models of Church–State relations, who deny that this entails illegitimate restrictions on religious freedom, but who often fail to convince that this culturally specific argument is any more than a justification of privilege and the denial of rights to others, which most would see as incompatible with democratic governance. This is a problem that crops up again and again, for example in the speeches and articles of Metropolitan Kirill of Smolensk and Kaliningrad who has led the campaign against what he sees as attempts to impose a Western liberal model on the new Russian reality. For this eminent Russian clergyman:

> The fundamental contradiction of our epoch and the main challenge to the human community in the twenty-first century, is the opposition of liberal civilized standards on the one hand, and the values of national, cultural and religious identity on the other.

The roots of the former lie in:

> liberal ideas which have united within themselves pagan anthropocentrism, which entered European culture at the time of the renaissance, Protestant theology, and Jewish philosophical thought. These ideas came to a head in the era of enlightenment in a certain complex of liberal principles. The French Revolution was the culminating act of this spiritual and philosophical revolution … It is no accident that this revolution began with the Reformation, for it was the Reformation that rejected the normative significance of tradition in the sphere of Christian doctrine … It is quite obvious that the introduction of the female priesthood and acknowledgement of homosexuality occurred under the influence of liberal ideas and the rights of the individual.

Whilst he praises some contributions of the liberal order, including the notion of freedom of speech and freedom of conscience, Kirill remains wary of their uncritical acceptance in Russia. He appears to suggest that civil liberties and freedom of conscience are important in so far as they benefit the Orthodox Church, but that they do not require unlimited entry into the Russian religious market-place by other religious actors.

As Alexander Agadjanian and Kathy Rousselet have suggested, Kirill's position is not one of simple hostility to liberal ideas, but he does focus very heavily on the tension between traditionalism and liberalism. For Kirill, the latter's focus on absolute individual freedom fails to take into account the limitations imposed by the Church's understanding of sin and its view of the 'unique human person' as located in a particular community. This is not an assertion that Orthodox understandings should prevail throughout the world, but an argument that each person is situated in a country with its own spiritual traditions and in a world made up of distinctive cultures.[6] Kirill claims to want a way of reconciling the positive aspects of liberalism with respect for tradition and religious values as interpreted by the Russian Orthodox Church.[7] Above all, however, church spokesmen have persistently warned that Orthodox nations emerging from communism should be wary of integrating into a Western civilisation whose values may be very different from their own.

Yet whilst the critique of liberalism and the rejection of a slavish imitation of Western ways is coherent and understandable, until recently the positive side of the argument was less clearly articulated, i.e. what is to replace liberalism and unthinking pluralism, what does encouragement of national cultural values mean in practice, and what are the mechanisms by which this can be reconciled with the rights and freedoms that go with a democratic form of governance that these churchmen formally accept, albeit with varying degrees of enthusiasm? Only in 2006 did the Russian Orthodox Church attempt to produce a coherent statement setting out what an Orthodox understanding of human rights would look like, in a document prepared for the annual meeting of the World Council of the Russian People. This stressed the prior right of 'internal freedom from evil' and the need to ensure that individual rights did not 'trample upon religious or moral traditions, insult religious or national feelings'. It also spoke of the Church as collaborating with the State in 'preserving the rights of nations and ethnic groups to their individual religion',[8] but was somewhat evasive in setting out what this meant for the right of individuals to make their own religious choices.

This frequently negative, anti-liberal approach is often tied into an anti-ecumenical and anti-Western stance that has deep historical roots, going back to the East–West schism and the fact that, in subsequent years, the East was cut off from the events and ideas that formed modern Western society. This isolation, often seen as a blessing by Orthodox commentators, has also meant that the values of the Western world are often seen as alien. Even in Greece, Archbishop Christodoulos of Athens warned that:

> Europe may eventually fill our pockets; it may also empty our souls. We must struggle for this not to happen here because, if it does, it will lead our country into decline and deterioration. We are at the heart of Europe … We are first Orthodox Christians and then Europeans. First comes the national identity, then come all the others.[9]

What is feared is that globalisation, and its local manifestation in Europeanisation, will bring with it a secular world-view that serves to restrict faith to the private sphere. This argument was reiterated in debates over the draft European Constitution when the archbishop joined other religious leaders in criticising the failure of the European Union to recognise that the preamble should offer a proper rendering of the 'honour due to history and civilization', i.e. a recognition that Europe was a Christian cultural reality.[10]

This attitude to the outside world has also been seen in internal religious debates over ecumenism with anti-ecumenical sentiments increasingly voiced in many of the Orthodox churches and the Georgian and Bulgarian Orthodox churches leaving the World Council of Churches in 1997–98.[11] We cannot possibly do justice here to all the arguments surrounding the Orthodox engagement with the external world and we should stress that each of these individual churches has a multiplicity of voices, some of which are open to change and flexible in their response to the new challenges that face them. Nonetheless, at the time of writing it is possible to say that the dominant voices within Orthodoxy tend to be deeply conservative, suspicious of the forces of liberalism and globalisation, and inclined to respond by building defensive walls.[12] And this in turn impacts upon their attitudes towards and engagement with the ideas and practice of democracy, especially to the extent that the models of pluralism being promoted are seen as external impositions. What is less clear is what is meant in practice by the nationally specific forms of democracy they sometimes claim to promote.

The problem with pluralism

For all religious institutions the pluralism associated with democratic political orders creates real problems. In established democracies they have, over time, come to terms with the variety of ideas and practices on offer, even where they find some abhorrent, and they have learnt how to promote their own ideas and values through the media, pressure groups and political parties. For religious communities in transitional societies adapting to pluralism has proved far more problematic. Under the old communist systems, conservative values prevailed, competition of ideas was constrained and, to some extent, the Orthodox churches enjoyed a semi-official status as national churches, albeit under the tight control of the State. With the collapse of authoritarianism, churches weakened by years of repression and harassment found themselves in a market-place of ideas, and faced a much freer media that appeared to know no limits. In consequence, conservative politicians and churchmen tended to associate the collapse of strong authority with a growing sexual permissiveness, an intrusive press, and the onslaught of new ideas that undermined traditional values, though in part these changes simply allowed into the open ideas and activities previously hidden. In consequence, the churches often argued for a 'managed pluralism', described as combining a commitment to tolerance with a recognition that the traditional values of a nation cannot simply be over-ridden by elite imposition of value systems and ways of life typical of the older democracies.

The rest of this section looks at how the Orthodox churches have handled two aspects of pluralism in the wider society and within the religious sphere.[13] Much of the concern of all traditional churches is with the changing attitudes towards sexuality that tend to accompany the opening up of hitherto authoritarian countries. After Franco's death Spanish churchmen expressed concern at the appearance of tiny bikinis or topless women on Spanish beaches, at the arrival of pornography on the news stands, and the increasingly casual public acceptance of sexual activity outside of marriage. Many of these same issues have arisen in the post-communist world, though it is the question of homosexuality that has particularly agitated Orthodox spokespersons.

Within the church context, and perhaps even more importantly, in terms of the message that it sends out, is the question of how dominant religious institutions respond to the emergence of a religious free market for it could be argued that an institution committed to pluralism and tolerance should be able to accept and adapt to difference in its own bailiwick. Here the argument is not about whether churches have to accept liberal assumptions on these issues for clearly, like all social institutions and organisations in a democracy, they have the right to make the case that their moral values or opinions should shape legislation. Rather we are concerned with the ways in which they seek their objectives and the extent to which their framing of the arguments and policy options is compatible with democratic assumptions about the rights of the individual and about tolerance of private behaviour. At the same time it is about the messages sent to the wider society by a significant and often widely respected institution, and whether these messages help to reinforce or undermine democratic development.

Coping with sexual difference

Issues of sexuality have always proved problematic for the Christian churches in so far as their absolutist stand on many of these issues sits uneasily with the pluralism that tends to emerge within democratic societies. For the Roman Catholic Church and some Protestants the defining issue has often been abortion, with the promotion of an understanding of life as beginning at conception clashing with the notion of the individual woman's right to choose. In the post-communist world the Orthodox churches have by and large adopted the same position, including the tendency to link abortion with sexual promiscuity and feminism, but they have not tended to initiate major campaigns on this issue. Instead they have turned their attention to the issue of homosexuality, with the Romanian and Russian Orthodox churches playing prominent roles in attempting to prevent the decriminalisation and wider public acceptance of homosexual activity. As with other traditional religious communities this stems first and foremost from their theological understanding that same-sex activity is simply sinful, contrary to God's plans for humanity, and a denial that the primary aim of sexual activity is procreation.[14] But there are also other factors at play, from prejudice and fear of difference which mirrors that of the wider society – e.g. in linking homosexuality to paedophilia – through pragmatic concerns about demographic decline, to a wider concern about the likely social impact of a rapid liberalisation of social mores in times of change and uncertainty. Above all they see this as representing an attempt to impose external, inappropriate liberal values on societies and churches committed to traditional 'family values', and to encourage acceptance of practices that are allegedly not currently to be found within their own churches or societies.[15]

In the Soviet bloc countries homosexual activity was simply criminalised, and heavy penalties imposed on those involved, but with the collapse of communism there have been attempts in most of these countries (a) to decriminalise homosexual activity and (b) to end discrimination against those in same-sex relationships. In the Russian case the anti-gay campaign has developed domestically, in attacks on attempts to 'promote' homosexuality within the new Russia – homosexual activity was decriminalised in 1993 – and externally, in conflicts within the ecumenical movement where Russian conservatism has come into conflict with the more open attitude adopted by some of the liberal Protestant denominations that make up the World Council of Churches. For Patriarch Aleksii, supporting Moscow Mayor Luzhkov's banning of a gay pride march in 2006, the Church has 'invariably supported the institution of the family and condemned untraditional relations, seeing them as a vicious deviation from God-given human nature'. Given the demographic crisis in Russia and the need to strengthen the family 'as the foundation of a strong state', the Patriarch could not support any activity that served to legitimise homosexual activity. Whilst he claimed that the Church remained committed to pastoral care for such people, this was focused on the need to change behaviour rather than accept it.[16]

Welcoming a 2005 Vatican decision not to allow practising homosexuals to enter its seminaries, the head of the Moscow Patriarchate's Commission for Inter-Christian Dialogue Fr Igor Vyzhanov argued that 'homosexuals should be viewed as people suffering from a serious illness . . . If laypeople are forbidden to engage in homosexual acts, so much more should priesthood candidates and Church people seek not political correctness, but a firm foundation for their faith in life'.[17] Though in 2007 Metropolitan Kirill could tell a group of Moscow university students that whilst discrimination against gays was not acceptable, he suggested that sexual minorities should not be able to dictate their views to majorities or propagate untraditional views in public demonstrations.[18] Such statements were very much in line with other pronouncements of Orthodox hierarchs who saw the acceptance of sexual difference as just another consequence of a rushed acceptance of every aspect of a Western-based liberalism that had little resonance with Russian traditions.

For Romania, acceptance into the Council of Europe, achieved in 1993, came with the proviso that homosexuality be decriminalised, a promise that was opposed by many in the wider society and by the Orthodox hierarchy in particular – according to Ramet this subject stimulated its political engagement in a way that issues such as human rights or crime or corruption did not.[19] In launching this campaign the Church reflected the view of the majority of Romanians, with surveys in 1993 showing that around 80% of the population believing homosexual acts could never be justified, and other polls demonstrating considerable levels of intolerance. In 1996 a partial liberalisation criminalised only those acts that caused a public scandal (a phrase that proved virtually impossible to operationalise) or were carried out in public, and allowed for punishment of those 'proselytising for homosexuality'. This proved unsatisfactory from the European perspective and in 2000 the government proposed changes to the Criminal Code that would fully decriminalise homosexual behaviour, whilst trying to avoid responsibility for this shift by effectively blaming the European Union. When the proposal was publicised, Patriarch Teoctist called upon the president not to sign the law which would justify 'degradingly abnormal and unnatural lifestyles', which undermined attempts to strengthen the family. Archbishop Anania commented that 'Europe asks us to accept sex, homosexuality, vices, drugs, abortions and genetic engineering' and attacked an 'impoverished Europe ... built exclusively on politics and economics, lacking any trace of spirituality'. In a last-ditch attempt to prevent the legislation he unsuccessfully called for a referendum that would permit the democratic majority to decide.[20]

Throughout these debates it should be stressed that at one, very formal, level, Orthodox campaigns against homosexuality were not undemocratic in the sense that they argued for a particular set of values and in many of these countries had majority support in doing so. What was more problematic was the manner in which they promoted their case, for example by placing the campaign against homosexuality in the context of attacking paedophilia, pornography, drug abuse etc., which were then contrasted with the more positive 'family values'. Equally there was failure to accept that if what is being created is a liberal democracy then some tolerance and acceptance of difference in private lifestyles is generally taken as read. No one has to view others' behaviour as desirable or morally acceptable, but generally democracies do not criminalise or discriminate against those with other lifestyles except where they harm others. Against this, Orthodox church leaders would have suggested that all societies engage in processes of moral 'boundary maintenance' and that an individualistic focus on the right to free expression was not easily reconciled with their understanding of the needs of the wider community.

Coping with religious pluralism

Liberal democracy works on the assumption that elites and wider populations are accepting of difference, tolerant of a variety of social and political viewpoints, and committed to some notion of individual rights – though the content may vary depending upon social and cultural context, and there remains a debate about the role of communal rights within democratic polities. It is not that everyone has to agree with alternative ways of seeing the world, or even accept the changes brought about by democratic change, but that there has to be some acceptance of the right to differ. In practice this is more complex, for every society has to make 'moral' judgements about what is appropriate behaviour in the creation of a stable society, and these judgements will always be contested, but the basic democratic principle remains that any restrictions in liberty should be justified. This means that in the religious field the default position is that in a democracy all religious communities should have the right to 'free exercise' so long as their activities do not breach the law, though this does not require a parrot-style imitation of US-style separation of Church and State. Equally it would suggest that whilst religious actors may legitimately seek to expand their own area of freedom, they will not seek to pressurise the State to restrict the rights of their competitors. And in terms of encouraging rather than discouraging a societal acceptance of pluralism, one might expect them to allow some degree of pluralism within their own ranks, though inevitably there will be limits set by church traditions and doctrines.

The traditionally dominant churches responded in a variety of ways to religious pluralism in the wider society, but when we examine the record of the Orthodox churches in this area we find that almost without exception their institutional leaderships engaged in some attempts to limit religious competition and restrict the rights of religious minorities. This was especially noticeable in the post-Soviet and Balkan states where Orthodoxy predominates, but even in Greece, with its longer tradition of democratic governance. Though under challenge, both domestically and in the context of the European Union, Greece still has on paper more restrictive legislation and practice affecting religious minorities than most West European countries – though arguably some of the recent anti-sect campaigns in France, Belgium and elsewhere have threatened to undermine religious liberty in these countries. The 1975 Greek constitution guaranteed freedom of worship and belief, but ambiguities within the text, as well as other legislative and administrative acts, frequently served to compromise the full realisation of religious liberty. Article 13 of the constitution offered religious freedom only to an undefined category of 'known religions', and several groups including Adventists and Jehovah's Witnesses have faced problems because they were not accepted as 'known'. In addition, a raft of legislation left over from the Metaxas era remains in place and impacts upon the activities of minorities. This includes the requirement that the opening of any place of worship needs approval from the local Orthodox bishop and most controversially, the ban on proselytism. In consequence of the latter ban, over 20,000 Jehovah's Witnesses served prison terms from 1939 onwards, though this has been enforced with decreasing rigour in recent years, in part because several cases found their way to the European Court. Other problems have arisen in relation to employment rights, conscientious objection, custody over children in divorce cases where one parent comes from a religious minority, and state surveillance over some religious groups. Though central state agencies are proving more reluctant to pursue these cases, local administrations, sometimes encouraged by some Orthodox hierarchs, are still to be found constraining the activities of religious minorities and the central Orthodox leadership can still be found defending such activities. Against that one should note that in urban areas many Greeks are unconcerned with what others do with their lives whilst the State has proved increasingly reluctant to defend such restrictions in the face of criticism from the European Court.[21]

In the post-Soviet states the situation has proved even more complex, and in Russia, Bulgaria and Romania, Orthodox leaderships have encouraged the state to approve legislation that to varying degrees constrains the activities of other religious groups. For reasons of space we can only look at the Russian case, though it should be stressed that this perhaps represents an exceptional case. At the end of 1990 the Russian Federation adopted a new law on freedom of conscience that did away with the old Soviet era controls and effectively created an open space in the religious field. In consequence of this free market situation, existing groups were able to flourish and develop, opening new churches and educational institutions, freely educating their clergy, engaging in teaching and charitable activities, and spreading their message through the media and in public places. The vast majority of these groups were home-grown, though because some were previously 'underground' and much maligned by the Soviet media they often appeared exotic or strange to many Russians. At the same time a variety of religious groups outside the country were now allowed to evangelise or to support their religious counterparts within the country. Though most of the religious groups involved were indigenous, the variety of such groups and their new presence in the media led some to speak of an 'invasion of the sects' (or 'totalitarian sects') and 'unfair competition' coming from well-financed international operations which was leading to the breakup of families, social conflict, and an undermining of the traditional church of the Russian people. In consequence Orthodox leaders and nationalist politicians began to argue for changes to the law that would 'protect' the Orthodox Church and deal with the problem of assertive minorities.

The details of what followed are well covered elsewhere,[22] but the culmination of this campaign was the passage of a 1997 law on religion which not only offered a primacy of status to Russia's 'traditional' religious communities, but also included several provisions whose effect was potentially restrictive for religious minorities. In particular it required a re-registration of religious groups that made it difficult for 'new' groups to gain legal recognition, restricted the right of communities to invite foreign preachers and co-religionists, and gave local officials considerable discretion in interpreting the law. Consequently, over the next ten years there were repeated cases of local officials, sometimes encouraged by dominant religious leaders – primarily, but not solely, Orthodox – attempting to restrict or prevent minority religious activity in their regions. Thought the claim was that such legislation would counter the activities of 'totalitarian sects', many of the cases recorded affected existing religious communities, such as Baptists, Pentecostals and Catholics, or other 'sects' such as Jehovah's Witnesses, who had a considerably history of activity within the former Soviet Union.[23]

Though such restrictions would appear to challenge pluralist assumptions, they were defended by religious and political leaders on a number of grounds. Firstly, it was suggested that privileging the national church was simply recognising the sociological reality that this was the church of the majority – 'equality of religions before the law does not mean their equality before the culture and history of Russia'.[24] Others spoke of the need for some institution to provide a degree of continuity and moral guardianship in times of great uncertainty, and to prevent an unsettled population from falling into the hands of 'destructive sects'. Such arguments also tied into nationalist arguments that may be positive – we need to strengthen the sense of national belonging and the traditionally dominant churches can play a key role here – or extremely negative, if not chauvinistic, rooted in an anti-foreigner mentality and rejection of any community that is deemed to have its roots outside Russia.[25] It should, of course, be stressed that the Russian Orthodox Church is formally committed to freedom of conscience and recognises it as enabling the existence of the Church in a largely secular world. Nonetheless, the 2000 *Social Concept* argued that 'the adoption of the freedom of conscience as a legal principle points to the fact that society has lost its religious goals and values and become massively apostate and actually indifferent to the task of the Church and to overcoming of sin', hardly a ringing endorsement of freedom of conscience comparable to Vatican II's *Dignitatis Humanae*.[26]

We should, of course, be wary of exaggerating the impact of the law and contemporary practice on religious liberty in the sense that only in exceptional cases can we find attacks on religious liberty comparable to those of the Soviet period, and the situation varies considerably in different regions of the Russian Federation. Equally, the 1997 law, although not always ideally phrased, does not explicitly introduce many formal restrictions on religious liberty and at this level Russian Orthodox Church leaders were partially correct when they said that freedom of conscience was protected by the law. But their frequent attempts to lump virtually all religious minority groups together, and the Patriarchate's complete denial that individual Orthodox leaders are seeking to restrict minority rights flies in the face of many well-documented cases from various parts of the Russian Federation. For Patriarchal spokesman Fr Vsevolod Chaplin these so-called cases represent the fantasies of 'our human rights defenders of the Soviet generation who do not like Russia', whose activities are based on 'a hatred of Russia', and who all too often are serving the interests of foreign powers who wish to see the disintegration of Russia.[27] To those minority communities still on the receiving end of restrictions and constraints on how they choose to worship, however, these are hard realities that serve to make their life more difficult, to the extent that in 2005 one Pentecostal leader suggested that if the worst came to the worst they might have to resort to the underground activities characteristic of the Soviet era.[28]

The key point, however, is that whatever legitimate concerns there may be about the activities of 'sects' and 'cults', the Russian Orthodox Church leadership (as opposed to individuals within the Church) has never fully accepted the basic democratic principle that all should be free to worship as they wish and that, whatever the cultural particularities of a country that might permit some recognition of national churches, this should not entail restriction of minority rights. Equally important is the fact that in most of the countries where Orthodoxy has been traditionally dominant, official attitudes towards religious pluralism, as well as to dissent within church ranks, gives out the message that the churches have at best a lukewarm commitment to social and political pluralism. From some perspectives this may be theologically understandable, but it also means that in societies where the future of democracy may still be at issue the churches rarely appear as leading advocates of democratic governance, instead tending to serve as reluctant followers of broader political trends – whether they tend towards further democratisation, as in Romania or Bulgaria, or to what, from an Orthodox leadership perspective, seems the more attractive vision of managed or illiberal democracy that emerged in Russia under Vladimir Putin.

A positive role for Orthodoxy?

Much of what we have said so far suggests that Eastern Orthodoxy has struggled with the democratic experiment in countries where it has traditionally been dominant. Yet, as we shall see, the experience of the USA indicates that minority Orthodox churches can adapt to democracy, whilst that of Greece suggests that, despite nostalgia for a closer Church–State *symphonia* and ambivalence about aspects of pluralism, these churches can learn to play the political game according to democratic 'rules'. In the rest of the Orthodox world several commentators have expressed optimism about the possibility of the Orthodox Church contributing towards democratisation and stabilisation. Some point to the possibility of the Church acting as an agent of reconciliation within society, though the example of the former Yugoslavia gives little cause for optimism. Equally, the oft-quoted example of the Russian Orthodox Church offering to mediate in the 1993 Moscow stand-off between parliament and president clearly over-estimates the significance of this action. In such situations the perception of the Church as somehow above politics may prove useful for secular politicians seeking a way out of crisis, though in the Russian case it seems that the participation of religious leaders served as a screen behind which more radical solutions could be prepared.[29]

More importantly, some hope has also been pinned on the idea that the Orthodox Church can make a contribution to the creation of a civil society that would underpin democratic development and consolidation. When looking at the more hopeful signs we might also point to the importance of time and context, remembering that, unlike the Roman Catholic and Protestant traditions, the Eastern churches have a very limited experience of responding to and living within democratic political orders. And in the case of the former communist countries it might be the case that ecclesiastical generational change could have an impact, though the evidence from both Greece and Russia suggests that young hierarchs are not necessarily more accepting of difference or less defensive in relation to the outside world. Nonetheless, assuming these countries continue their democratic development – a questionable assumption in the Russian case – one might expect that daily experience of working within the constraints of a system where bargaining, negotiation and compromise are at a premium, will over time encourage not a simple replication of 'Western' models of democracy but at least an accommodation with those elements that are essential to any meaningful pluralist and democratic polity.

Russian Orthodoxy and civil society

As Zoe Knox has noted, there is a tendency in the literature on contemporary Russian Orthodoxy to focus on the traditionalist, largely conservative leadership, whilst ignoring civic initiatives, and the fact of pluralism within the Orthodox community. In similar vein, Nikolai Gvosdev has suggested that whilst the Church may appear monolithic to outsiders, there is actually a good deal of internal debate and autonomous social activity.[30] In the light of these claims can we find evidence to suggest that Russian Orthodoxy is making some of the contributions to a 'civil society' that Alexis de Tocqueville saw made by religious associations in early nineteenth-century America? Or, perhaps more appropriately, is it making a contribution to a specifically Russian model of civil society that builds upon older traditions of communal self-governance?

In the literature on established democracies the underlying assumption is that the very existence of a rich associational life will provide some sort of bedrock for a democracy by: encouraging participation in and debate about public affairs; strengthening organisational and leadership skills; promoting civility and teaching people to handle difference in a tolerant manner that is rooted in a degree of trust both within the community and in the relationship between the community and the government; and contributing to the development of pro-democratic attitudes. Needless to say this model is something of an ideal type with regard to mature democracies, but the basic idea remains that civil co-operation and communication reinforce democratic virtues. It is also sometimes said that this concept is essentially Western, rooted in the idea of the centrality of the individual citizen and insensitive to the needs of societies where communal identities are more important. Yet arguably many of the traits associated with this model must apply to any model of democracy that assumes participation, choice and tolerance – even allowing for debates about the importance of cultural context.

During the early 1990s the expectation was that the Church would grasp its new opportunities in developing charitable, education and communications activities, though it was recognised that seventy years of oppression had constrained its capacity for new initiatives. In particular it had no experience of social activity or even unrestricted parish life, its financial position was poor, and its relatively small number of clergy lacked the experience to participate in many of the activities taken for granted by many European clergy. Nonetheless, a host of initiatives sprung up, both formal charitable activities funded by the Moscow Patriarchate, and individual parish or lay activities concerned with feeding the homeless, caring for the disabled, organising religious discussion groups, etc. Interviewed in 2004, Metropolitan Kirill of Smolensk and Kaliningrad offered concrete examples from the Moscow diocese, noting that 'the "Life Giving Spring" in the Tsaritsyno district is a center successfully giving aid to crippled children. In the St Nicholas Church in Moscow suburb of Zdekhovo construction is under way of a village for elderly people'. He also pointed to church work with AIDs victims, soup kitchens, homes for the homeless and orphanages run by the Moscow Patriarchate.[31] Whilst the central church authorities have been involved in some of these activities, many are local initiatives coming from individual priests or groups of laypeople and operating with varying degrees of support from the church hierarchy. Some of these are discussed in Wallace Daniel's recent book on Orthodoxy and civil society in Russia, though his case studies largely focus on Moscow-based intellectual religious and lay figures whose activities may not be fully representative of what is going on in within the wider Orthodox community.[32] And these various initiatives are supported in the Patriarchate's *Social Concept* which speaks of the importance of 'autonomous spheres' in society.

Whilst the mere presence of social initiatives and associations helps to expand an autonomous social sphere that can constrain the activities of an overbearing state, there is still a requirement that these contribute towards a degree of civility in social relationships. Some religious-based activities clearly do so, whether in the general revitalisation of parish life evident in at least some areas or in the case of aid given to the marginalised within the new Russia, whereby religious communities can help to give people the means not just for survival but also help to develop a sense of self-worth. Civility is also encouraged by the very act of participating in these activities or in co-operating with others, both religious and secular, in seeking to meet the needs of a wider society. Against this, one should also stress that not all forms of religious self-organisation contribute towards civility, and several writers have pointed to the various Orthodox brotherhoods, many (though not all) of which have promoted a xenophobic, anti-Western and anti-Semitic vision of Orthodoxy that is both defensive and aggressive, and that hardly contributes towards a vision of a transformed and pluralist society.[33] Moreover, as Daniel has pointed out, there are different conceptions of civil society operating within the church, and he suggests that the debate over the 1997 law on religion indicated a belief that in Russia the emergence of civil society should have less to do with a cacophony of competing voices than a rediscovery of a moral centre rooted in national traditions.[34]

Minority Orthodoxy and democracy: the American case

Our focus so far has been on countries where Orthodoxy represents the traditionally dominant religion, but another way of exploring the Orthodox engagement would be to look at how Orthodox communities have adapted to pluralism in societies where they represent a minority – and it is worth noting here a corresponding question raised in the literature on Islam and democracy which suggests that the experience of many believers living as minorities in non-Muslim countries has had some impact on the debate about whether democracy can serve Muslim political needs. As the 'foundational' liberal democracy the United States represents perhaps the best example, with around two million Orthodox grouped in some 2,400 parishes loyal to a variety of jurisdictions. Orthodoxy first came to North America in 1794 when Russian Orthodox missionaries landed in what was then Russian Alaska.[35] By 1900 there were around 50,000 Orthodox in America, but the numbers grew exponentially after the Russian Revolution and then again after the communist takeover of Eastern Europe. These mostly Slavic exiles joined a growing Greek community but also, during the second half of the twentieth century and after, were joined by more Armenians, Orthodox Arabs, Copts and Malankara Orthodox Christians from India. The basic divisions within this community are between what might be called Byzantine Orthodox (Greek, Russian, Bulgarian, etc.) who adhere to 'standard' Trinitarian doctrine and Oriental churches (Copts, Armenians, Syrian, Malankara, Eritrean, Ethiopian) who have inherited a 'Neo-Chalcedonian' theological position.[36] This is not the place to explore the various jurisdictions, their peculiarities and divisions, but simply to note that amongst the more significant are the Greek Orthodox Archdiocese of America, the Orthodox Church in America (granted autocephaly from the Moscow Patriarchate in 1970), and the Antiochian Orthodox Christian Archdiocese – between them, these three claim the loyalty of up to 750,000 American Orthodox.[37]

For the first generation of Orthodox immigrants the Church was a place that provided them with stability and order in the seeming chaos of the new society they were entering, and they often expressed no desire to participate in

American public life because they did not really see themselves as part of that society. As new generations settled in,
questions began to be raised about whether the Church could
or should be equated with an ethnic enclave. What some saw
as a strength others saw as a weakness for a body ostensibly
committed to worship and mission regardless of ethnicity.
New arguments emerged about whether the multitude of
jurisdictions really served the interest of the Orthodox
Church, and there were periodic suggestions of the need for a
united Orthodox witness in America, though these usually
fell at the first hurdle as traditionalists and 'mother
churches' proved reluctant to let go. Much of the impetus for
change came from second- and third-generation Orthodox
and from converts who argued for celebrating the liturgy in
English or simplifying the demands made upon believers,
though ecclesiastical reform movements should not necessarily be equated with the theological liberalism of many
Protestant and Catholic communities in America. For
members of the 'oriental' churches, often fleeing from persecution in the Middle East, living as a defensive minority
came naturally and the lack of social engagement was understandable, but the new generation of Orthodox had become
accustomed to American ways and sought to adapt church
practices to those of the host country. Yet this tension
between 'belonging' and 'visiting' remains, with Thomas
Hopko suggesting to his co-religionists that all too often 'we'
view our church membership primarily in terms of our
ancestry, whilst the mother churches look on us as an ecclesiastical diaspora; in consequence we 'use our ecclesiastical
structures for nationalistic, cultural, ethnic and ideological
ends. We employ our church buildings as shrines of national
heritage, museums for cultural exhibitions . . . meeting places
for patriotic and political programmes'.[38]

The extent to which these churches have become 'democ-
ratised' and 'Americanised' varies considerably, but in
addition to serving the liturgy and maintaining parish life, all
of the major churches operate a variety of social and welfare
organisations, carry out charitable and educational activity,
and maintain journals and sophisticated websites very
similar to those of many Western Christian churches.[39]
Despite all this, and despite the fact that ethnic Orthodox
have often done very well in academia, the media and busi-

ness, Prodromou has noted a tendency for the Orthodox to be less civically and politically engaged in public affairs, beyond concerns with community 'defence'.[40] Krindatch also points to survey evidence suggesting lower levels of political engagement and the fact that the social services on offer tend to be available only to members of the ethnic group rather than to the wider society, though of course there are exceptions.[41] In another study he also notes reluctance on the part of Orthodox clergy to engage with social and political issues in their sermons.[42]

Yet overall, an impressionistic survey of the Orthodox experience in America largely mirrors that of the much larger Catholic community, which started as a despised immigrant community but which eventually became an accepted part of the American scene and one whose members adapted to and played a full part in the life of American democracy. As beneficiaries of pluralism and 'free exercise' they have mostly become acclimatised to working within democratic structures regardless of the reservations expressed by individual theologians and pastors. A sceptical response would be to suggest that it is easy to accept a particular political order when you are in a minority position, but harder to do so when you are a majority church in a country where you have been the traditionally dominant religious. Yet the American story does point, as have other stories told in this book, to the adaptability of religious communities and their ability to modify (often very slowly and reluctantly) their attitudes towards the imperfect reality of democratic politics.

★ ★ ★ ★ ★

Our argument in these two chapters has suggested that in countries where Eastern Orthodoxy represents the majority tradition there is a hesitation about the full embrace of a Western-oriented model of liberal democracy, with reservations about both the liberal and the majority rule dimensions of this form of governance. In consequence we are claiming not that Orthodoxy is inherently undemocratic but that at the present time its 'centre of gravity' has qualified the potential for these churches to be active supporters or promoters of democratic change. Whilst Orthodox social teaching does not preclude or oppose democratisation, there are elements within its actual outworking at the present moment – focusing on the unity of society, the necessary link between faith and nation, distrust of difference – that are not always helpful for democratic development. Whether this matters very much depends to some extent upon the context. The presence of less auspicious elements in the Greek Orthodox tradition has had a very limited impact upon a Greek polity firmly committed to democracy, whilst the largely marginalised Bulgarian Orthodox Church has been unable seriously to affect political developments. By way of contrast it might be suggested that the Russian Orthodox Church's political presence and anti-pluralist stance in a context of incomplete or 'managed' democratisation has been one of a number of factors that have hindered the full acceptance of social and political pluralism in Russia. The same might well be said about the Serbian Orthodox Church's obsession with issues surrounding ethnicity during the 1990s which prevented it making any significant contribution to more liberal visions of the political order.

One way of looking at Orthodox attitudes might be to focus on two questions: are the Orthodox churches in these countries convinced of the value of democracy as a general concept, and are they willing to accept a certain degree of pluralism and tolerate the fact that democracy means the acceptance of difference within society? In both cases the answer is ambiguous. Indeed, one should stress that the answer is ambiguous for all religious institutions because there must always be a tension between the proclamation of some notion of spiritual truth versus the democratic acceptance that policy is often the product of bargains, compromises and imperfect knowledge. Yet one could still argue that in the recent period, when the Orthodox have for the first time had to respond to democracy as a form of government, they have struggled more than some churches to adapt. On the one hand, there is the tendency to view all forms of government as provisional, though both the Greek and the post-communist churches offer formal support for democratisation. In Greece the church has broadly accepted pluralism and learnt to operate as a very significant pressure group when its values and interests are challenged.

Within the post-communist world the picture is more mixed, and we have already noted the view of the Russian Orthodox *Social Concept* which saw democracy as less desirable than certain other forms of governance – though it does not call for opposition to democracy. Fr Vsevolod Chaplin of the Moscow Patriarchate is much more outspoken. In an article published in 2004 he spoke of democracy as a form of government which 'rejects religious authority and declares the government independent from God ... it is rooted in competition ... The Church's ideal is the nation as a living organism, a unified body that sees disagreements as unnatural and unhealthy'. Moreover, in terms of priorities, the primary aim of the Church should be less with democratic development than 'uniting its forces in service to the fatherland and the nation'.[43] By 2007 he was becoming even more hostile, stating that 'Orthodox civilization stands in opposition to western democracy, whose downfall is not far off' and suggesting that 'Multiconfessionality, multiparty systems, separation of powers, competition, administrative conflicts – all that the present political system takes such pride in – are symptoms of spiritual unhealthiness. The very existence of a pluralistic democracy is none other than a direct result of sin'.[44]

Of course, there is a danger that by focusing heavily on the religious hierarchy and its institutional statements we miss the much greater diversity of views within the Orthodox churches. All of these churches have individual hierarchs, priests and laypeople who appear more committed to an open, inclusive vision of Orthodoxy that seeks to engage with the world (and with the consequences of democracy) and with other religious communities. At the same time we have to recognise that within 'actually existing' Orthodoxy, within the Orthodox Church as a whole and within individual jurisdictions, these are very much a minority, and in many cases are barely tolerated. Zoe Knox and others have noted that though there is pluralism within the Russian Orthodox Church, its expression since the early 1990s had tended to be very one-sided as the Moscow Patriarchate has largely adopted a 'softly softly' approach to Orthodox religious groups promoting nationalistic, chauvinist and anti-Semitic agendas, while seeking to restrict the activities of young priests promoting a reformist agenda and sometimes attracting large and young congregations.[45] This again suggests that in Russia in particular, the Orthodox centre of gravity remains wary of pluralism, whether within its own ranks or, as we have already seen, in the wider society. This is tied in with a rejection of liberalism, with its focus on the rights of the autonomous individual, and an emphasis on the rights of nations and communities. It also fits with the 'democratic' model – favoured by President Putin in Russia – where the competitive and critical element is reduced, and there is an emphasis on state, nation and national unity as the presiding values. And whilst Russian Orthodoxy offers perhaps the best documented examples, similar views have been expressed by Orthodox leaders in the Balkans, who have tended to focus on the Church as intimately tied to the nation, with the form of government under which it exists as secondary to the need for a government sympathetic to Eastern Christianity.

If we seek to explain the Orthodox contribution, or more accurately its relative lack of contribution so far, to democratisation, there is nothing comparable to the 'inadvertent' Protestant contribution to the emergence of democracy suggested by Bruce or the 'altruism' posited by Huntington. There may, however, be an explanation that focuses on historical experience – mirroring Weber's suggestion that capitalism was the product of very specific circumstances in which some of the ideas and understandings generated by the Reformation played a part – but also on theological development. An impressionistic survey of the post-communist countries indicates that by and large those located within the Western Christian tradition have found it easier to democratise than those with an Orthodox or Islamic heritage. As with the development of capitalism after the Reformation, there are all sorts of reasons for this – the 'Orthodox-Islamic' countries were generally the less developed parts of the communist world, they in many cases experienced more thorough-going repression, they had less experience of the 'West' and they were geographically furthest from the influence of the capitalist democracies and more 'alien' to potential investors.

Having said that, can we also say that political cultures, shaped by historical and religious experience, played a part in limiting the Orthodox contribution to democratisation. We noted earlier that for most of their modern history the most important Orthodox churches have existed under authoritarian rule and, apart from a short period in Greece, none had any significant experience of democratic rule prior to the 1990s. Under the Ottomans the status of the churches had

been given a protection, albeit somewhat precarious for religious leaders, whilst under many of the national regimes
emerging in the nineteenth century they had seen their role
as national churches promoted and their status and rights
protected. Equally importantly, these circumstance meant
that none had developed a substantial body of social theology
and none had been forced to engage in any serious way
with what democracy might mean for the Church. It has
been said many times before but is worth repeating that
whereas the Western Church had faced the challenges of the
Renaissance, Reformation, Enlightenment, American and
French Revolutions, and the gradual evolution of democracy,
most of these developments passed the Orthodox churches
by. One would not want to suggest that they were unaware of
such developments, and many see having avoided them as a
positive thing, but it did mean that the central authorities of
these ecclesiastical bodies had not really engaged with them.
There had been movements for reform, and the 1918
Russian Sobor just *might* have led to the creation of a more
socially conscious and less defensive Orthodox Church,
though its potentialities have sometimes been exaggerated in
the light of the horrors that followed. For all this, however,
when political transition came, the Orthodox churches as
institutions were not really prepared, and so adopted defensive and often negative public positions. Whilst delighted to
see the end of communist repression, they felt unsure about
how to handle the new situation, especially given their past
compromises with the old regimes which laid them open to
criticism, and their unfamiliarity with a religious market
situation. Whilst a few of the more knowledgeable might
look to the experience of the Orthodox in the USA or
Western Europe, the temptation to seek dominance was too
great for many and they turned to what one writer has called
the Orthodox version of Catholic social theology rooted in
'the combination of nationalism, cooperation with the state,
and preference for collectivism' and an emphasis on the
freedom of community as more important than individual
rights.[46]

Our other two 'models of explanation' focused on self-
interest, on the pursuit of hegemony and the maintenance of
market share. During the identity card debate in Greece
much of the rhetoric of Orthodox leaders was about the

intrinsic link of Orthodoxy and Greekness. In altruistic terms this was about a simple recognition that the sociological majority of the population adhered to Orthodoxy and therefore the Church could not be excluded from public life; in hegemonic terms this was about preserving power and influence and preventing membership of the European Union and the wider consequences of globalisation chipping away at this dominance. The situation in the communist world was a little different, for here all the churches had been subordinate to political authority, though in those countries where Orthodoxy was traditionally dominant they had sometimes enjoyed a higher status in the late communist period. With the collapse of communism they formally spoke of their support for democracy but this commitment was often expressed in lukewarm tones, as much a product of an ecclesiastical tradition which gave support to whoever was in power as any more positive belief in the values of democracy.

At the same time Orthodox support for democracy reflected a desire to distance the Church from past compromises, as in Greece where the Church had failed to offer any serious resistance to the military junta. Equally, in Russia, Bulgaria and Romania the churches remembered all too well the persecution, harassment and compromises associated with the old system. In such circumstances they were quick to offer their formal commitment to the new order and all denied that they were seeking a restoration of old State–Church ties. Yet as we have seen, most did in fact seek some sort of recognition as church of the nation, and gave the appearance of wanting protection from the State against ideological challengers in their own sphere.

The pursuit of hegemony was in part about preserving power and influence, but it was also about using that power to maintain some degree of control over the religious market place. In all of the countries where Orthodoxy was dominant the Orthodox churches have to varying degrees used their access to the State to seek controls and restrictions on the rights of religious competitors. Though they might not use the language of the market-place, preferring to speak about special rights in 'their' canonical territory or about defending the population from the temptations offered by 'totalitarian sects' or exotic Eastern religions, the underlying concern was often about maintaining market share in the new competitive context. Unused to handling opposition or competition, and used to seeing the state apparatus controlling minority groups, they often sought to resurrect old controls and restrictions. Yet for all these efforts, in many of these countries the presence of restrictions has failed to prevent the emergence of competition and states have mostly been unwilling to back dominant churches up with rigorous enforcement of restrictive legislation.

For a variety of reasons, Eastern Orthodoxy's current 'centre of gravity', at least in those countries where it remains the dominant tradition, is characterised by a certain hesitation about democracy that is conditioned by both its historical experience and its theological suspicions of the liberal baggage that comes with the models of democracy that have been promoted in many of these countries. This hesitation is certainly not an insuperable barrier to democratisation in countries where the Church's real political influence is limited. Moreover, most surveys of the political attitudes of religious believers in these countries generally show only slight difference from other citizens in their acceptance of democratic norms.[47] And in many of these countries one can find examples of civil society activity and political engagement that may lay the grounds for a fuller civic involvement in the future. Yet in countries like Russia there is also little evidence to suggest an active pro-democratic engagement on the part of the religious population and in general one has the impression that religious hierarchies are very comfortable with the sort of 'managed democracy' promoted by President Putin. To some extent the issue of whether Orthodoxy can be supportive of democracy depends upon where you look, and in both the former communist world and the wider Orthodox world there are plenty of positive examples. The problem, as with the search for liberal Islam, is assessing how representative of the tradition and the community these examples are. In our view the 'centre of gravity' of the tradition remains deeply hesitant, if not sceptical, about aspects of political democracy, but this is likely to change over time in response to the pragmatic need to engage with the democratic political orders that are likely to persist, with perhaps some exceptions in the former Soviet territories, in most of the traditionally Orthodox countries.

Notes

1 S. Ramet, 'The way we were – and should be again? European Orthodox Churches and the "idyllic past"', in T. Byrnes and P. Katzenstein (ed.), *Religion in an Expanding Europe* (Cambridge: Cambridge University Press, 2006), p. 152.

2 T. Hopko, 'Orthodoxy in post-modern pluralist societies', *Ecumenical Review*, 51:4 (1999), p. 364.

3 E. Prodromou, 'The ambivalent Orthodox', *The Journal of Democracy*, 15:2 (April 2004), pp. 62–75.

4 Ibid., p. 66.

5 Ibid., p. 73.

6 A. Agadjanian and K. Rousselet, 'Globalization and identity discourse in Russian Orthodoxy', in V. Roudemetoff, V. Agadjanian and J. Pankhurst (ed.), *Eastern Orthodoxy in a Global Age: Tradition Faces the Twenty-First Century* (Lanham: Rowman and Littlefield, 2005), pp. 29–57.

7 *Nezavisimaya gazeta*, 16–17 February 2000.

8 In a document entitled 'Russian Declaration of Human Rights' adopted by the World Council of Russian People 'on behalf of the distinct Russian civilization', and appearing around the same time that the Kremlin pushed through a controversial law on NGOs. The text can be found at: www.sras.org/news2.phtml?m=608andprint=1 (accessed 10 June 2007).

9 *Athens News*, 30 May 2000.

10 'Address by Archbishop Christodoulos to the Eurodeputies', www. ecclesia/gr/English/archbishop/speeches/address_europe. html (accessed 14 July 2006); though these types of argument are often seen as the preserve of the conservative leaders within the Church, during the 1980s the country witnessed the emergence of a neo-Orthodoxy that also engaged left-wing intellectuals in looking to religious ideas as a way of creating a Greek identity separate from that of the West. V. Makrides, 'Byzantium in contemporary Greece: the Neo-Orthodox current of ideas', in D. Ricks and P. Magdalino (ed.), *Byzantium and the Greek Identity* (Aldershot: Ashgate, 1998), pp. 141–54.

11 Ramet, 'The way we were', pp. 155–9.

12 Cf. Agadjanian and Rousselet, 'Globalization and identity discourse in Russian Orthodoxy'; K. Buchenau, 'From hot war to global integration? Serbian Orthodox voices on globalization and the European Union', in Roudemetoff, Agadjanian and Pankhurst, *Eastern Orthodoxy in a Global Age*, pp. 58–83; Ramet, 'The way we were', pp. 148–75; V. Perica, 'The politics of ambivalence: Europeanization and the Serbian Orthodox Church', in Byrnes and Katzenstein, *Religion in an Expanding Europe*, pp. 176–203.

13 I have dealt with the latter theme more fully with regard to Russia, Bulgaria and Greece, in J. Anderson, *Religious Liberty in Transitional Societies: The Politics of Religion* (Cambridge: Cambridge University Press, 2003).

14 S. Harakas, 'The stand of the Orthodox Church on controversial issues', at www.goarch.org/en/ourfaith/articles/article7101.asp (accessed 1 July 2006), pp. 4–5.

15 During the course of 2004–5 the Archbishop of Athens, who in recent years has tried to raise the moral tone of Greek society by encouraging a

return to Orthodox values, had to face up to a series of sex and corruption scandals involving high-level clerics, some of whom were engaging in homosexual activity. *The Guardian*, 19 February 2005.

16 www.times10.org/cvr0321104.htm (accessed 1 July 2006); in 2003 the Nizhny Novgorod authorities defrocked a priest who carried out a same-sex marriage: http://news.bbc.co. uk/1/hi/world/europe/3081252.stm (accessed 1 July 2006).

17 www.virtueonline.org/portal/modules/news/article.php?storyid=3392 (accessed 17 July 2006).

18 *Mir religii*, 19 October 2006 and 28 February 2007.

19 Ramet, 'The way we were', p. 168.

20 This section is based heavily on L. Turcescu and L. Stan, 'Religion, politics and sexuality in Romania', *Europe-Asia Studies*, 57:2 (2005), pp. 291–303; cf: http://news.bbc.co.uk/1/hi/world/europe/5045352.stm (accessed 1 July 2006) on the breaking up of a gay rights march in Budapest in June 2006.

21 See Anderson, *Religious Liberty in Transitional Societies*, chapter 2 for more details and sources.

22 See various chapters in J. Witte and M. Bourdeaux (ed.), *Proselytism and Orthodoxy in Russia – The New War for Souls* (New York: Orbis, 1999).

23 Anderson, *Religious Liberty in Transitional Societies*, pp. 126–38.

24 A. Kuraev, 'Ot strany pobedishvshego ateizma k obshchestvu torrzhestvuyshchego yazychestvo' ('From a country of victorious atheism to a society of triumphant paganism'), in S. Filatov (ed.), *Religiya i politika v postkommunisticheskoi Rossii* (*Religion and Politics in Post-Communist Russia*) (Moscow, 1994), p. 210.

25 Anderson, *Religious Liberty in Transitional Societies*, pp. 166–88 for a much fuller discussion of these arguments.

26 www.mospat.ru/index.php?mid=90 (accessed 30 June 2007).

27 www.stetson.edu/~psteeves/relnews/0501a.html#02 (accessed 2 May 2007).

28 *Nezavisimaya gazeta – religii*, 2 June 2005.

29 J. Ellis, *The Russian Orthodox Church: Triumphalism and Defensiveness* (London: Macmillan, 1996), pp. 152–4.

30 Z. Knox, 'Civil society, Russian Orthodoxy and democracy: theoretical framework/conceptual clarification', and N. Gvosdev, 'Unity in diversity: Civil society, democracy, and Orthodoxy in contemporary Russia', in C. Marsh (ed.), *Burden or Blessing? Russian Orthodoxy and the Construction of Civil Society and Democracy* (Boston: Institute on Culture, Religion and World Affairs, 2004), pp. 9–16 and 25–30.

31 *Argumenty i fakty – dolgozhitel*, 17 June 2004, PS.

32 W. Daniel, *The Orthodox Church and Civil Society in Russia* (College Station: Texas A and M University Press, 2006).

33 S. Rock, 'Fraternal strife: nationalist fundamentalists in the contemporary Russian Orthodox brotherhood movement', in J. Sutton and W. van den Bercken (ed.), *Orthodox Christianity and Contemporary Europe* (Leuven: Peeters, 2003), pp. 319–42.

34 Daniel, *The Orthodox Church and Civil Society in Russia*, p. 71.

35 An excellent overview of the position of the Orthodox in America can be

found in: A. Krindatch, 'The Orthodox (Eastern Christian) Churches in the USA at the beginning of a new millennium': http://hirr .hartsem/edu/research_orthodoxpaper.html (accessed 2 July 2007).

36 Neo-Chalcedonian refers loosely to those churches who emphasised the single (divine) nature of Christ rather than his dual (human and divine) nature as defined by the Council of Chalcedon (451).

37 For a general survey see J. Erickson, *Orthodox Christians in America* (New York: Oxford University Press, 1999).

38 T. Hopko, 'The narrow way of Orthodoxy: a message from Orthodoxy in America to Eastern Europe', *Christian Century*, 15 March 1995.

39 For example see the website of the Orthodox Church of America at www.oca.org/.

40 E. Prodromou, 'Religious pluralism in twenty-first century America: problematizing the implications for Orthodox Christianity', *Journal of the American Academy of Religion*, 72:3 (2004), pp. 733–57.

41 A. Krindatch, 'What makes the Orthodox churches strangers to American mainstream Christianity': http://hirr.hartsem. edu/research /orthodoxarticle1.html) (accessed 2 July 2007).

42 A. Krindatch, '"American Orthodoxy" or "Orthodoxy in America"? Profiling the Next Generation of Eastern Christian Clergy in the USA', at http://hirr.hartsem.edu/research/orthodoxarticle2.html (accessed 2 July 2007).

43 V. Chaplin, 'Orthodoxy and the societal ideal', in Marsh, *Burden or Blessing?*, pp. 31–46.

44 *Blagovest-info*, 17 August 2007, PS.

45 See Knox, 'Civil society, Russian Orthodoxy and democracy'.

46 M. Radu, 'The burden of Eastern Orthodoxy', *Orbis*, Spring 1998, pp. 283–300.

47 A 1999 study found that 'Responses to survey questions indicate that religious sentiments do provide a partial foundation for political partici- pation in Russia; however, religious beliefs do not appear to provide the basis for any major attitudinal or ideological cleavages. In the Russian setting, we venture to argue that Orthodoxy is serving as an integrating as well as a motivating ideology. Religious believers vote at higher rates than nonbelievers. Religious believers also support the incumbent leader (Yeltsin) at higher rates than nonbelievers. High religiosity, however, does not imply unconditional acceptance of representative institutions and officials of the government. Religiosity also does not imply political intolerance': V. Hesli, E. Erdem, W. Reisinger and A. Miller, 'The Patriarch and the President: religion and political choice Russia', in *Demokratizatsiya*, 7.1 (1999).

7

The Protestant ethic revisited: conservative Christianity and the quality of American democracy

We have already discussed the role of Protestantism in facilitating the emergence of democratic ideas and practices, but most of this discussion focused on its role in the period from the Reformation until the mid-nineteenth century. After that, the gradual rise of religious pluralism in North America and much of Europe, alongside the fragmented nature of Protestantism as a religious tradition, meant that its political consequences were sometimes downplayed, especially during the 'third wave' which occurred primarily in Catholic-dominated countries. True, Samuel Huntington in his discussion of the 'third wave' continued to emphasise the modernising and democratising role of Protestantism, noting the case of South Korea where liberalisation paralleled the rapid expansion of Protestant Christianity. By and large, however, the Protestant relationship with democratisation was neglected until scholars began to suggest that two key developments of the 1980s onwards might have some consequences for the nature and quality of democracy in both a well-established democracy and in countries within the developing world, some of which were undergoing political transition.

One was the rise, fall and rise of the so-called Christian Right in the USA which sought to change the American political agenda and that has, under President George W. Bush, seen its discourse become more widely accepted and its influence seemingly grow in the domestic and foreign policy thinking of a Republican administration. Whilst critics claimed that this revitalised movement was in danger of subverting American liberties and undermining the traditional separation of Church and State, supporters argued that it involved a return to the sort of religious influences that helped to shape American democracy in the first place. Into this debate about 'a nation with the soul of a church' weighed Samuel Huntington, though his concerns extended beyond the religious issue to wider questions about American identity. Painting with typical broad-brush strokes, he expressed the fear that a variety of trends might be undermining the 'Anglo-Protestant culture' which underpinned American democracy and even American 'civilisation' itself.[1]

The second development, sometimes wrongly linked causally to the first, is the rapid globalisation of Pentecostalism, with some sources suggesting that there are now some 250–500 million 'Pentecostals', mostly located in the developing world. Their greatest expansion has been in Latin America and Africa, and to a lesser extent in parts of Asia, but they have made virtually no impact on the Middle East. Given their size, they can be seen as representing potentially the largest form of social movement in the modern world, and as the most significant contributor to what Peter Berger calls the 'popular movement' culture that is one of the key features of contemporary globalisation.[2] Though generally neglected by much of the political science literature outside of area studies, a few scholars have started to explore the likely impact of this movement upon politics. In the last substantive chapter we focus in particular on its role in promoting or hindering the spread of democracy.

In this chapter we explore the first of these developments, with particular reference to its likely consequences for the evolution of American democracy. The rise of the Christian Right from the late 1970s onwards has become the subject of a huge literature, but it is more recent developments that have raised issues of democracy more prominently to the fore. In particular there is the suggestion that whilst earlier movements such as the Moral Majority in the 1980s and the Christian Coalition in the 1990s helped to put issues of concern to conservative Christians on the political agenda, since the end of the 1990s the much greater influence of the Christian Right on the Republican Party and on the administration of George W. Bush is in danger of changing the very nature of American democracy and pushing it in a more 'theocratic' direction. What is now on offer, some suggest, goes beyond the vaguely Protestant 'civil religion' that characterised American public life during much of the nineteenth and twentieth centuries, and seeks to impose a single vision of truth on a pluralist America – though arguably, the very vocal and visible presence of the Christian Right disguises the far more influential role played by business interests in the Bush administration. To explore this further we examine the nature of America's Protestant democracy and outline some of the ways in which the Christian Right has sought to return the United States to a mythical 'golden age'; we look at the alleged 'threats' posed to democracy by this movement as well as the counter-arguments which suggest that its actions have actually strengthened democracy by encouraging wider participation. We conclude with a brief discussion of Huntington's suggestion that without 'Anglo-Protestant culture' the new America will be a very different sort of democracy.

America's 'Protestant' democracy

As suggested in the second chapter, for many of the early settlers a primary motivation for making the dangerous crossing across the Atlantic was the desire to flee religious intolerance in Europe and create some form of Christian-based political order in the New World. In principle they were not necessarily any more tolerant of religious difference than the rulers of the states they fled, but the circumstances in which they found themselves did not always allow for the imposition of a single religious vision over the long term. This was especially the case as the original settler communities were expanded through the addition of many who came to seek their fortune or escape impoverishment at home, whilst the spread of settlement westward was often characterised by a wild, lawless frontier mentality in which religion was often marginalised.[3] Nonetheless, this remained a nominally Protestant society, and the makers of the American Revolution combined Enlightenment liberalism and dissenting traditions in their campaign against the British king. After the revolution the federal state may have moved to the formal separation of Church and State, but the underlying assumption of most of the governing classes was that a strong religious presence was central to good governance and to tempering political excess on the part of a democratically inclined citizenry. Moreover, for many of the founders separation was about protecting religion from the State and preventing religious differences dividing the body politic.[4]

If the original religious impulse was distinctively Protestant, it was also very much a non-denominational phenomenon that by the mid-twentieth century had evolved into a rather vague 'civil religion'. Though not all are happy with this concept,[5] its general meaning was well understood and often seen as rooted in De Tocqueville's suggestion that:

> In the United States, religion exercises but little influence upon the laws and upon the details of public opinion, but it directs the customs of the community, and by regulating domestic life, it regulates the state.

For De Tocqueville it was not so much that religion contributed directly to democracy as that it imposed moral constraints in a system that was built on individual liberty. In similar fashion Wald claimed that 'certain patterns of religious thought, habitual ways of reasoning about God and humankind, made it easier for certain ways to take root in American society'.[6] Or in the rather less subtle words of President Eisenhower, 'Our government makes no sense unless it is founded on a deep felt religious faith – and I don't care what it is'.[7] In practice this civil religion represented a sort of watered-down Protestantism that encompassed slogans such as 'in God we trust' or 'one nation under God', permitted military chaplains and oaths on the Bible despite formal Church–State separation, granted Billy Graham a role as almost the unofficial pastor of the nation for several decades, yet permitted no specific mention of Christ. This was a form of state religion that could be signed up to by most citizens with a deistic inclination, reassuring but not too challenging.[8]

Though this broad, loosely Christian consensus was accepted by most citizens, it was increasingly challenged in the post-war years, by Supreme Court judgements which raised the 'wall of separation' and attempted to remove religion from the public arena in a variety of ways, and by the rapid social changes of the 1960s which led many to question the rather cosy consensus of 1950s America. Perhaps inevitably there was a reaction to this turn of events, as the courts sought to impose a radical separation on a nation that was more religious than any of the other developed countries and multiculturalism was increasingly interpreted as allowing no public recognition that many citizens were religious. More surprising was the fact that this response was led by an evangelical and fundamentalist community which had traditionally preferred not to dirty its hand with political engagement and that this new movement was able to draw in sections of the Roman Catholic Church, traditionally the subject of Protestant hostility.

The story of the Christian Right

For much of the twentieth century, and especially after the Scopes 'monkey' trial (which, whilst convicting Scopes for teaching evolution, made a laughing stock of conservative Christians in the media and elite circles), conservative Protestants in America had tended to eschew politics, preferring to concentrate on the pursuit of salvation, evangelism, and the creation of community boundaries that would protect their own life worlds. Individuals had been involved in anti-communist campaigns and attempts to combat assorted social ills, but by and large evangelicals and Pentecostals saw the realm of 'the world' as of secondary interest. All this began to change in the 1960s and 1970s as changes within society began to make a greater impact on their communities and affect their ability to hold onto their own young. Equally, conservative organisers close to the Republican Party began to see the utility of mobilising this substantial constituency, especially in the traditionally Democratic strongholds of the South where 'fundamentalism' was strongest. And whereas in Europe, many evangelicals seem capable of distinguishing their moral-theological objections to the permissive society from socio-economic and political positions, in the United States conservative evangelicals until very recently appeared more likely to buy into the whole socio-economic agenda of the Right, including arguments for unrestrained capitalism, limited environmental controls, high defence spending, capital punishment etc.

The factors contributing to the emergence of the Christian Right have been well documented elsewhere, and in some respects they correspond to those underlying the wider rise of political religion in various parts of the world, as communities sought to preserve themselves from the 'mixed offerings' of modernity, by retreating into particular identities, and offering a voice for those uncomfortable with the pace of change.[9] In the US context the key elements appear to have been the increasing questioning of authority at all levels emerging in the 1960s, growing sexual permissiveness, the perceived liberalisation of the mainstream churches, the *Roe vs Wade* Supreme Court decision which legalised abortion, the attempt to approve an Equal Rights Amendment, the growing acceptance of homosexuality, and a series of Supreme Court decisions which appeared to raise the 'wall of separation' higher than was appropriate in a society where religion still played a major role. All of these were encompassed under the broad umbrella of 'secular humanism', an ideology which was said to be pervading American public life and undermining its Christian traditions by denying the notion of moral absolutes and even leading to the persecution of those who persisted in wanting to practise and promote their Christian values. According to Bruce:

> The increasing permissiveness of American culture was a threat to the fundamentalist way of life, not only because it rejected the principles of control and discipline which fundamentalists held dear, but also because it had roots in the increasing affluence which many fundamentalists shared and which presented them with new temptations ... The other great change in American life was the promotion and acceptance of group rights ... they ran counter to the individualism of conservative Protestants ... the success of any such claims would likely result in major changes in power, influence and authority.[10]

For some this resurrection of Christian engagement with politics reflected a wider 'culture war' within an American society that was deeply divided along class, regional, gender and religious lines with competing impulses of 'orthodoxy' and 'progressivism'; for others it represented a last-ditch attempt to halt the slide to secularisation by re-creating an idealised Christian past (often rooted in nineteenth- or mid-twentieth-century American customs rather than those of early Christianity) as well as an identifiable 'enemy' in the form of 'secular humanism'; whilst others saw it as simply a cyclical phenomenon, in the sense that religious revival has periodically revitalised the public engagement of American Christianity.[11]

Whatever the case, the period since the early 1980s has seen a major intervention in public affairs by conservative Christians that has gone through perhaps three major stages. The first primarily encompassed the Reagan years and was associated with the Moral Majority organisation, though a host of other groups were involved, including Christian Voice, the Religious Roundtable, and Focus on the Family. The story is well known but, to recap very briefly, in the late 1970s, focusing on the perceived failures of the evangelical but liberal Jimmy Carter, a group of conservative activists became aware of the potential for mobilising the evangelical constituency behind the Republicans. They in turn were able to tie in with the organization of Baptist preacher Jerry Falwell,[12] hitherto sceptical about political engagement, and this led to the creation of the Moral Majority organisation, whose very name aimed to suggest that there was a silent majority in America that was being swamped by the new permissive atmosphere dominating the USA. Utilising their extensive mailing list and media access, this movement sought first of all to ensure that Christian voters were registered and then that they voted the right way. In particular they campaigned on specific issues such as abortion, homosexual rights, traditional family structures and feminism, whilst targeting congressmen and congresswomen who voted 'the wrong way' on these issues. Yet by the late 1980s disillusionment with the actual achievements of the Reagan years alongside a series of scandals involving televangelists appeared to have undermined the movement, and in 1987 Jerry Falwell wound up the Moral Majority and announced his return to a primary focus on preaching the Gospel. The first phase was over and the movement had seemingly been defeated by divisions within, and the very nature of the American political system, that required compromise to achieve results when the movement's key supporters tended to absolutist positions.[13]

The second phase can probably be dated from the 1988 presidential campaign, when Pentecostal televangelist Pat Robertson made an unsuccessful bid for the White House.

Initially he enjoyed some success, taking second place in the Iowa primary, but eventually reached the Republican convention with just 120 delegates, despite spending $26 million, and he soon gave his endorsement to George Bush. What Robertson's campaign demonstrated, and what some of the later poll evidence suggested, was that even many of those religiously identified with the Christian Right remained sceptical about ministers campaigning directly, preferring instead mainstream 'secular' candidates who took the right position on the issues they cared about – even in the southern primaries only about 14% of conservative Protestants voted for Robertson.[14] Nonetheless, out of this campaign emerged the Christian Coalition, organised by Ralph Reed, a body that gradually developed more sophisticated techniques for exerting influence on both Republican agendas and political reality.[15]

Whilst continuing the emphasis on national campaigns and seeking to influence Republican agendas, they also paid a lot more attention to taking over local Republican organisations and provided members with advice on how to fight specific battles at the local level. Of particular concern was the fighting of legal battles in the courts over issues such as prayer in school, the teaching of creationism, the censoring of literature and school textbooks, and cleaning up the media. Yet Ralph Reed's political antennae increasingly brought him into conflict with his core constituency, as he seemed prepared to go for small gains rather than grand victories, and as he attempted to shift the perception of the Christian Right as a primarily negative community – anti-abortion, anti-gay, etc. – to one that promoted traditional family values, offered support for pregnant women as an alternative to abortion, and supported racial reconciliation. With the Christian Coalition under federal investigation for alleged violations of the electoral law, Reed resigned from the organisation in 1997, whilst continuing to claim that Christians were being persecuted for getting involved in politics. Though his strategy of compromise had created divisions within the movement, by the end of the 1990s, 15–20 state Republican organisations were reportedly controlled by Christian Right activists.[16]

Although we have so far spoken of the Christian Right in terms of Protestantism, one if its earliest political goals was to reach out to a wider constituency, to the perceived 'moral majority' who adhered to any faith or even none. Of particular concern were conservative Jews, Afro-American Protestants and Roman Catholics, all of whom had tended to be more sympathetic to Democrats but who often shared a conservative moral vision. Courting all of these groups often proved problematic – Jews appreciated the evangelical sympathy for Israel but remained suspicious of eschatological visions which required Jewish conversion; black Protestants tended to share conservative positions on issues of sexuality but remained wary of a southern-based white Christianity that in the past had been less than sympathetic to their struggles for equality and social justice; Catholics could not but note the continued prevalence of anti-Catholicism within many Protestant communities. Yet on issues such as abortion, homosexuality and 'family values' the Catholic Church appeared to share many of the same concerns as the conservative Protestants. In consequence it was hardly surprising to see successive organisations such as the Moral Majority and the Christian Coalition seeking to build bridges with the Catholic community. For their part the so-called Catholic 'theocons' – men such as Richard Neuhaus, Michael Novak and George Weigel – began to see the utility of conservative Protestantism as an ally in promoting the re-Christianisation of America. With their central concern for combating the 'culture of death' – whilst glossing over Pope John Paul II's inclusion of war and the death penalty in this 'culture' – they shared the same starting point as many of their Protestant allies. Some have gone further still and suggested that they played as important a role as conservative Protestants in ushering in the third stage of Christian Right development.[17]

This third phase can be dated from the selection of George W. Bush as Republican presidential candidate, as for the first time there was a candidate and then president who appeared genuinely committed to much of the Christian's Right's language and policy agenda – unlike predecessors who paid lip service to it for electoral gain. President Eisenhower may have proclaimed that 'our government makes no sense unless it is founded on a deeply felt religious faith', but President Bush was to be far more specific about the type of faith this was to be and willing to describe himself as motivated by a religious calling. Drawing on a population 40% of which claims to believe in the literal truth of the Bible, and a demographically expanding conservative Christian constituency the majority of which voted for the Republicans in 2000 and 2004, the President had no trouble in using the language of America as a chosen nation keen to spread righteousness at home and abroad. Thus in a country with separation of Church and State, Attorney General John Ashcroft could hold semi-voluntary prayer meeting at the beginning of the working day and the President could some-times slip into crusading language when speaking of 'the war on terror'. According to some critics, this biblical and sometimes apocalyptic rhetoric was encouraging American foreign policy-makers to determine objectives with greater reference to biblical prophecy than American interests, especially when it came to dealing with the Middle East.[18] Less clear was whether this new phase in Christian Right development would be any more successful in pushing policy change and whether its victories would survive the election of a less religiously inclined President.

The nature of the beast

We have so far been speaking of conservative Christians or conservative Protestants in very general terms and before proceeding with our main analysis we perhaps should make it clear who we are talking about as this has some bearing on our later comments about divisions within the movement. At one level, when we refer to the Christian Right we are speaking of key individuals – Phyllis Schlafly, Jerry Falwell, Pat Robertson, Ralph Reed, James Dobson – and key organisations – Moral Majority, Christian Coalition, Focus on the Family – involved in the attempt to 'restore' America's Christian heritage. These are the vocal individuals and groups who argued their case in the public arena, who linked up with a variety of other individ-uals and groups to promote 'moral' agendas, and who claimed to speak for Christian America – we shall return later to the question of whether they truly represent their core constituencies. Beyond that we need to look at the wide body of conservative Christians variously described as fundamen-talists, evangelicals, Pentecostals and charismatics, all terms that are used very loosely in much of the polemical literature. Again, it is not our intent to get into lengthy definitions, but very crudely one can perhaps isolate the following categories of conservative Protestants:

- Reconstructionists – a very small minority of thinkers who wish to return America to its Christian roots and who promote a 'dominion theology' which argues for rule by Christians and suggests that Old Testament law should prevail in a Christian America.
- Fundamentalists – whose name comes from the series of pamphlets published early in the twentieth century which restated what was described as traditional Christianity over and against the 'false gospel' being promoted by liberalised mainstream churches. In particular there was an emphasis on the inerrancy of Scripture as literally understood, on the salvation work of Christ who died once and for all for mankind, and on evangelism. Alongside this went a general wariness of the world which encouraged those involved to 'separate' out from the world and from nominal Christians.
- Evangelicals – a broader category, who often shared key theological tenets with fundamentalists, but some of whom would take a slightly less literalist understanding of Scripture that did not, for example, commit them to a six-day creation as an essential article of faith or to quite such a radically separatist view of engagement with the world. In practice the difference was often slight and many of the Christian Right's leaders would probably describe themselves as evangelical whilst accepting a relatively fundamentalist view of Scripture. And within the evangelical community there is also a small political 'left' which often shares the position of many conservatives on issues such as abortion, but is generally more socially progressive on socio-economic issues relating to poverty, corporate privilege, climate change etc.
- Pentecostals – emerging from religious revivals at the beginning of the twentieth century, here the emphasis was both on biblical teaching and on the direct experience of the spirit, manifested in speaking in tongues, prophesying, and other spiritual 'manifestations' of the work of the Holy Spirit. Some also speak of 'neo-Pentecostals, often separate from the traditional Pentecostal denominations, who are much more experience- than doctrine-based, focusing very heavily on healing and the material benefits of 'baptism in the spirit'.
- Charismatics – a movement similar to Pentecostalism

focusing very much on the ongoing work of the Spirit, but rather than leading to the creation of specific denominations tending to affect all the major Christian traditions, including Roman Catholicism.

And as already suggested, in practice the boundaries between these categories often overlap, as does the degree of commitment of many of those claiming allegiance to conservative Christianity.

As to the number of Americans who could be considered 'conservative Protestants', figures differ and depend to some extent on the nature of the measure used – self-identified evangelical, members of conservative denominations, adherence to core beliefs. Most sources suggest that around 25% of the population adhere to a white conservative church, about 18–20% to the 'mainline churches', about 8% to African-American based churches (which are usually theologically conservative but socially progressive) and around 25% to the Roman Catholic Church. Within each of these churches there are those who would be considered 'conservative', and some surveys suggest that up to 40% of the population have an instinctive conservative Protestant orientation – for example, in their claimed attitudes to the veracity of the Bible – but that commitment is probably less than often claimed, with several polls finding that actual church-going is considerably lower than claimed church-going, and only around 7% of the population identifying themselves completely with the religious Right's agenda.[19]

A danger to democracy?

For many critical commentators the Christian Right threatened American democracy because:

> it presents a fundamental threat to a pluralist society. From the republic's founding, they contend, the dangers of a triumphant religious sectarianism have been kept at bay by laws and practices that protect the rights of believers and non-believers alike. Above all, the First Amendment erects a 'wall of separation' between Church and State. The Christian Right, it is claimed, is seeking to replace a secular state with an evangelical authoritarianism.[20]

In particular, it was suggested that the movement sought to go beyond promoting a vaguely theistic civil religion in imposing a particular, quasi-denominational interpretation of religious and moral values on all American citizens. Whilst critics perhaps idealised the liberalism of 'civil religion', their main claim was that should such conservative groups come to dominate American political life they would inevitably curtail some of the basic freedoms associated with the American tradition and encourage an intolerance of difference. At the heart of the critique lay the argument that the Christian Right promoted a socially conservative agenda, that it encouraged intolerance, that it challenged the constitutional separation of state that was essential to the maintenance of America's democratic system, that it acted illegitimately in the public sphere by appealing to 'special revelation', that it placed Christianity in the service of one political party, and that it supported foreign policy agendas that were neither in the interests of the USA nor contributed positively to peace and development. All of these charges may, of course, be true, and many of their policy prescriptions may be undesirable, but this is not the same as saying that the movement is undemocratic.

The first charge, that the Christian Right promotes a socially conservative agenda, is undoubtedly true. At the heart of their programme are issues of morality and values though, as the more radical evangelical Jim Wallis has pointed out, when they speak of morality they are not talking of war, poverty or the environment, but primarily about what goes on in the home and the bedroom.[21] The rise of politicised conservative Christianity is often seen primarily in terms of a reaction to the 1973 *Roe vs. Wade* Supreme Court decision which legalised abortion, and the campaign in the late 1970s to prevent the Equal Rights Amendment being approved. In time this broadened out to encompass not just anti-abortion, but also attempts to promote sexual fidelity, abstinence, 'traditional family values' (in practice the family values referred to were often those of 1950s America or colonial New England, albeit dressed up in biblical language), and more negative campaigns against permissiveness in general, pornography, feminism and homosexuality – all allegedly encouraged by the 'secular humanist' takeover of America. In response the Christian Right often spoke in terms of 'taking back America' or of the need to 'remake contemporary culture in the image of Christian Scripture'.[22] Yet that they pushed this social conservatism in itself is neither here nor there when it comes to evaluating their democratic commitment. Here all that matters is the extent to which they promoted that agenda through constitutional avenues and according to common understandings of the democratic process. They have sought to promote and legislate particular moral understandings on issues relating to sexuality, reproduction, lifestyles, education and science, and these understandings might in some cases be reprehensible, but the very fact of promoting them is not undemocratic.

Where things become more problematic, however, is when the promotion of these agendas encourages intolerance, and an unwillingness to compromise or to accept difference as a natural feature of democratic politics. Thus critics claim that the Christian Right

> has mobilized into politics a group of religious bigots who lack the norms of civility and tolerance and who despise the very idea of compromise and cooperation. The movement is portrayed as undermining democracy by elevating the importance of an unrepresentative group of activists in the political process, intimidating opponents, and polarizing political discourse. The source of the movement's greatest strength – the certitude of its members that they are doing God's work – is seen as its greatest problem. Individuals bent on doing God's work are unlikely to find common ground with those who oppose them.[23]

This raises the question of whether in achieving their goals they would seek to impose their understandings on the wider population, i.e. to regulate private lives outside their congregations as well as within them. Again, to the extent that all legislation represents the imposition of someone's values on the wider community this is not intrinsically undemocratic unless it reaches the point of transgressing the basic freedoms protected by the Constitution and Bill of Rights.

What does appear clear is that the more active leaders and supporters of the Christian Right do wish to impose their values on the whole of society and there is some evidence to suggest that they are more intolerant of 'cultural outsiders'.[24] Several surveys do tend to support the common view that the doctrinal orthodoxy and the possession of theocratic beliefs, rather than religious adherence and participation as such, tends to be associated with intolerance in the sense of an unwillingness to extend civil liberties to 'out-groups'. Whilst holding that certain practices may be morally wrong is not itself problematic; if groups are denied basic rights because of their different lifestyles then issues are raised for liberal democratic polities. Studies of tolerance amongst evangelicals tend to produce ambiguous results, with Christian Smith concluding that whilst evangelicals were not going to be 'pacesetting advocates for multiculturalist diversity, tolerance, racial integration or absolute freedom of speech ... neither are conservative Christians shown to be consistently or militantly exclusivist and intolerant'. Only on the issue of homosexuality and the claimed influence of homosexual elites did they find themselves particularly uncomfortable with tolerating difference.[25] In similar vein Greeley and Hout found that they were only slightly more intolerant than other Americans.[26]

Yet whilst these surveys are useful in demonstrating that Christian Right leaders cannot claim to speak for all of their claimed constituency they do not get rid of the suspicion of many that an excessive Christian Right influence on politics or the successful acquisition of real power by their leaders might shift America away from a culture of accepting otherness and tolerance, just as elite liberal dominance in other periods could change attitudes by changing policy – for example, the civil rights movement in the USA. In that sense the fear remains that Christian Right leaders wish above all 'to remake society in the light of one particular reading of Christian doctrine' and that however tolerant individual evangelicals may be, they also would not be averse in practice should legislation shift public policy in directions that conform with their gut instincts.

A further argument revolves around the question of whether by challenging recent judicial interpretations of the First Amendment the Christian Right is seeking to overthrow the separation of Church and State often deemed vital to American democracy. From the European side of the Atlantic this argument sometimes appears fanciful in so far as it assumes that separation per se is central to democracy – although European states with established churches are no less democratic than the United States – but in America debates about the establishment clause have a particularly sharp resonance. Put briefly, the argument of the Christian Right is that post-war 'judicial tyranny' has reinterpreted the

First Amendment in such as way as to distort the intention of the founders by creating ever larger hurdles to religious involvement in politics. In consequence the law has come to favour the irreligious, the secular humanists who have dominated elite thinking and excluded the religious majority from the public square. The liberal response is that only by maintaining a strict exclusion of religion from political life can we ensure that religious divisions don't serve to create those radical confrontations from which the original American settlers were fleeing.

The meaning of the First Amendment's injunction that 'Congress shall make no law respecting an establishment of religion, or prohibiting the free exercise thereof ... ' has been the subject of fierce debate over recent decades. On the one hand the 'separationists' have suggested that the founders' intent was to keep religion out of the public sphere so as to avoid dividing society and prevent uncivil religious interventions. 'Accommodationists' respond that on the whole religion is a positive influence in society, that the founders never intended to exclude religion completely from the public sphere and that the rigid separationist interpretations emerging from the courts in recent years effectively gives religious people less rights than other citizens.[27] Much of the argument revolves around claims and counter-claims about the intent of the founding fathers, though assessing their intentions has proved deeply problematic and, as Jelen points out, it is not entirely clear quite how eighteenth- and early nineteenth-century understandings can or should be operative in a far more religiously plural America two centuries later.[28]

For critics of the Christian Right the concern is that under a thin veneer of respect for constitutional separation they are actually seeking to undermine separation in their attempts to bring about a Christian nation. To the argument that the Christian Right is merely trying to correct the balance between Church and State that has been disturbed by over-zealous judges during the last sixty years, they respond that many of these judgements arose from recognition of the growing pluralism and religious diversity of modern America. For their part religious activists claim merely to want a place at the table, a recognition that in a country where most believe it does not make sense to arbitrarily exclude their concerns from politics – as Congressmen Mark Souder asked, am I supposed to 'check my Christian beliefs at the public door ... when I serve as a congressman'?[29] Nonetheless, the charge is that in recent years, and especially under the Bush administration, the Christian Right has systematically sought to undermine the strict separation of Church and State by increasing the leeway available to the government in funding faith-based social initiatives, in seeking through the courts to permit the public display of religious symbols on state and federal property, in attempting to censor textbooks and teach science in ways they promote, to permit prayer in public schools, to gain access to government departments and institutions in their efforts to promote a particular vision of sexual morality and to combat the activities of those who take a different viewpoint. For critics this is more than about a place at the table and Kaplan points to Jerry Falwell's comment that 'we must never allow our children to forget that this is a Christian nation. We must take back what is rightfully ours'.[30]

A further argument ties into a wider debate about the legitimacy or otherwise of religious interventions in the political realm, and the suggestion that the Christian Right's interventions, whilst seeming reasonable at one level, in fact go beyond what is legitimate. Over recent years there has been some debate about religious participation in politics, with most agreeing that there is no reason why religious citizens should not be involved in politics, but considerable disagreement about whether religious-based argument should be used. Of particular concern was the issue of whether 'special revelation' should have any status in public debate, leading to a suggestion that religious-based argumentation should be left out of politics. Thus, when Christian Right spokespersons make the argument that certain types of policy are right or wrong because 'God told me' or 'the Bible says so' they are making illegitimate arguments. In the first place they are not arguments that will appeal to those who don't share the same religious viewpoint – and why should they be treated any more seriously than someone saying 'my ethnic tradition requires' or 'the pixies told me that'? Others have suggested that such arguments are too restrictive, to the extent that they appear to say that everyone can bring their own values (however derived) to the public square except religious people, thus requiring the latter to be essentially dishonest in thinking up secular reasons for their arguments – though appealing to wider audiences may have advantages for prudential reasons.[31] Nonetheless, liberal critics in the USA often remain wary of religious argumentation in political life and express the fear that appealing to God's authority is a dangerous precedent for democratic governance.

Where this charge of illegitimacy is clearer, however, has been in the growing assumption of most Christian Right activists that only one party is deserving of support and in its consequent penetration of numerous Republican Party organisations. Liberal leaning evangelical leader Jim Wallis may take the view that God is neither a Republican nor a Democrat, but this is not a view shared by many Christian Right leaders. Prior to the 2004 presidential election Jerry Falwell spoke of the responsibility of 'every political conservative, every evangelical Christian, every pro-life Catholic, every traditional Jew, every Reagan democrat, and everyone in between to get serious about re-electing President Bush'.[32] And he probably would have sympathised with conservative Catholic Richard Neuhaus's suggestion that it was almost impossible to be a good Catholic and a good Democrat, a view apparently shared by several Catholic bishops who wanted the Democrat candidate denied Communion because of his pro-choice position on abortion.[33] What is clear is that since the 1980s Christian Right activists have sought to gain influence in state-level Republican organisations and have become very influential in some of these. Yet whilst this has definitely shifted the agenda and discourse of the Republican Party, several studies suggest that its impact upon public policy has been more limited as once in power their activists have often had to compromise with other interests within the party and excessively overt promotion of Christian Right agendas can attract new voters but it can also alienate existing supporters.[34]

Having gradually acquired greater influence within the Republican Party the other key goal of the movement has been to make itself an indispensable voting bloc for the Republicans to the extent that the party will not be able to ignore the Christian Right agenda as happened under Ronald Reagan. During the 1990s the Christian Coalition in particular spent a large amount of time mobilising and registering conservative Christian voters, distributing voter guides about their candidates' performance in office – though some of these guides were of doubtful veracity – and promoting 'pro-family candidates' in any way they could. Though they claimed not to provide formal endorsements, in 1996 the Federal Elections Commission sued the Coalition for illegal campaign contributions that had effectively endorsed individual campaigns. For some commentators this close linkage with the Republicans has already given the Christian Right a position as controllers of the party's future. Anatol Lieven locates this strength in the centrality of Christian voting patterns to continued conservative political success, pointing out that white evangelicals vote Republican by a majority of two-to-one, whilst Esther Kaplan suggests that 40% of President Bush's 2000 electorate was made up of this same group.[35] Others suggest that this trend continued in 2004 and claim that the 'moral values' campaign won the election for the incumbent. Others are less convinced, with Greeley and Hout noting that whilst 89% of affluent white conservative Protestants voted Republican, less than half of poor white Protestants did so – a trend that indicates that income and class may still be more important predictors than religion.[36] Regardless of how one interprets the data, it is clear that the Christian Right itself sees the Republicans as their natural allies and has put considerable effort into increasing its role and influence within that party, and that even though that party may fail to deliver on the Christian agenda this alliance is likely to remain an enduring one. And if the alliance remains strong critics suggest that, combined with an often illiberal social agenda, it has the potential to push America in the direction of theocracy.

The Christian Right as democratic support?

To the suggestion that the Christian Right poses a significant threat to American democracy there have been two types of response. The first suggests that on the contrary they have helped to improve the quality of democracy by encouraging participation and drawing in a hitherto under-represented group; the second argues that the 'threat' element is vastly over-stated and that in any case there are structural factors within both the American system and their own movement that prevent them from imposing a narrow theocratic agenda on the wider population. From a Christian Right perspective all they are doing is seeking to return to the ideals of the early American experiment which they believe was very much shaped by religious imperatives and traditional moral values, and where the rigid separationism of the post-war Supreme Court would have been unthinkable. Religion has always been engaged with public life and they point to the attitudes of the founding fathers, to the religious rhetoric of Abraham Lincoln during the civil war, and the campaign for civil rights during the 1960s – though just as liberals tend to praise the political involvement of black Christians in this political movement whilst condemning contemporary conservative involvement, Christian Right activists often conveniently forget that many of their spiritual forbears were all too often on the 'wrong' side of the battle-lines during that same period. Whilst organisationally they are merely seeking a place at the table, they are also making the more important point that it is simply undemocratic to exclude religious people from the political process, to ask them to 'check in' their beliefs at the door as Mark Souder puts it. Being socially conservative is not undemocratic, being Christian is not undemocratic, nor in practice is there any supposedly neutral language of politics. All bring to politics a value system, a set of beliefs about the good society derived from a variety of sources, so why should conservative Christians somehow be treated differently? And if they succeed in persuading the majority of their views, why should they not alter legislation in ways that seek to implement their particular value system?

A further argument of this type revolves around the suggestion that the Christian Right has drawn a new section of the population into politics and thus contributed towards the building of social capital and extending democratic representation. For Mary Segers religious engagement with politics is positive because it broadens participation and representation, encourages voting, promotes democratic citizenship by giving people important organisational and leadership skills and, through a strong sense of sin, ensures a certain wariness of concentrated government power[37] – though a cynic might qualify this with 'unless that power aids the right causes'. Yet it remains the case that the activism of the Christian Right organisations has brought into political life a hitherto under-represented section of the population by (selectively) promoting voter registration of their own potential constituencies and encouraging political participation by conservative Christians. It might be less than desirable that much of this engagement should identify with a single political party, but it could also be pointed out that black Christians and a small minority of liberal-leaning evangelicals have tended to identify pretty solidly with the Democrats.

There is also an argument which points to the ways in which engagement in politics has forced Christian Right leaders to adapt to the democratic system. Thus Ralph Reed sought to extend its appeal to groups beyond the core constituency, though the danger remained of alienating key supporters by making compromises or bargaining. Jon Shields has pointed to the growing sophistication of Christian Right activists, noting, on the one hand, literature directed at their base constituencies which tends to use highly coloured language about 'radical special interests', 'militant homosexuals', and 'ultra-feminists' whose primary concern is with attacking Christianity. But having persuaded people to engage with politics, these same groups ask people to engage in politics in a very different way, emphasising civility, the exclusion of religious arguments in favour of 'common-sense arguments', and an emphasis on moral reasoning. Of course this does not mean that conservative Christians change their faith-based views in response to better arguments, but it does mean that they are engaging with the basic deliberative process that underpins a democratic society. And in this they follow tactics favoured by many social movements which overplay the 'threat' or 'problem' to garner support but then act more 'reasonably' when dealing with the 'unconverted' or with political elites.[38]

The second category of arguments suggests that for a variety of reasons the 'threat' posed by the Christian Right is considerably exaggerated and that the very nature of the American political system will always prevent them from attaining many of their objectives. Writing at the end of the first phase of their activity Steve Bruce had already pointed to some of the problems they faced in building a broad coalition, which as it became larger found it harder to satisfy its core constituencies. Drawing in Catholics meant playing down traditional anti-Catholic rhetoric, drawing in Jews required distancing themselves from those whose focus was on converting Jews, allying with other types of conservatives in the grand Republican coalition meant doing deals and making compromises, as did participation in elected institutions. And all this had to be done whilst trying to assure the 'base' that they had not given up on fundamental theological principles.

They also faced the problem of the numerous checks and balances built into the American system which meant that getting a district or state to legislate your way could not guarantee implementation, as electoral turnover, federal over-rides or judicial intervention could all limit or reverse hard-won victories.[39] Indeed, some argued that by being prepared to compromise with Catholics or even with Protestants adhering to different theological principles, and by participating in political institutions, they had perforce to acquire new skills of bargaining, negotiating and compromise. During the 1990s this issue became a subject of considerable debate as organisers like Ralph Reed tended to promote a 'small steps' approach focusing on incremental achievements whilst others preferred an all 'or nothing' approach. For example, the purists would argue that if abortion was wrong then Christians could be satisfied with nothing less than a complete ban, whilst those less absolutist felt that this was not achievable and that it was worth making concessions and engaging in bargaining in order to incrementally chip away at the circumstances in which abortion could be permitted so as to gradually reduce the number of abortions taking place.[40] For some commentators the very need to bargain, compromise and work within a political order where power was fragmented would always limit their success, though in 2003 Anatol Lieven wondered whether a situation had been reached where these self-correcting mechanisms were capable of constraining this new religious-based American nationalism both at home and abroad.[41]

If the movement's potential is constrained by the very nature of the political system, it is also undermined by the fissiparous nature of the constituency it claims to represent. A number of recent works based on survey evidence suggest that, in Alan Wolfe's words, 'America's conservative Christians are as American as they are conservative

Christian' and that the culture has transformed them as much as they have transformed the culture. Wolfe's study goes on to show that in many areas of life what conservative Christians say and do are two different things, and that whilst some, including the leaders of the Christian Right, appear rigid and intolerant, their 'base' is much more variegated with many wary of the world but also more tolerant of what others do in their private lives. Moreover, in a whole host of ways self-identified evangelicals differ little from those around them, for example being slightly less likely to engage in premarital sex but just as likely to divorce as other Americans.[42]

These findings have been reinforced by Christian Smith's *Christian America: What Evangelicals Really Want* (2000) and Andrew Greeley and Michael Hout's *The Truth About Conservative Christians: What They Think and What They Believe* (2006). It is impossible to do justice to these studies here but for our purposes the interesting conclusion is the suggestion that the Christian Right leadership can only doubtfully be said to be speaking for their own perceived and claimed constituency, let alone a 'moral majority'. On social and political issues conservative Christians appear to be just as divided as they often are theologically. Smith found that whilst many agreed with the Christian Right's diagnosis of America's failings many were averse to noisy political campaigns, preferring instead to rely on personal contacts, evangelism and general good-neighbourliness to transform their own corners of American society. He also notes certain disjunctions between Christian Right rhetoric and actual experience, with many of his respondents buying into the belief that Christians experienced hostility or persecution in the wider culture, yet with a large majority unable to identify any personal experience of animosity. Whilst evangelicals shared many of the concerns about public schooling, family breakdowns, and homosexuality, few wanted to withdraw from social engagement or to contradict the claim that all citizens should enjoy the same rights. Similarly, although they used conventional language about male headship in the family and about the importance of family values, very few questioned the right of women to work and most indicated that in practice running a household was a shared responsibility.[43]

Greeley and Hout's book confirms many of these findings, but goes further in arguing that moral values played a far smaller part than sometimes claimed in the 2004 presidential election and suggesting that old-fashioned issues like income and class are as likely to determine political attitudes and behaviour as religion. More importantly they note that even on core issues like abortion the evangelical position is a little less black and white than their self-proclaimed leaders would suggest, with few in favour of completely outlawing abortions and varying in the extent to which they might allow health or social circumstances to affect the legality of terminations. This study bears out some suppositions made about conservative Christians – that they are more likely to live in the south, have less education and be poorer than average, and that they are slightly less egalitarian and more nationalistic than the average American – but also suggests that these are differences of degree not kind and that, perhaps not surprisingly given the size of the constituency, they are not very different from most other Americans in their attitudes and political behaviour. Even on voting this study suggests that they are only 6% more likely to vote Republican than the population as a whole – in other words they have enough clout to swing a close election, but their influence should not be over-stated.[44]

So broadly speaking the argument is that whilst some of the rhetoric, programmes and policies promoted by the Christian Right may pose dangers to the maintenance of a liberal American polity, this threat can be exaggerated. Those involved are too tainted by individualism and the American way of life to represent a true threat to democracy, they are constrained by the very structure (formal and informal) of the political system, and they lack the degree of support in society that would enable them to impose their views – even if their core constituency is instinctively conservative. Moreover, they are overly dependent upon the vagaries of the American political system, and in particular upon presidential elections which require the building of large political coalitions and which will rarely throw up a presidential candidate like George W. Bush with a degree of commitment to the Christian Right agenda. Against that one should also note the question marks that remain about conservative Christian agendas that survey-based studies do not entirely dispel. Yes the constituency is more tolerant and diverse than the leaders would suggest, but it remains the case that they are still instinctively wary of many of the trends affecting American society. So whilst they may prefer the path of setting an example through personal behaviour and conversation and in that sense do not actively seek to impose their way of life, in the extremely unlikely event of there appearing a president truly committed to a theocratic agenda it is doubtful that this constituency would actively oppose illiberal policies.

The future of Protestant American democracy

Critics of the Christian Right suggest that their intent is to subvert the separation of Church and State, if not American democracy itself, by imposing a particular religious understanding of life on the whole of America. Conservative Christian spokesmen respond that all they are seeking to do is ensure that religious believers are not excluded from the public sphere and that due recognition is given to the fact that they represent a sociological majority within a country that has been fundamentally shaped by Christianity. Though rejecting their more particularistic interpretation, Samuel Huntington appeared to reinforce aspects of this argument in his 2004 book *Who Are We? America's Great Debate* where he points to the significance of what he calls 'Anglo-Protestant culture' (as opposed to Anglo-Protestant people)[45] for the preservation of American identity. For Huntington this is less about doctrinal Protestantism than a more diffuse belief system, perhaps not unlike earlier elaboration of civil religion as Christianity without Christ, and

> combines political and social institutions and practices inherited from England, including most notably the English language, together with the concepts and values of dissenting Protestantism, which faded in England but which the settlers brought with them and which took on a new life in the new continent ... With adaptations and modifications, this original culture persisted for three hundred years.[46]

This society was very different, in the first place because 'America was born Protestant and did not have to become so',[47] and this Protestantism made a significant contribution to what he calls the American Creed because:

> almost all the central ideas of the Creed have their origins in dissenting Protestantism. The Protestant emphasis on the individual conscience and the responsibility of individuals to learn God's truth directly from the Bible promoted American commitment to individual equality, and the rights to freedom of opinion and conscience. Protestantism stressed the work ethic and the responsibility of the individual for his own success or failure in life. With its congregational form of church organization, Protestantism fostered opposition to hierarchy and the assumption that similar democratic forms should be employed in government. It also promoted moralistic efforts to reform society and to secure peace and justice at home and throughout the world ... The American Creed, in short, is Protestantism without God.[48]

He goes on to discuss the basic American assumption that despite separation most Americans still believed religion to be central to public well-being and accepted the basic assumptions of a civil religion rooted in belief in a deity, celebration of certain national rituals, and the use of religious language and symbols.[49] Having said all this he goes on to claim that due to the new wave of immigration from Latin America and Asia and the growing commitment of political and social elites to cosmopolitanism and multiculturalism, the American Anglo-Protestant identity, which hitherto has successfully absorbed incomers, is in danger of disappearing, with consequences for the very survival of American civilisation.

It is not my intent to discuss Huntington's book, but for our purposes there is an interesting parallel between his argument that Anglo-Protestant culture is somehow central to American identity and Christian Right claims that good governance requires Christian input into the political process. For Huntington this religious tradition provided the seedbed out of which democracy grew – though, unlike the Christian Right, he would also give some of the credit to Enlightenment ideas. Of course, his religion is a rather vague, almost content-less civil religion to which the legendary 'all people of good-will' might subscribe, but it remains an argument that the continuance of American democracy requires some sort of religious basis. As with the earlier *Clash of Civilizations* Huntington's tendency to paint with a very broad brush has given critics a field day and, amongst other things, they have suggested that he underestimates the contribution of other religious traditions, including those of enslaved blacks and Catholic settlers, overestimates the extent to which Catholics have been 'Protestantised', and pays little attention to history by understating the extent to which religion has been as much a cause of division as unity in American society.[50]

For Huntington, the ideal America dates from an earlier, perhaps mythical period, when Anglo-Protestant religion dominated public life. To his critics this vision represents a distorted view of the past, and ignores the reality of a modern, plural and multicultural society whose very existence and growth appears to have sparked his polemic. Leaders of the Christian Right share a historical memory of a time when America was shaped by its Protestant heritage but they promote a vision that is much more particularistic, albeit one that can occasionally stretch, somewhat uncomfortably, to embrace some Catholics and Jews. In doing so they claim that this is not about imposing a theocratic set of policies in the public sphere but about gaining a rightful place at the table for a sizeable section of the American population excluded from public life by a post-war judiciary which has raised the Church–State separation bar far too high and an elite-promoted secular humanism that denied religious people a right to be heard. From this perspective the rise of the Christian Right can then at least in part be explained as an attempt to re-democratise the American polity, through encouraging more people to participate, to campaign, to vote, and to seek office – conservative Protestant political engagement thus represents an attempt to redress one side of the democratic deficit affecting many pluralist polities.

Yet as critics suggest, there is an ambiguity at the heart of this revitalisation of conservative Christian politics that returns us to previous discussions of the tensions between liberalism and democracy. Christian Right leaders are right when they claim to have brought more citizens into the political arena, but at the same time this engagement has been highly partisan and often aimed at promoting what many would see as highly illiberal agendas. Critics are also right when they suggest that much of this democratic engagement has far less to do with encouraging democracy – i.e. it is not about altruism in the sense suggested in our Catholic case studies – than about preserving hegemony. Christian Right leaders are concerned with their loss of power and authority, symbolised by a declining respect for the authority of Scripture – though most surveys dealing with public attitudes to the Bible suggest that this is hardly the threat it is made out to be – by the lack of respect for traditional authority figures, by the loss of control over younger generations, and about the loss of male authority over women. In this sense their engagement with democracy is rather like that ascribed to African church leaders by Jeffrey Haynes, that is, it is about preserving ideological power and influence.

To some degree any final assessment of the impact of the Christian Right on American democracy will depend upon the commentator's ideological perspective and views on the appropriate place of religious discourse and action in the public arena. Indeed, it might be argued that the increasing formal exclusion of religion from the public sphere, however exaggerated by conservative spokespersons, often served to breed the more militant and sometimes intolerant attitudes personified by sections of the Christian Right. And it might also be the case that the growth of Hispanic immigration that causes Huntington such anxiety might if anything increase the need for religious representation if these communities are to be truly integrated in 'the American way of life'. In addition, there is a suggestion that Pentecostalism is making significant inroads in these communities and that this might have some impact upon both their integration within American society and the political orientations of new Hispanic citizens. Though it might seem an odd thing to say, given the extensive history of Protestant involvement in American politics, it is perhaps too early to assess the political impact of the latest wave of conservative Protestant engagement. It is doubtful that it has enriched the liberal qualities of the American tradition or encouraged a radically critical perspective on American public life – except in so far as it has offered a critique of an alleged liberal orthodoxy. But neither has it so far led to the destruction of that democracy or the replacement of democracy, nor is it likely to do so. As already suggested, the very structures of the political system and the need for the parties to build broad coalitions of support militate against that, as do the divisions within conservative Christianity. We have already pointed to the fact that Christian Right organisations are not as representative of their constituency as they claim to be, but there are also signs, however small, of divisions at the leadership level. Since around 2004, several leaders of the evangelical community have started to distance themselves from the Christian Right and to opt for broader definitions of morality that encompass issues like poverty and war.[51] If anything, this pluralisation of the conservative Protestant community has to be a good thing for American democracy, on the one hand in providing an independent and critical perspective on American reality, but also in so far as it succeeds in creating a system of checks and balances within the religious constituency that mirrors that found in the wider society and governmental structures.

Notes

1 S. Huntington, *Who Are We? America's Great Debate* (London: Simon and Schuster, 2004), p. 69.

2 P. Berger, 'Introduction: the cultural dynamics of globalization', in P. Berger and S. Huntington (ed.), *Many Globalizations: Cultural Diversity in the Contemporary World* (Oxford: Oxford University Press, 2002), pp. 1–16. Berger suggests that there is an emerging global culture diffused through both elite and popular vehicles, and it can be subdivided into the 'Davos culture' of the business world, the 'faculty club culture' of the world of NGOs, academia etc., the 'popular culture' associated with Disney, McDonalds, the music industry etc., and 'the popular movement culture' of environmentalists, feminists, and including 'evangelical' movements.

3 For a useful if controversial discussion of American religiosity see R. Finke and R. Stark, *The Churching of America, 1776–2005*, Revised edition (New Brunswick: Rutgers University Press, 2005).

4 Some useful context, as well as an important corrective to the view that the founders' intentions can be easily divined, is provided in N. Feldman, *Divided by God: America's Church–State Problem and What We Should Do About It* (New York: Farrah, Strauss and Giroux, 2005), pp. 19–56.

5 P. Kelly, *Politics and Religious Consciousness in America* (New Brunswick: Transaction Publishers, 1984), pp. 4 and 215. Kelly suggests that the Puritan civil religion was very much of the state-sponsored kind, and that only in the 50 years following the civil war can one really speak meaningfully of a civil religion.

6 Both quoted in C. Wilcox and T. Jelen, 'Religion and politics in an open market: religious mobilization in the United States', in C. Wilcox and T. Jelen (ed.), *Religion and Politics in Comparative Perspective: The One, the Few and the Many* (Cambridge: Cambridge University Press, 2002), p. 294.

7   Quoted in A. Lieven, *America Right or Wrong: An Anatomy of American Nationalism* (Oxford: Oxford University Press, 2005), p. 54.

8   For a general discussion see G. Parsons, *Perspectives on Civil Religion* (Aldershot: Ashgate, 2002).

9   M. Marty, 'Fundamentalism as a social phenomenon', in G. Marsden (ed.), *Evangelicalism and Modern America* (Grand Rapids: William B. Eerdmans, 1984), pp. 56–68.

10   S. Bruce, *The Rise and Fall of the New Christian Right: Conservative Protestant Politics in America, 1978–1988* (Oxford: Clarendon, 1988), pp. 32–3.

11   See the overview of the arguments presented in the conclusion to R. Fowler, A. Hertzke and L. Olson, *Religion and Politics in America: Faith, Culture and Strategic Choices*, 2nd edition (Boulder: Westview, 1999); James Davison Hunter, *Culture Wars: The Struggle to Define America* (New York: Basic Books, 1991); Bruce, *The Rise and Fall of the New Christian Right*.

12   For an interesting analysis of Falwell's changing discourses on political life see S. Harding, *The Book of Jerry Falwell* (Princeton: Princeton University Press, 2000).

13   D. Marley, 'Ronald Reagan and the splintering of the Christian Right', *Journal of Church and State*, 48:1 (2006), pp. 851–70.

14   S. Bruce, *Fundamentalism* (Cambridge: Polity, 2000), p. 73.

15   For a general study of the Christian Coalition see J. Watson, *The Christian Coalition: Dreams of Restoration, Demands for Recognition* (Basingstoke: MacMillan, 1999).

16   R. Hopson and D. Smith, 'Changing fortunes: an analysis of Christian Right ascendance within American political discourse', *Journal for the Scientific Study of Religion*, 38:1 (1999), pp. 1–13; others have noted that whilst conservative Christians have enjoyed some success in gaining influence on Republican state organisations, this has not translated easily into policy success. See J. Green, M. Rozell and C. Wilcox (ed.), *The Christian Right in America – Marching to the Millennium* (Washington DC: Georgetown University Press, 2003).

17   On the Catholic contribution see D. Linker, *The Theocons: Secular America under Siege* (New York: Doubleday, 2006).

18   Ibid.; see also K. Phillips, *American Theocracy: The Perils and Politics of Radical Religion, Oil and Borrowed Money in the 21st Century* (New York: Viking Books, 2006). I haven't discussed the Christian Right's influence on foreign policy here because this is not directly relevant to American democracy, but one could note that over the years its influence may have encouraged administrations to support non-democratic groups such as the Nicaraguan Contras during late communist period, and pursue policies in the Middle East, including offering uncritical support to Israel, that undermined proclaimed attempts to democratise that region.

19   The sources vary but these are the sort of figures most often quoted for the period since the early 1990s, though arguably the Christian Right influence is increased by the fact that their constituency is more thoroughly mobilised. On the figures see S. Diamond, *Not by Politics Alone: The Enduring Influence of the Christian Right* (New York: The Guilford Press, 1998), p. 8; C. Smith, *Christian America: What Evangelicals Really Want* (Berkeley: California University Press, 2002), pp. 15–18; A.

Greeley and M. Hout, *The Truth About Conservative Christians: What They Think and What They Believe* (Chicago: Chicago University Press, 2006), p. 7.

20 M. Durham, *The Christian Right, The Far Right and the Boundaries of American Conservatism* (Manchester: Manchester University Press, 2000), p. 105.

21 J. Wallis, *God's Politics: Why the American Right Gets it Wrong and the Left Doesn't Get It* (Oxford: Lion, 2005), p. 7.

22 Diamond, *Not by Politics Alone*, p. 1.

23 J. Green, M. Rozell and C. Wilcox, 'The meaning of the march: directions for future research', in Green, Rozell and Wilcox, *The Christian Right in America*, pp. 277–8.

24 Cf. V. Karpov, 'Religiosity and tolerance in the United States and Poland', *Journal for the Scientific Study of Religion*, 41:2 (2002), pp. 267–88; Hopson and Smith, 'Changing fortunes'.

25 Smith, *Christian America*, pp. 244–7.

26 Greeley and Hout, *The Truth About Conservative Christians*, p. 64.

27 One version of this debate can be found in M. Segers and T. Jelen, *Wall of Separation? Debating the Public Role of Religion* (Lanham: Rowman and Littlefield, 1998).

28 T. Jelen, 'In defense of religious minimalism', in Segers and Jelen, *Wall of Separation*, p. 10; see also D. Davis and M. McMearty, 'America's "forsaken roots": the use and abuse of founders' quotations', *Journal of Church and State* 47:3 (2005), pp. 449–72.

29 Mark Souder, 'A conservative Christian's view on public life' in E. Dionne, J. Elshtain and K. Drogosz (ed.), *One Electorate Under God – A Dialogue on Religion and American Politics* (Washington DC: Brookings Institute Press, 2004), p. 21.

30 Quoted in E. Kaplan, *With God on Their Side: George W. Bush and the Christian Right* (New York: The New Press, 2005), p. 61.

31 See the discussion in T. Cuneo (ed.), *Religion in the Liberal Polity* (Notre Dame: Notre Dame University Press, 2005), especially the chapters by Stout, Eberle and Mouw. Cochran suggests that there are five conditions that should underlie religious participation in democratic discourse: that those who wish to participate should permit democratic discourse within their own internal life (which is not the same as to say they should be democratically organised), they should not have to abandon their specific theological language for some impossible neutral moral language, they should avoid the temptations of civil religion when they appear in public, they must do their homework to be taken seriously, and they must apply internally principles and standards they wish to impose on others. C. Cochran, 'Introduction', Segers and Jelen, *Wall of Separation*, pp. xvii–xviii.

32 Quoted in Wallis, *God's Politics*, p. xxviii.

33 Linker, *The Theocons*, pp. 166–74.

34 See the essays in Green, Rozell and Wilcox, *The Christian Right in America*.

35 Kaplan, *With God on Their Side*, p. 3.

36 Greeley and Hout, *The Truth About Conservative Christians*, chapter 3.

37 M. Segers, 'In defence of religious freedom', in Segers and Jelen, *Wall of*

Separation, pp. 80–8.

38 J. Shields, 'Between passion and deliberation: the Christian Right and democratic ideals', *Political Science Quarterly*, 122:1 (2007), pp. 89–113; see H. Heclo, *Christianity and American Democracy* (Harvard: Harvard University Press, 2007), p. 121.

39 Bruce, *The Rise and Fall of the New Christian Right*, pp. 70–6.

40 Diamond, *Not by Politics Alone*, pp. 131ff.

41 Lieven, *America Right or Wrong*, p. 217.

42 A. Wolfe, 'Dieting for Jesus', *Prospect*, January 2004, pp. 52–7; he makes this argument at greater length in A. Wolfe, *The Transformation of American Religion: How We Actually Live Our Faith* (Chicago: Chicago University Press, 2003).

43 Smith, *Christian America*.

44 Greeley and Hout, *The Truth About Conservative Christians*, p. 179.

45 Huntington, *Who Are We?*, p. xvii.

46 Ibid., pp. 59–60.

47 Ibid., p. 63.

48 Ibid., pp. 68–9.

49 Ibid., pp. 104–6.

50 Cf. J. Zmirak and J. Black, 'Problems of identity in America: two views', a review of Huntington's book in *Modern Age*, 47:3 (Summer 2005), pp. 278ff.

51 F. Fitzgerald, 'The evangelical surprise', *New York Review of Books*, LIV:7 (26 April 2007), pp. 31–4.

8

The Protestant ethic revisited: the Pentecostal explosion as democratic hindrance or support?

The impact of global Pentecostalism on democratisation is almost as hotly debated as the influence of the Christian Right on the American polity, and in some analyses the two movements are seen as connected. Initial studies tended to assume that Pentecostals were politically conservative and quiescent, inclined to other-worldly values that simply accepted the political order in the countries where they lived and worshipped. Several writers pointed to the support that Pentecostal leaders offered to General Pinochet in Chile, or to the comments of preachers who likened Arap Moi's Kenya to an earthly version of heaven. Some suggested a link between these churches and the activities of the American intelligence agencies or the Christian Right. Others pointed to the internal structures of Pentecostal churches in Africa, Asia and Latin America which tended to mirror that of traditional society, with the authoritarian pastor taking the role of the landowner in controlling the daily life of those belonging to the community. Whilst all of these arguments had an element of truth, since the mid-1990s a more nuanced picture has begun to emerge with scholars stressing the indigenous roots and nature of most of these churches, making distinctions between the political attitudes of leaders and led, exploring the ambiguous impact of Pentecostalism on gender relations, and looking at the role of some of these communities in fostering involvement in both civil society activities and more direct engagement with politics. Writers such as Peter Berger and David Martin have made even larger claims for the movement, suggesting that the logic of its development might just be analogous to that of Protestantism in Western Europe and North America in producing a new Protestant ethic that will support the emergence of a democratic capitalism that might help to finally resolve the seemingly eternal development problems facing many in the Majority World.[1]

In this chapter we explore some of the political implications of the global Pentecostal phenomenon, focusing in the first instance on the extent, nature and scope of the movement and on charges that it represents a foreign implantation that serves the interests of the 'West' in the developing world. We then turn to the claim that the movement essentially acts as an apolitical, conservative force in societies where it is successful. Here the charge is that Pentecostalism encourages an other-worldliness that effectively supports the status quo and that, in some cases, goes beyond this to offer individual and institutional backing to authoritarian regimes. One area of particular interest in this debate relates to gender, with scholars noting the paradox that whilst Pentecostal churches may serve to perpetuate patriarchal relationships within families and communities, the immediate practical consequence of conversion often serves to provide a new sense of identity for women and to limit the excesses of *machismo*. The third section focuses more on Pentecostal engagements with the public realm and the extent to which these can be said to be promoting or hindering democratic development. On the one hand the very style of Pentecostalism is participatory - it offers believers the possibility of involvement and may promote organisational and leadership skills - but in many contexts it is also very leader dominated. Some Pentecostal leaders do develop a social critique of society and culture that goes beyond a narrow focus on 'personal sin', but there is as yet nothing comparable to the institutional support for human rights that characterised the Roman Catholic Church during the 'third wave'. In a few cases Pentecostal leaders have engaged more directly in politics, supporting or creating political parties to pursue a 'Christian' agenda or defend their institutional interests, but all too often they have found themselves corrupted by the client–patron relationships that predominate in many political assemblies of the developing world. A final section returns to Berger and Martin's cultural logic argument, suggesting that the jury remains out on the likely long-term impact of globalised Pentecostalism, and also to the question of whether we can isolate a 'centre of gravity' within the tradition that does have implications for democratic development in the short term.

The phenomenon of globalised Pentecostalism

Though the modern Pentecostal phenomenon has its roots in an American religious revival at the beginning of the twentieth century, its spread in many parts of the globe quickly took on a local character and in many countries the role of external missionary activity was minimal. The more recent expansion that has occurred since the 1970s has been far more significant numerically, with some sources claiming that up to 500 million of the world's population can now be described as Pentecostal, a figure that represents perhaps a quarter of the world's Christians and makes them the largest group after Roman Catholics. Almost inevitably, given the highly fragmented nature of the movement, reliable statistics are hard to come by, but in 2000 it seems that there were around 140 million 'Pentecostals' in Latin America, with perhaps 15% of the population in Brazil, 20% of the population in Chile and around 25% in Guatemala identifying themselves as Protestant (again mostly Pentecostal).[2] Figures for Africa are even harder to come by, and a host of 'spirit-filled churches' are commonly lumped together as Pentecostal, but most sources suggest that over 100 million people adhered to some form of Pentecostalism in 2000, representing around 10–12% of the continent's population and with strong concentrations in Zimbabwe, Kenya, Nigeria, Ghana and Zambia.[3] In Asia there are perhaps 140 million Pentecostals, with significant communities in South Korea, the Philippines and China, though reliable information on Chinese churches remains difficult to find. Moreover, this general survey of statistical data ignores the ways in which features of the Pentecostal movement have impacted upon other Christian communities, most obviously in more emotional styles of worship.

Though there may be half a billion 'Pentecostals', mostly located within the Majority World, we need to be aware of differences within this tradition. Many of the sources use 'evangelical', 'Pentecostal', 'charismatic' and 'neo-

Pentecostal' interchangeably and, as we noted in the previous chapter, in practice the boundaries between them are often fluid. Though Pentecostals differ over detail, most take the view that there is a distinctive stage of 'baptism of the spirit' that occurs at some stage after initial conversion. The 'charismatic movement' which became more prominent within Protestant churches and then some Catholic ones in North America and Western Europe during the 1970s and 1980s, and married Pentecostal experiences to traditional church teaching, often tended to attract more middle-class adherents than the traditional lower-class Pentecostals. Finally 'neo-Pentecostalism' has come to be associated with the 'wealth and prosperity', 'name it and claim it' and 'deliverance' theology coming out of the United States over the last thirty years – though it also resonated strongly with indigenous religious traditions in many parts of the developing world. Here the ties with a traditional 'Protestant ethic' were broken, as neo-Pentecostal preachers taught that poverty or ill-health were the result of insufficient faith and low levels of spiritual (and sometimes financial) commitment to the Church, or alternatively the product of demon possession. Of course, this analysis is overly simplistic, and the extremely fissiparous and fragmentary nature of Pentecostal organisation means that one cannot identity a unified movement, whilst some of the African Independent Churches with their adaptation of pre-Christian traditions do not always fit easily into this category. Nonetheless there are 'family' resemblances in the heavy emphasis on experience over doctrine, and oral communication over the written word, features which have proved to be extremely influential in parts of the developing world and capable of adapting to local expectations of what a religious faith should provide.

One explanation of Pentecostal expansion focuses on the role of foreign missionaries in exporting an American style of Christianity in order to provide ideological support for Western imperialism, capitalism and the agenda of the Christian Right. Writers within the region sometimes speak of 'an invasion of the sects', and 'underlying the denunciations is the suspicion that Protestant expansion is another form of American imperialism. Many critics in the Catholic Church and on the left presume that the CIA is bankrolling evangelism, to soften up popular resistance to US foreign policy'.[4] Though the language may be exaggerated, such authors do make a strong case for foreign interest in the spread of a religious trend that appears likely to encourage an apolitical attitude, with Brouwer and his colleagues arguing that 'the universalising of faith is intertwined with the homogenising influences of consumerism, mass communication, and production in ways that are compatible with the creation of an international market by global capitalist institutions'.[5] They note the role of Christian Right activists such as Pat Robertson in raising money for the Guatemalan 'pacification' campaigns in the 1980s that destroyed many families and villages, and opening up local cultures to Protestant influences, and suggest that the new Protestant ethic involves a strong commitment to 'order'.[6]

That there has been external involvement is clear, with foreign missionaries sometimes involved in setting up or supporting Pentecostal churches in their early stages of development, and with local street pastors keen to build their influence through real and pretended links to international religious groups. During the Cold War, organisations like Campus Crusade for Christ played a role in promoting faith as an antidote to communism and groups within the Christian Right helped to fund the activities of the Nicaraguan 'contras'. Paul Gifford notes that in several African countries many Pentecostal churches have developed networks with US and European religious groups, though he points out that there is nothing inherently sinister in this connection which, for many Africans, represents an effort to plug into global networks that largely bypass Africa.[7] And Brian Smith suggests that claims of foreign involvement are hardly damning given that much the same could be said of the Roman Catholic Church in Latin America, which receives extensive funding from Europe and half of whose priests were foreign born by the end of the twentieth century.[8]

For all this, and despite both theological influences and some well-publicised interventions in the politics of developing countries, most sources indicate that Protestant-Pentecostal growth is largely indigenous in nature. Chile provides one of the clearest examples, with Pentecostalism making an early impact at around the same time as the emergence of the movement in the USA, leading to a schism within the Chilean Methodist Church in 1910. During the 1940s further growth appeared as the Pentecostal Methodists were joined by other groups, and by 1960 it was estimated that around 10% of the population was Protestant (mostly Pentecostal) with particular strength in the central valley and lower-class suburbs of Santiago. According to Cleary and Sepulveda, in recent years Pentecostalism has been most influential amongst groups suffering from social exclusion and lacking access to services.[9] Wilson makes similar comments regarding Guatemala, noting a Protestant history going back to the late nineteenth century and pointing to the growing influence of Pentecostalism, resulting in significant sections of the population adhering to 'enthusiastic' Christianity. Whilst foreign influences have played some role here, he suggests that they cannot account for such significant growth, and along with other authors suggests that even when external actors have stimulated or supported Pentecostalism the tendency to split and create new churches undermines any sense of common purpose.[10] Discussing Brazil, Freston makes the same point, noting that with 15% of the population, Brazilian Protestantism (dominated by Pentecostalism) is 'national, popular and rapidly expanding'.[11] Foreign involvement may be there, but it is the ability of this religious tradition to meet – or at least promise to meet - the religious needs of the populations of the Majority World that account for its spread at a time when local nationalism has often failed to deliver and the forces of globalisation threaten traditional understandings of the world. Yet this is not necessarily a movement of resistance to globalisation but a particular 'popular' means of engaging with it and perhaps benefiting from what it appears to offer.

Apolitical conservatives – supporters of authoritarianism?

A common stereotype of Pentecostals suggests that their focus on the other-worldly means that they are unlikely to engage fully with the political arena, neither offering any critique of authoritarianism or contributing to the building of new democratic orders. Sometimes they are depicted as local branches of the American Christian Right, promoting socially conservative agendas and in practice supporting authoritarian regimes in much of the developing world. In effect they embodied Marx's description of religion as the 'opium of the people', encouraging passivity and other-worldliness in the face of oppression and injustice. With regard to the influence of American conservative Protestantism, clearly there were attempts by groups within the Christian Right to promote their message in Central America, and several North American televangelists have enjoyed considerable access to the airwaves in parts of the developing world. On issues relating to the family and sexuality, Pentecostal churches and their representatives within local legislatures have tended to adopt traditional positions akin to those promoted by the Christian Right. In a few cases Christian Right involvement was more direct, as in the case of Pat Robertson whose ostensibly humanitarian Operation Lovelift effectively subsidised Guatemalan President Rios Montt's 'pacification' campaigns.[12] Yet, as Freston suggests, the 'fragmentation of evangelicalism means its direct political impact is always smaller than might be hoped or feared. No evangelical neo-Christendom potentially dangerous to democracy is feasible … Also it does not seem that Third World evangelicalism will line up with the First World Christian Right on many issues: while it may do so on abortion and homosexuality, it is far more fractured on questions of gender and economics, and distant from the Christian Right on geopolitical issues'.[13]

As a result of their own internal leader-focused structures it is sometimes suggested that Pentecostals feel at home with authoritarian styles of political rule, whether embodied in military dictatorships at state level or in patron–client style relations at local level. For Jean-Pierre Bastian their activities reinforced 'caudillist models of religious and social control' and had nothing 'to do with political and social reform'.[14] Another early study of Latin American Pentecostals in the 1960s by Christian Lalive d'Epinay suggested that pastoral leadership in these churches was akin to that of the *patron* on the rural *haciendas* where the boss provided security but at the cost of total control over the lives of the community. In consequence, they may have not identified with authoritarian political orders during the 1960s, but their effective isolation from the wider society meant that they had no significant political impact beyond reinforcing existing authority relations.[15] Despite the emphasis on spiritual equality, Hoffnagel suggested that on joining the community a female believer has to subordinate herself to its authority in terms of social engagement, marriage, and participation in social activities like cinema or dance. Speaking of Latin American Pentecostals she notes that in the Assemblies of God (the leading Pentecostal denomination in many parts of the world) ordinary members have very little say in choosing their leader and at the national level church leaders exercise considerable influence over the decision-making of the denomination.[16]

Several studies demonstrate the shift towards authoritarianism that affects many Pentecostal groups as charismatic leaders, who have succeeded in building up a significant religious movement, begin to distance themselves from their roots and to enjoy the trappings and rewards of office. In this context any criticism of the leader is interpreted as disloyalty and even as rejection of a God who speaks through the leader, and the would-be dissident is presented with a choice: 'either you follow me or leave'.[17] David Maxwell, in his introduction to a study of the Zimbabwean Assemblies of God of Africa (ZAOGA), notes the tendency of contemporary Pentecostalism 'to produce oligarchic governments whose leaders often retain power for decades before passing it on to their immediate kin. Some of these leaders have formed cosy alliances with equally authoritarian secular politicians'.[18] His own study provides clear evidence of this from Zimbabwe, though his study also reinforces the point made by David Martin that the attitudes of believers should not be read out of the statements of their pastors,[19] and also indicates that the inherently pluralistic nature of Pentecostalism means that it is not difficult for those who break away to set up their own congregations and perhaps even develop their own personality cults. For many authors the combination of hierarchical authority patterns within these religious communities and their sectarian tendency to separate from 'the world' hardly make them friends of democratisation, a process that assumes the questioning of authority and collaboration with non-believers, as well as bargaining and compromise within communities.

One consequence of this was that during the period when military dictatorships dominated Latin America, as well as parts of Asia and Africa, evangelicals in general and Pentecostals in particular tended to be quiescent if not supportive of such regimes. In part this stemmed from a doctrinal commitment, rooted in St Paul's comments in the book of Roman, to obeying those set in authority by God – rulers could only be resisted when they asked believers to deny their faith or act against their conscience. One of the most quoted examples of this came from Chile where a group of Pentecostal church leaders offered some support to the regime and in return were favoured by political leaders weary of Catholic critiques of human rights abuses. Following the military coup the leadership of the Pentecostal Methodist Church of Chile described the intervention as 'the answer of God to the prayer of all believers who see Marxism as the Satanic force of darkness *par excellence*', and they later invited General Pinochet to open their new cathedral. He agreed on condition that they expressed their support for his regime, a condition that was met in December 1974 when 32 Pentecostal pastors gave their backing in the name of all Chile's Protestant churches. Following this letter, Pinochet attended a Te Deum to celebrate the opening of a new Pentecostal 'cathedral' in Santiago and attended subsequent events organised by the Pentecostals. Yet one needs to be wary of reading too much into this, as reportedly some pastors expressed concern that they were being used by the regime, and some sources suggest that the majority within the largely working-class Pentecostal community opposed military rule. Indeed, in the early 1980s another Pentecostal group, the *Confraternidad Christiana de Iglesias*, which brought together a range of Protestant pastors and churches, explicitly repudiated these statements of support and issued a series of documents condemning the impact of neo-liberal economic policies on the poor and the marginalised.[20]

Similar trends could be observed in Africa where leading Pentecostal pastors played a role in legitimising the new 'democratic' version of President Rawlings in 1992 and 1994, with Nicholas Duncan-Williams of Christian Action Faith Ministries playing a leading role in a service of thanksgiving in 1994, and praising the political leadership for turning to God.[21] In Kenya President Arap Moi made much of his religious credentials and in response one Pentecostal leader could suggest in 1992 that 'in heaven it is just like Kenya has been for many years. There is only one party – and God never makes a mistake', and he went on to praise the president for the peace prevailing in the country.[22] Yet whilst these sort of attitudes often led to support for authoritarian leaders, several authors have noted that the reasons underlying this support were often pragmatic rather than principled, including 'a desire for the respectability conferred by government recognition, and for the material rewards a well-disposed President can dispense'.[23] In countries where specific denominations enjoyed historically close links to the state, the gains for newcomers from alliance with an authoritarian regime might include a more liberal attitude towards opening new churches and the curtailing of legislative and administrative favouritism accorded to the dominant religious community.

This was evident in Zimbabwe where until the late 1990s the Pentecostal movement (ZAOGA) led by Ezekial Guti increasingly sought the approval of President Mugabe's regime, both because of shared values – an authoritarian style cultural nationalism and opposition to sexual license and homosexuality – but also because the church leadership sought recognition and incorporation into elite circles. Yet whilst one can focus on church elites seeking upward social mobility, it also tied in with their core theological commitment to creating the best conditions for evangelisation and church growth, a goal that was placed well above commitments to human rights or particular political regimes. And when Mugabe's policies led to an economic decline that affected their core constituency at the turn of the century, in particular by undermining the promise of prosperity offered as a consequence of conversion, church leaders quickly distanced themselves from the regime and, on occasions, even appeared to favour the opposition.[24]

Even where Pentecostals are not offering overt support to dictators, some commentators have suggested that their other-worldly, apolitical attitudes and social conservatism are hardly conducive to a vision of democracy that goes beyond occasional voting. Burdick notes that some Brazilian Pentecostals directly attributed their conversion to what they saw as excessive politicisation of the local Catholic community, whilst Ireland notes that many are wary of mobilisation into political campaigns.[25] Many of the theological beliefs associated with Pentecostalism tend to encourage a certain respect for political authority, except where it denies believers the right to practise their faith, whilst the 'deliverance' belief that characterises at least some African churches tends to see political problems in terms of the activities of demonic spiritual forces and focus on religious revitalisation as the only solution to a nation's difficulties.[26] There is also a preference for avoiding forms of political engagement that might lead to conflict or violence, a view that arises from both theological commitment to obeying the 'powers that be' and a historically shaped inclination of the Protestant churches to 'keep their heads down' that dates from the days when they were often a tiny, sometimes persecuted religious movement.[27] Yet as we shall see, whilst this apolitical and other-worldly orientation is very definitely a significant characteristic of Pentecostal Christianity, in reality the Pentecostal engagement with the political order is more complex and ambiguous in nature.

The other charge sometimes made is that Pentecostalism encourages a socially conservative political agenda though, as we suggested with regard to the Christian Right in the USA, this tells us very little about Pentecostals' attitude to democratic politics. In common with most conservative Protestants they tend to be opposed to abortion and to any public recognition of homosexuality as a legitimate sexual choice, and they promote traditional ideas about family relations. A survey of Pentecostals in ten countries – USA, Brazil, Chile, Guatemala, Kenya, Nigeria, South Africa, India, the Philippines and South Korea – published by the Pew Forum on Religion and Public Life in 2006, exploring the attitude of 'renewalists' to social and moral issues, demonstrated that they were generally more conservative than both the general population and 'other Christians'. On the question of homosexuality all tended to be more conservative than the general population, with between 64% (Chile) and 99% (Kenya) of Pentecostals saying homosexual behaviour could never be justified. They were also typically more opposed to abortion than most other groups (though in some cases ambiguous as to whether governments should actively prevent women obtaining abortions). Interestingly, however, when asked if divorce could never be justified the figures ranged from 37% in Brazil to 84% in the Philippines, with most Pentecostals taking a far more negative view of drinking alcohol than of divorce. This survey appears to support many of the case studies which point to a moral conservatism that is occasionally qualified in response to specific cultural circumstances – for example, the African Pentecostals were almost unanimously opposed to homosexuality but the majority opposing polygamy was much lower than in the other countries surveyed. On gender issues they tended not to differ that much from the wide population, though Pentecostals were more willing to accept women pastors or ministers than other Christians in all but one (Brazil) of the countries surveyed – the figures here ranged from 39% in India to 90% in South Korea. But whilst there were variations in their general attitude to gender equality, on balance they were only very slightly less egalitarian than the general population.[28]

Whilst these figures do confirm the view of Pentecostals as social conservatives when it comes to 'traditional family values', they also indicate ambiguities in some areas, most notably in relationship to gender issues. This confirms conclusions reached by scholars carrying out more detailed case studies of the role of women in Pentecostalism more generally, who have noted ambiguities that are masked by simple assertions about Pentecostalism reinforcing patriarchal lifestyles. At one level it has been noted that in Latin America conversion to Pentecostalism provides women with a new sense of worth and that the teaching of the equality of all before God subverts traditional notions of subordination. In addition when the men follow suit it often provides a counter to the traditional culture as well as improving the material position of households once men start spending money on their families rather that on drink or prostitutes. Thus Elizabeth Brusco researching in Columbia during the early 1980s states:

> I found that Columbian evangelicalism reforms gender roles in a way that enhances female status. It promotes female interests not only in simple, practical ways but also through its potential as an antidote to machismo.[29]

When both partners are converted, women have the power 'to speak out in the name of God and seek support in collective prayer', and to appeal to scriptures when domestic troubles loom or when seeking to influence male behaviour.[30]

Pentecostalism also provides women with a sense of community and belonging, and one in which they are sometimes offered:

> unaccustomed opportunities for official and unofficial leadership and new roles in the religious community. Leadership roles within women's groups are especially common, perhaps as a result of women's predominance within many Pentecostal churches ... Women are also usually the leaders and primary participants in *cultos o domicilio*, worship services held in individual homes. Many of these group activities – social welfare, prayer, church maintenance and cleaning – simply replicate women's domestic roles. They may nonetheless be a source of status within the church. Moreover, such groups may give women new skills, such as public speaking or fundraising, and enhance their sense of efficacy in bringing about change.[31]

Though leadership remains predominantly male, Pentecostal churches have historically accorded women a greater role in preaching and teaching than the other Christian churches. In this sense Pentecostalism does not fundamentally challenge traditional gender roles, but does create new opportunities for women to participate in both the private and public sphere that may in the long term undermine more conservative perceptions of gender roles.

Though some hope that this may eventually contribute to changes in political culture that will encourage a more participatory vision of both family relations and public life, others are more sceptical, pointing to the danger that women might also become more tolerant of men's bad behaviour which can now be blamed on the devil,[32] and others have noted that these churches often serve as places to seek clean-living marriage partners.[33] Steigenga and Smilde's study of Central America does not find that Pentecostalism is making significant changes in the direction of gender equality though, perhaps counter-intuitively, their surveys suggested that whilst the religiously conservative were more likely to be politically quiescent, they were also more likely to accept equal political rights for women than the wider population.[34] Another study focusing on Chile – where divorce was only legalised in 2004 – has found deeply conservative attitudes prevailing, with the majority taking the view that women working damages family life, even though many families cannot support themselves without two incomes – or that of the woman alone where she is bringing up children on her own. This in turn leads some scholars to argue that Pentecostalism is having an impact in changing the attitude of men, and that it is also offering an alternative response to globalisation that is critical of the consequences of global trends but that is rooted in a strong family-based ethical conservatism.[35] For our purposes, the key point is that whilst the global Pentecostal movement may be socially conservative in many respects, this tells us very little in itself about its commitment to political democracy and, as we have seen, there may be ambiguities in the social consequences of the movement that could potentially work either for or against democratisation in those countries where it has become influential.

Pentecostal political engagements

Social critique and attitudes to political involvement

In our discussion of the 'Catholic third wave' we noted that the Church contributed to democratisation through developing a public critique of authoritarianism. This entailed a social critique of the injustices perpetuated by both the regimes and the international system. In its more radical form this critique was represented by liberation theology, but in its more common form by a 'centrist' focus on human rights that grew in part out of the theological re-orientation that came from the Second Vatican Council. In the case of the Pentecostals this critical function has been largely absent, in part because of the very nature of the tradition, which lacks transnational institutional structures (though it is based on extensive international networking), but also because these were predominantly churches of the poor and marginalised whose world-view tended to stress experience over theology – which is not to deny the socially engaged thinking going on in Pentecostal research centres and religious colleges. One consequence of this fragmentation has been that although individual pastors and church leaders may occasionally preach critical social messages, which would not be surprising given that most represent and preside over congregations of the poor, this rarely gains a public attention of the sort available to Catholic or mainstream Protestant church leaders. Where they do get publicity the focus has tended to be on their promises of wealth, healing and deliverance, as well as the general show-business dynamics of some of their services. And in these contexts, to the extent that they engage with the public sphere, the emphasis of many preachers is often on the role of spiritual forces in creating negative political situations and the importance of religious renewal for the rebuilding of public life, rather than on the structural causes of social ills.

Of course, there are exceptions, and one of the more interesting of these is Ghana's Mensa Otabil, a former Anglican who set up the International Central Gospel Church in Accra in 1984. At first sight this is just another 'faith church' promising spiritual and material rewards in return for sacrificial giving. Otabil's books focus on 'winning' and achieving success, and his congregation tends to be young, upwardly mobile and middle class, full of people keen to rise above their circumstances. But there is another side to Otabil, discussed at some length by Paul Gifford, which does offer something resembling a social critique of the situation facing African Christians and Africans in general. Central to this is the promotion of black pride and the need for blacks to take control of their own churches. At the same time Otabil has developed an analysis of the situation facing black Africa that goes beyond relying on changing lives to change society – 'we can get everyone in Africa saved, but that won't solve our problem'. He rejects the notion that if people give they will get richer as simplistic and unrealistic in the presence of unjust economic structures and oppressive rulers. For Otabil the whole history of colonialism is about exploitation for economic gain, and in the post-colonial world this exploitative role has been taken over by the multinationals. In particular, he suggested that Western policies ensured that 'we will always be running but never catch up' and attacked local leaders 'for selling us for generations yet to come'. At the same time, whilst stressing external factors he rejects the tendency to blame everything on external forces and points to the internal causes of African problems, arguing that Africa is held back by an inferiority complex, by tribalism, cultural stagnation, idolatry, fetishism, a village mentality, corruption and poor leadership. Whilst this social analysis often remains undeveloped and he remains committed to a faith gospel preaching that those who sow will reap rich rewards, this attempt to explore the cultural factors underlying Africa's problems and his acceptance that a simple focus on personal salvation is not enough represents an interesting attempt to engage with the political sphere.[36]

Alongside this overtly critical approach we see the emergence of what Miller and Yamamori describe as a 'progressive Pentecostalism' that adopts a more holistic approach that stresses the need to deal with people's material and physical well-being as well as their spiritual condition. Such groups are not progressive in the sense of being overtly political or left-wing, but they have a social orientation that is evident in their engagement with activities that may contribute to social transformation from the bottom up by stressing human dignity and the right of all to a decent quality of life. To this end they develop an array of social programmes aimed at poverty reduction, education, medical assistance, development etc. Above all they are coming to recognise that whilst an individualistic approach that focuses on changing individual lives may help, it will not deal with deep-seated structural problems such as poverty and AIDs.[37]

In terms of Pentecostal attitudes to political involvement it is extremely difficult to make generalisations about this diverse and fragmented movement. Though much of the emphasis on personal salvation and on exploring the 'gifts of the spirit' could be said to distract believers from civic engagement, simply by participating in faith communities some are learning for the first time what it means to experience collective action and others are acquiring organisational and leadership skills. They can then go on to use these in political settings, and a number of scholars have pointed to the role played by some Brazilian Pentecostals in the activities of the Workers Party during the 1990s - providing up to 10% of the party's membership in some districts.[38] Though case studies tend to show up differing results, certain patterns can be observed in Pentecostal attitudes to political engagement. Where these are churches of the very poor or extremely marginalised the very social circumstances tend to preclude civic engagement as the struggle for survival takes precedence, but when a certain degree of security has been ensured, many studies suggest that Pentecostals are as likely to get involved as others. Steigenga's analysis of Costa Rica and Guatemala indicated that often those with the most conservative theologies were the most likely to vote.[39]

The other common feature of Pentecostal involvement, as already noted, is that whilst willing to participate, Pentecostals generally preferred to avoid conflictual situations that might lead to violence, though in Brazil Burdick suggested that though less likely to join trade unions, when they did so Pentecostals tended to want to see labour conflict through to the end.[40] Overall the evidence is still too partial and fragmentary to draw definitive conclusions but the general pattern emerging, and confirmed to some degree by the 2006 Pew Forum survey, suggests that Pentecostals are not vastly different from the rest of the population in their attitudes towards religious involvement in politics, though they were much more likely to want their political leaders to have strong religious convictions.[41] More generally it suggests that whilst they are not likely to be found at the forefront of campaigns for democratisation or the deepening of democracy, neither are they becoming a major obstacle to this process in most of the countries where they are strong.

Direct political involvement

If the evidence on attitudes towards social engagement and involvement in social organisations enables us to draw few definitive conclusions about the likely impact of the Pentecostal explosion on democratic political development, the same could be said about their more direct involvement in the political arena. At the level of executive power we have seen the election or selection of several Pentecostal heads of state, some of whose activities in office worked against the promotion of liberal democratic visions of political order. The most notorious of these was General Efrian Rios Montt in Guatemala, who came to power in a military coup in 1982 and whose 'pacification campaign', as already noted, was financed in part by Pat Robertson's 'Operation Lovelift'. Some critics argued that Rioss Mont, who belonged to a neo-Pentecostal congregation, saw this campaign not just about combatting subversives but also as undermining traditional Mayan/Catholic communities by breaking up villages and making the dislocated populations more open to Protestant evangelisation. Neo-Pentecostalism also spread quickly amongst the upper classes, and tended to reinforce their preference for public order and tranquillity over social justice.[42] Though Rios Montt was put in power by other officers and there was no primarily Pentecostal impulse behind his seizure of power, both he and Jorge Serrano (president from 1991–93) – who in 1993 sought to dissolve parliament and suspend the constitution – came from Pentecostal churches and liked to claim at least some religious motivation for their activities. Yet Freston suggests that neither of these candidates was really socialised in the evangelical tradition and their political attitudes and engagements were not primarily motivated by religion.[43]

A more overt case of taking one's religion into the public sphere was provided by Zambia's Frederick Chiluba who succeeded Kenneth Kuanda in 1991. Two months after taking the presidency Chiluba proclaimed Zambia 'a Christian nation that will seek to be governed by the righteous principles of the Word of God', a statement welcomed by some of the evangelical churches but seen as divisive by both the mainstream Christian denominations and the Muslim community. In subsequent months Chiluba broke off relations with Iran, established diplomatic relations with Israel, and started visiting churches to re-emphasise his government's commitment to Christian values and evangelisation. This move on Chiluba's part probably reflected a personal commitment but also an electoral imperative, whilst for the 'evangelicals' it offered the promise of parity with the more established denominations.[44] Yet as Gifford has pointed out, Chiluba found it as hard as his predecessor to prevent his government getting mired in corruption and many Christian churches were disappointed that their influence had not grown in what was constitutionally proclaimed a Christian nation in 1996.[45]

In a number of developing countries Pentecostals have also sought influence by standing for legislatures, with Brazil as perhaps the best example of both their success and the limitations of this engagement from both the democratic and the Pentecostal perspective. Following the military's retreat from power in the mid-1980s some 33 *evangelicos* were elected to the 1986 Constituent Assembly, of which 18 were Pentecostals. This trend continued in subsequent elections with 29 elected in 1992, 30 in 1994 and 49 in the 1998 elections, with about two-thirds representing a variety of

Pentecostal churches. Up until the late 1990s the vast majority of these associated with parties of the Right though, as is common in the Brazilian party system, many of the Christian deputies regularly changed their affiliation. They also initially appear to have been primarily motivated by a desire to raise the profile of the Pentecostal movement and to increase their following. With time, however, they started to focus on developing a 'family values' agenda and to forge alliances with other conservative deputies. Towards the end of the 1990s a small minority begun to associate with the Workers Party of President Lula and a small evangelical left wing sought to promote a wider social agenda.

For most, however, the focus of their activities has tended to concentrate on protecting their own church interests, ensuring that Catholic dominance was not written into the constitution, and taking conservative positions on traditional 'moral' issues. As the years progressed the most prominent group of deputies became those associated with the rather controversial Universal Church of the Kingdom of God (IURD), who seemingly concentrated primarily on using political involvement to further the Church's economic and media interests.[46] Overall the impact of this Christian intervention was mixed – it mobilised and provided a voice for those who might not have participated in the past, but its impact was undermined by squabbles within the legislative group and by the activities of a few who were drawn into selling votes for favours.[47]

A new Protestant ethic?

Beyond the discussion of context-specific Pentecostal contributions to civic engagement and political life, there is a wider debate about the long-term implications of the global expansion of this 'enthusiastic' social movement. On the one hand there is the argument that the primarily other-worldly nature of Pentecostalism is likely to discourage political engagement and that its internal authoritarianism might well parallel a similar acceptance of the political status quo in the political arena. John Foster, for example, suggests that:

> the cost of inflation, the brunt of neo-liberal economic policies, and the overall degradation of traditional community life caused

the poor to seek out shelter in these religious movements. Unlike their predecessors in the religious marketplace, conservative evangelicals and Pentecostals mirrored the cultural heritage of the Latin American poor. Functioning as a refuge from the anomie that most poor people experience in the face of a seemingly uncontrollable world, this second wave of Protestantism is deeply rooted in the experience of the destitute.

He goes on to argue that whilst a rigorous moral ethic might help individuals to overcome the squalor of poverty and drunkenness, Pentecostal groups with their authoritarian leaders are more likely to replicate the clientelistic patterns of existing political orders – indeed, he sees one of the reasons for their success in Latin America as stemming from their greater cultural affinity to the life of the poor with its oral culture and acceptance of authoritarian leadership.[48]

Against this it has been asked whether, despite the fact that individual Pentecostals may be more or less politically active, there are political consequences of this movement that might be comparable to that of earlier religious 'waves', whether the Reformation 'ethic' identified by Max Weber that contributed to the 'spirit of capitalism' or the post-Vatican II 'democratic turn' in Catholicism identified by Samuel Huntington. This argument is perhaps most clearly associated with David Martin who in his 1990 book *Tongues of Fire* argued that just as 'Methodism widened the rent in the "scared canopy" which the Anglican Church tried to maintain over English society' and 'helped destroy what remnants of the sacred canopy remained in the United States ... Pentecostalism now performs similar roles with respect to Roman Catholicism in Latin America'.[49] Martin also raises the question of whether Pentecostalism might have a Weberian effect in transforming behaviour and culture, whether it might be able to 'implant new discipline, re-order priorities, counter corruption and destructive machismo and reverse the indifferent and injurious hierarchies of the outside world'.[50] And in the same way that Protestantism came to be associated with democracy, the very divisiveness of Pentecostalism might play a role in destroying monopolistic religious situations and opening up social spaces for new forms of association, authority and dissent.[51]

Peter Berger takes this argument one stage further, noting that whilst Pentecostalism is a tradition with Anglo-Saxon roots, 'it has been successfully indigenised everywhere it has penetrated. It does not typically use the English language, and its worship (especially in its music) takes over many indigenous forms'. Yet its spirit retains Anglo-Saxon traits:

> especially in its powerful combination of individualistic self-expression, egalitarianism … and the capacity for creating voluntary association. Thus it not only facilitates social mobility in developing market economies … but also facilitates actual or anticipated participation in the new global economy. To this must be added the fact that among the leaders of the movement there is a consciousness of being part of a global movement, with increasing cross-national contacts between them and with the centers of evangelicalism in the United States.[52]

In other words this new socio-religious movement has affinities with both democracy and capitalism, and with these phenomena in their modern globalised manifestations. On this assumption the long-term impact of Pentecostalism might be the promotion of a liberal-capitalist and democratic ethos and, despite the tradition's predominant roots amongst the poor, it is more likely to be found in the ranks of the forces favouring globalisation than those resisting its more questionable impacts.

Because this debate revolves around long-term consequences, the questions raised cannot be answered definitively, but a few general comments can be made. In terms of the creation of a new capitalist ethic the evidence appears to be contradictory, with anecdotal evidence supporting the claim that conversion does encourage a better use of income amongst believing families, particularly where it encourages men to contribute more to family affairs, both financially and in terms of engagement. There is also survey evidence to support the suggestion that many Pentecostals believe themselves to have become better off as a result of conversion, with Steigenga's study of two Central American countries reporting that over half of those polled felt that conversion had helped them economically even though it had not brought real economic change or greater upward mobility.[53] Miller and Yamamori also note a growing middle-class Pentecostal constituency which may arise from an upward social mobility stimulated by the better use of resources,[54] though their evidence is largely impressionistic and perhaps ignores the vast majority of street-based Pentecostal communities where fundamental shifts in income and social position are less evident. Clearly this is a subject that needs further investigation, but the assumption that Pentecostalism might encourage the sort of work ethic that might promote liberal capitalism has also come under question. Paul Gifford's analysis of Pentecostalism in Ghana notes the complaint that many of these new churches encourage a seven-days-a-week commitment that actually undermines a work ethic, as well as promoting a reliance on divine solutions to poverty rather than solutions rooted in hard work.

Whilst many of these studies are essentially impressionistic or rooted in local case studies, Anthony Gill sought to explore this question through data analysis using the 1990 World Values Survey. His conclusion was that 'Weber is not at work in Latin America, at least in terms of the cultural defining role of Protestantism'. The evidence he produces suggested that denominational affiliation (Catholic or Protestant) had little impact upon economic and political attitudes. These were far more likely to be determined by age, gender and socio-economic status, although on the political front he found that what is more important is regular church involvement, as those active in religious groups are more likely to participate in social groups, and in some countries more likely to trust government than those who do not.[55]

This study would appear to confirm the work of others which suggests that whilst Pentecostal conversions may transform individual lives, the evidence remains inconclusive on whether the cumulative effect of such personal changes can have a significant political impact upon the wider society. Where Pentecostal communities are rooted in middle-class or even semi-elite circles as in Guatemala and elsewhere, conversion and engagement in these churches may bring or reinforce prosperity; where these churches serve the genuinely poor and marginalised some studies would suggest that, despite perceptions of greater prosperity, the socio-economic conditions of those involved has not fundamentally changed. And in the short term the latter may not have the energy or inclination to engage in an active way with processes of democratisation, whilst the former may be inclined to prefer a status quo that protects their own position. Having said that, we still know far too little about the

Pentecostal explosion and its possible political consequences, a position perhaps best summed up in Steigenga's words:

> Without question, the most interesting and substantial political effects of Protestantism in Latin America are those that tend to remain under the radar of many political science analyses. Religion often serves to motivate social and political changes that are difficult to discern at the level of national politics. While Protestant political parties, evangelical presidents and right wing televangelists provide tangible and familiar subjects for analysis, the household politics of gender, church related community volunteerism and religiously motivated attitudes towards citizenship can be more difficult to measure and evaluate.[56]

And as Maxwell puts it, whilst many of the arguments about Pentecostalism's democratising impact are speculative, focused on long-term cultural consequences, it is at the day-to-day, micro-level that Pentecostalism may be helping to democratise civil society. At this level there are signs of an 'alternative pluralist and egalitarian political culture' where the meaning of Scripture is debated with a degree of civility, where women and young people learn to participate and acquire organisational skills, and where local associations in theory enjoy a degree of autonomy and the ready ability to secede should they be unhappy with centralised bureaucracies or leaders. Much may also depend upon the outcome of the tensions between these democratic trends and the authoritarianism often associated with the charismatic leaders who created these groups. In the long term Pentecostalism will probably not be at the forefront of campaigns for political change, but neither is it likely to engender significant obstacles to democratisation and on occasions may offer resources for those seeking justice in this world as well as salvation in the next.

Notes

1 P. Berger, 'The cultural dynamics of globalization', in P. Berger and S. Huntington (ed.), *Many Civilizations: Cultural Diversity in the Contemporary World* (Oxford: Oxford University Press, 2002), pp. 1–16; D. Martin, *Tongues of Fire: The Explosion of Protestantism in Latin America* (London: Blackwell Publishers, 1990), especially chapters 2 and 13.

2 A. Anderson, *An Introduction to Pentecostalism: Global Charismatic Christianity* (Cambridge: Cambridge University Press, 2004), p. 63; K. Coleman *et al.*, 'Protestantism in El Salvador: conventional wisdom

versus the survey evidence', in V. Garrard-Burnett and D. Stoll (ed.), *Rethinking Protestantism in Latin America* (Philadelphia: Temple University Press, 1993), p. 112; P. Freston, *Evangelicals and Politics in Asia, Africa and Latin America* (Cambridge: Cambridge University Press, 2001), p. 1; B. Smith, *Religious Politics in Latin America: Pentecostal vs Catholic* (Notre Dame: University of Notre Dame Press, 1998), pp. 2–3.

3 Anderson, *An Introduction to Pentecostalism*, pp. 103–22; Allan Anderson, 'The globalization of Pentecostalism', found at http://allananderson.info/ (accessed 24 May 2006).

4 Coleman, 'Protestantism in El Salvador', p. 112.

5 S. Brouwer, P. Gifford and S. Rose, *Exporting the American Gospel – Global Christian Fundamentalism* (London: Routledge, 1996), p. 3.

6 Ibid., p. 229.

7 P. Gifford, *African Christianity: Its Public Role* (London: Hurst, 1998), chapter 6.

8 Smith, *Religious Politics in Latin America*, p. 23.

9 E. Cleary and J. Sepúlveda, 'Chilean Pentecostalism: coming of age', in E. Cleary and H. Stewart-Gambino (ed.), *Power, Politics and Pentecostals* (Boulder: Westview, 1998), pp. 97–121; according to Freston, in Chile some 1.6% of upper class, 12.5% of middle class, and 24.8% of lower class identify themselves as Pentecostals. Freston, *Evangelicals and Politics in Asia, Africa and Latin America*, pp. 212ff.

10 E. Wilson, 'Guatemalan Pentecostals: something of their own', in Cleary and Stewart-Gambino, *Power, Politics and Pentecostals*, pp. 139–62.

11 Freston, *Evangelicals and Politics in Asia, Africa and Latin America*, p. 11.

12 Brouwer, Gifford and Rose, *Exporting the American Gospel*, p. 56.

13 P. Freston, 'Evangelical Protestantism and democratisation in contemporary Latin America and Asia', in J. Anderson (ed.), *Religion, Democracy and Democratization* (London: Routledge, 2005), p. 39.

14 Quoted in D. Stoll, 'Introduction: rethinking Protestantism in Latin America', in Garrard-Burnett and Stoll, *Rethinking Protestantism in Latin America*, p. 11.

15 Ibid., pp. 6–7.

16 J. Hoffnagel, 'Pentecostalism: a revolutionary or conservative movement', in S. Glazier (ed.), *Perspectives on Pentecostalism* (New York: University of America Press, 1980), pp. 111–24.

17 D. Miller and T. Yamamori, *Global Pentecostalism: The New Face of Christian Social Engagement* (Berkeley: University of California Press, 2007), p. 185.

18 D. Maxwell, *African Gifts of the Spirit: Pentecostalism and the Rise of a Zimbabwean Transnational Religious Movement* (Oxford: James Currey, 2006), p. 9.

19 D. Martin, *Pentecostalism: The World their Parish* (Oxford: Blackwell, 2002), p. 89.

20 Cleary and Sepúlveda, 'Chilean Pentecostalism', p. 105; Anderson, *Introduction to Pentecostalism*, p. 7; F. Kamsteeg, 'Pentecostalism and political awakening in Pinochet's Chile and beyond', in C. Smith and J. Prokopy (ed.), *Latin American Religion in Motion* (London: Routledge, 1999), pp. 187–204.

21 Gifford, *African Christianity*, pp. 86–8.

22 Brouwer, Gifford and Rose, *Exporting the American Gospel*, p. 176.

23 Gifford, *African Christianity*, p. 87.

24 Maxwell, *African Gifts of the Spirit*, pp. 145–51.

25 J. Burdick, 'Struggling against the devil: Pentecostalism and social movements in urban Brazil', and R. Ireland, 'The *crentes* of Camp Alegre and the religious construction of Brazilian politics', in Garrard-Burnett and Stoll, *Rethinking Protestantism in Latin America*, pp. 20–44 and 45–65.

26 P. Gifford, *Ghana's New Christianity: Pentecostalism in a Globalising African Economy* (London: Hurst, 2004), pp. 161–3.

27 T. Steigenga, *The Politics of the Spirit: The Political Implications of Pentecostalized Religion in Costa Rica and Guatemala* (Lanham: Lexington Books, 2001), pp. 144–5.

28 This survey can be found at http://pewforum.org/surveys/pentecostal /?gclid=COvOiOe-hogCFQLTJAodZU8D4g (accessed 12 May 2007).

29 E. Brusco, 'The reformation of machismo: asceticism and masculinity among Columbian evangelicals', in Garrard-Burnett and Stoll, *Rethinking Protestantism in Latin America*, pp. 143–58.

30 Martin, *Pentecostalism*, pp. 98–9.

31 C. Drogus, 'Private power or public power: Pentecostalism, base communities and gender', in Cleary and Stewart-Gambino, *Power, Politics and Pentecostals in Latin America*, pp. 59–60.

32 C. Mariz and M. Machado, 'Pentecostalism and women in Brazil', in Cleary and Stewart-Gambino, *Power, Politics and Pentecostals in Latin America*, pp. 41–54.

33 Gifford, *Ghana's New Christianity*, p. 183.

34 T. Steigenga and D. Smilde, 'Wrapped in the holy shawl: the strange case of conservative Christians and gender equality in Latin America', in Smith and Prokopy, *Latin American Religion in Motion*, pp. 173–86.

35 A. F. Talavera, 'Trends towards globalization in Chile', in Berger and Huntington, *Many Globalizations: Cultural Diversity in the Contemporary World*, pp. 253–4.

36 This paragraph relies heavily on Gifford, *African Christianity*, pp. 80–4 and 237–40, and Gifford, *Ghana's New Christianity*, pp. 117–32.

37 Miller and Yamamori, *Global Pentecostalism*, especially pp. 31–4, 42–3, 67, 169–70.

38 J. Burdick, 'Struggling against the devil: Pentecostalism and social movements in urban Brazil', in Garrard-Burnett and Stoll, *Rethinking Protestantism in Latin America*, p. 34.

39 Steigenga, *The Politics of the Spirit*, pp. 141–4; cf. Steigenga and Smilde, 'Wrapped in the holy shawl'.

40 Burdick, 'Struggling against the devil', p. 32.

41 http://pewforum.org/surveys/pentecostal/?gclid=COvOiOe-hogCFQLT-JAodZU8D4g (accessed 12 May 2007).

42 Brouwer, Gifford and Rose, *Exporting the American Gospel*, pp. 56–7.

43 Freston, *Evangelicals and Politics in Asia, Africa and Latin America*, pp. 263ff.

44 Martin, *Pentecostalism*, pp. 150–1.

45 Gifford, *African Christianity*, pp. 181–245; Freston, *Evangelicals and Politics in Asia, Africa and Latin America*, pp. 154ff.

46 On their electoral involvement see N. Ivette Feliciano, 'Politics, Pentecostals and democratic consolidation in Brazil', a paper dated 3 July 2005 and found at www.acad.carleton.edu/curricular/POSC /faculty/montero/Ivette%20Feliciano.pdf (accessed 2 September 2007).

47 D. Lehmann, *Struggle for the Spirit: Religious Transformation and Popular Culture in Brazil and Latin America* (Cambridge: Polity Press, 1996), p. 215; Freston, 'Evangelical Protestantism and democratisation in contemporary Latin America and Asia', pp. 33–5.

48 J. Foster, 'A Church responsive: understanding and interpreting the changing composition of Christianity in Latin America', found at www2.davidson.edu/academics/acad_depts/rusk/prima/Vol3Issue1 /church.pdf (accessed 2 October 2007).

49 Martin, *Tongues of Fire*, p. 26.

50 Ibid., p. 284.

51 Martin as paraphrased by Stoll, 'Introduction', in Garrard-Burnett and Stoll, Rethinking Protestantism in Latin America, p. 12.

52 Berger, 'The cultural dynamics of globalization', p. 8.

53 Steigenga, *The Politics of the Spirit*, chapter 2.

54 Miller and Yamamori, *Global Pentecostalism*, p. 175.

55 A. Gill, 'Weber in Latin America: is Protestant growth enabling the consolidation of democratic capitalism?', in Anderson, *Religion, Democracy and Democratization*, pp. 42–65.

56 Steigenga, *The Politics of the Spirit*, p. 154.

9

Conclusion

Generalize to make sweeping conclusions, and one ignores
the detail. Pay attention to the detail and generalization
becomes impossible.

(Alan Wolfe)[1]

In this book we have offered a description and analysis of
some of the complex interactions between the various
Christian traditions and democracy, with a particular emphasis on the democratising processes that have been evident
since the mid-1970s. Inevitably, in attempting to cover all of
the major communities as they work out their relationship
with democracy in many parts of the globe and in very different cultural contexts, we have been forced to paint with a
very broad brush and consequently risk superficiality and
misunderstanding. Nonetheless, at this stage it is worth
summing up what seem to be the key conclusions and point
to possible future developments in this dynamic and changing relationship.

Our first aim was simply to *tell the story* of how the
Christian churches have responded to democracy and
inevitably we started with the much-touted Protestant relationship, though recognising that there were from the earliest
days of Christianity theological resources and practical exper-
iments which could be looked to by those believers
promoting a more pluralistic understanding of political order.
With Bruce we took the view that, whilst key features of the
Protestant Reformation helped to create the possibility of
democratic politics, this relationship was essentially inadvertent, a by-product rather than a direct consequence of the
Reformers' religious agenda. Moreover, whilst there remains

a statistical relationship between the significant presence of Protestantism and the successful consolidation of democratic governance (at least in its minimalist form), the flirtations of German Lutherans with Nazism and the ambiguous relationship of some Protestant groups to various contemporary authoritarian regimes cautions us against any over-simplification of this relationship.

In many respects the Roman Catholic relationship has been more complex, as from the time of the French Revolution up until the mid-twentieth century the Church remained a strong opponent of both democracy and some of its key features – freedom of conscience, expression, and pluralism in general. In response to the changing circumstances created by the rise of fascism and, more importantly by communism, as well as under the influence of men like John Courtney Murray and Jacques Maritain who pointed to the advantages of pluralism from a Catholic viewpoint, the Church gradually changed its position. At Vatican II the leaders of the tradition focused on the importance of human dignity and the rights of all, whether Catholic or not. In consequence, the Church began to play a key role in promoting human rights and civility in public life. Central here was the activity of Pope John Paul II who strongly emphasised the importance of human rights, although the extent to which he can be said to have promoted a transformative view of democracy may depend upon one's own ideological preferences. Yet whilst democracy might be favoured, it always tended to be seen as provisional and as a lesser evil, and the Church retained the right to criticise majority representatives where they promoted values opposed to the teachings of the Church or, the more cynical might suggest, where they challenged the Church's institutional interests. Nonetheless, and despite exceptions such as Argentina, there can be little doubt that during the 'third wave' the Catholic Church did become an institution that tended to support those arguing for an end to the abuse of human rights and the bringing down of authoritarian regimes.

With the partial exception of Greece, in those countries where Orthodoxy was dominant there had been little opportunity to engage with democratic governance, whether in a positive or negative fashion, until the collapse of communism in 1989–91. In consequence, and despite some Russian

Orthodox claims of a rich democratic heritage, little thought had been given to social and political matters in general, and the realities of more or less pluralistic societies often came as something of a shock. As in other contexts the general loosening up of social mores associated with political pluralism did little to encourage Orthodox enthusiasm for pluralism, whilst the emergence of a religious free market left religious communities, weakened by decades of communist repression and harassment, feeling vulnerable to what they saw as better financed and organised 'foreign sects' and religious competitors. As a result, much of their public activity appeared to focus on denouncing immorality or seeking restrictions on competitors, rather than promoting a more affirmative vision of both their religious tradition and its contribution to a more open society.

Finally, we returned to look at the impact of a revitalised Protestantism as represented by the predominantly evangelical Christian Right in the USA and the rapidly expanding global Pentecostal movement. In both cases we pointed to ambiguities, as religious leaders sometimes promoted illiberal policy agendas, yet the very fact of participating in politics often forced them to engage in the sort of bargaining and compromise that are an essential feature of democracy. Simultaneously, their followers often gained considerable experience in negotiating, organising and leading, all processes that had the potential to reinforce commitment to democratic politics. Meanwhile, the often fractious and fissiparous nature of Protestant communities meant that the Christian Right's more rhetorically outspoken religious leaders did not always speak for and were not always able to mobilise their claimed constituencies. In the case of Pentecostalism, while we saw some merit in the argument of Martin and others that a revitalised Protestantism might encourage patterns of behaviour that had the potential to promote a democratic-capitalist ethic, case studies and surveys provide insufficient evidence to build a strong case about the long-term impact of this development. Though these new forms of Protestantism may not pose a major impediment to democratisation – their very fractious nature makes it difficult for them to act as coherent forces in a way comparable to the Roman Catholic Church or even Orthodoxy – there is very little to suggest that they will be at the forefront of campaigns to promote further democratisation.

Though we have spoken about religious traditions as adopting particular postures in relation to public life, we have not meant to imply that their political stances are static nor to fall into the trap of 'essentialising' the political consequences of specific religious beliefs. Equally important is to note that what one sees depends partly upon where one looks, and our primary focus on religious elites and institutions may at times have blinded us to what is happening at the grass-roots level within religious communities. There are also important distinctions to be made between what surveys might indicate about the specific political commitments of individual believers and the longer-term role of religious traditions in shaping political cultures and ways of doing politics in specific contexts. For all that, we remain convinced that religious traditions do have some impact upon political outcomes because at particular points in time they have what we have called 'centres of gravity' that may work more or less in the direction of promoting democratic development. The Roman Catholic Church may not have been the primary contributor to democratic governance in Latin America, but the fundamental shift in the Church's position from the 1960s onwards certainly transformed it in most cases from a more or less keen defender of authoritarianism to a defender of the concept of human dignity regardless of religious or political belief. Equally, it might be argued in the Russian case that the Orthodox Church's scepticism about the merits of pluralism makes it one of those institutional actors reinforcing (but not determining) Vladimir Putin's development of 'managed democracy'.

A second concern of this book has been with *explaining religious responses to democracy and democratisation*. In dealing with the Catholic response to the 'third wave' we explored arguments that focused on theological change, the preservation of ideological and institutional hegemony, and on the protection of market share as factors impelling the churches to oppose or support democratisation. Our analysis suggested that ideas do matter, but that their impact can vary considerably. In the Catholic case we suggested that the major theological re-thinking that culminated in Vatican II fundamentally reshaped attitudes towards politics amongst clergy and laity alike, and that this shifted that particular church in a pro-democratic direction. This was not uniformly welcomed, but nonetheless contributed to the more critical stance on human rights and sympathetic attitude towards civil society campaigners that developed among many national Catholic hierarchies during the last quarter of the twentieth century.

Other commentators were more sceptical about the motives underlying such shifts, preferring to focus on the long history of religious adaptation to political change which reflected the need of churches to carry out their mission regardless of the nature of the political system, as well as pointing to the need to protect their institutional and value hegemony. Hence Jeffrey Haynes could argue that the Catholic contribution might be explained with reference to the need of leading bishops to retain their 'big-man' status as well as their institutional hegemony. The same types of argument might also be used to explain Orthodox campaigns to preserve their privileged status or the Christian Right's defence of 'traditional values', an agenda which though shaped by religious values could also be seen as a reaction to a loss of social power.

Similar arguments were proposed by rational choice theorists who saw religious commitments to democratisation as, at least in part, shaped by the need of these bodies to preserve their market share. Consequently, it was argued that in the face of competition from religious minorities that were proving successful amongst the poor and marginalised – whether Pentecostals in Latin America or a wide variety of 'sects' in the former communist world – Catholic hierarchies opted for identification with the needy whilst Orthodox leaders took the more traditional route of requesting the State to impose restrictions on market entry. Clearly all of these approaches have some merit and help us to understand the religious contribution to democratisation, but we can offer no single, over-arching explanatory model that will explain every case, and in reality much seems to depend upon the contingencies of time and place, on the domestic and international resources which individual religious communities can call upon, on the nature of leadership, on the relations between religious leaders and their own flock, and on their relationship with the wider population and the leaders of the State.

One issue that has repeatedly raised its head throughout this book is the inevitability of tension between the Christian churches and democratic political orders, a tension rooted in what I have called the *liberal-democracy paradox*. In part this tension stems from the fact that politics is ultimately not what the churches are about. Whilst they will intervene to defend their interests or promote particular faith-based agendas, such actions are generally very much subordinate to their goal of preaching the gospel, celebrating the sacraments, encouraging prayer and spirituality, and generally caring for the 'spiritual needs' of their flock. From this perspective, the form of government is largely secondary so long as it does not impinge upon the 'free exercise' of religious belief and practice, though most Christian churches in the 'West' have come to recognise that democracy in some shape or form provides the best conditions for their survival and growth.

The central tension, however, relates to the liberal-democracy paradox, the fact that liberal democracies tend to be rooted in a view of individual autonomy and rights that may clash with religious perceptions that emphasise absolute truths, some understanding of divine law as primary, and a notion of the 'common good' that can over-ride individual interests. In most established democracies religious groups have come to terms with this tension, though groups like the US Christian Right and the Catholic Church in Europe continue to reject the notion that majorities can decide everything and to argue for a greater 'recognition' of religious values in public life. At the same time there is a growing pressure, coming from both the Orthodox churches and some of the Protestant churches of the developing world, for a recognition of a modified democratisation in which individual rights are more keenly balanced (or perhaps constrained) by responsibilities, by Christian moral values, and by national traditions. In making these suggestions religious leaders have argued that they are not opposed to democratic governance or the concept of human rights that are often said to underpin democracy, but that they are simply suggesting (rather like De Tocqueville) that democracy cannot survive without moral restraint of the sort that religious communities can provide.

The problem in making this argument is not so much the

need to avoid the appearance of special pleading for their own values, which is what all lobbies do, but how to promote their perspective without seeming to promote restrictions on the legitimate rights of others – whether individuals or competing groups. The challenge for religious bodies, at least for those claiming to accept the importance of democracy, is to come up with a new model of democracy, one consonant with 'national traditions', one that places a greater role on responsibility, yet one that is still recognisable as democratic. And, as we suggested in our discussion of the Russian Orthodox Church, it has often proved difficult to disguise the fact that calls for a national model of democracy all too often seem to be about privilege for the dominant religious bodies and restrictions on the rights of minorities or individuals.

Clearly there is no definitive way of resolving this tension, but rather one has to accept that the relationship between religious bodies and democratic states is one that will be subject to constant renegotiation. In my view, and in response to a reviewer of the manuscript of this book who felt that I was perhaps too balanced in my approach, a number of general and unashamedly liberal conclusions can be drawn with regard to resolving this paradox. Firstly, a democratic state does not require a necessary separation of religion and state, though it would be harder to justify establishing a particular religion if one were creating democratic states from scratch and especially in multicultural and multi-religious contexts. A democratic state probably does have to be secular, not in the French or Turkish understanding that seeks to keep religion out of the public sphere at all costs, but in the sense of not permitting any religious institution to dominate the public square – whatever defenders of the rights of 'national religions' may suggest to the contrary.

Within the political arena religious bodies should be as free to act as other groups, to make their case heard, to put forward arguments that may be rooted in religious beliefs, and to seek legislative change through democratic avenues. This possibility will, however, be constrained by the liberal dimension of democracy that guards against majority tyranny, that requires all individuals to be treated equally and guarantees a high degree of individual freedom, so long as it is not used to harm others. In consequence, the democratic state will, for example, not restrict religious freedom but neither will it tolerate attacks on those who wish to change their religion; it will encourage respect for religion and discourage (if only on grounds of good taste and sensitivity to others) the public insulting of faith communities but will not engage in censorship of works of art that may give offence to believers – except in so far as these cross legal lines regarding libel, obscenity etc.; it will promote a common school curriculum that seeks to promote understanding and tolerance of difference, whilst embodying current scholarly understandings in its curriculum content; and whilst ensuring due respect for the views of religious communities and maximum opportunities to practise the faith, will not allow religion to be used to deny equal rights to all regardless of gender, sexual orientation, race and belief.

Of course, in practice this is rather simplistic, and very hard to operationalise in the real world, and there are very sophisticated arguments revolving around the need to recognise the needs and rights of groups and communities within multicultural societies. Nor do these debates – about religious exclusions and protections, about respect for minorities – permit easy solutions in practice. Nonetheless, the bottom line has to be that democracy (in the liberal vision) is about guaranteeing the maximum degree of human freedom possible, and this ultimately has to be tied into an emphasis that focuses on human autonomy. This can and probably should be rooted in a sense of responsibility or obligation, and some notion of moral restraint that religious bodies may help to sustain, but this can never be at the expense of freedom – even if we dislike the consequences. This freedom also includes the freedom to believe and practise one's faith, to promote the belief that true freedom lies in religious faith, and to seek to persuade others of this understanding, but this is not something a state can or should legislate for.

Looking to the future, several questions are worth noting. Firstly, will groups such as the Eastern Orthodox and the Pentecostals, who are in many cases just starting their engagement with democracy, successfully adapt to this new form of politics? Our historical survey suggests that religious communities 'learn on the job', from the very process of involvement, and there is no intrinsic reason why these communities should not follow suit and contribute in positive ways to a renegotiated (and perhaps redefined) understanding of democracy. Yet in the Orthodox case, much of the evidence we have presented indicates that in much of the post-communist world the leaders of the Church remain deeply conservative and defensive, suspicious of the values associated with liberal democracy.[2] They are also perhaps overly prone to fall for the 'twin temptations' of seeking alliances with state and nation rather than focusing on the development of civil society and individual autonomy. Though there have been discussions of an Orthodox model of democracy, as yet attempts to give this real substance have not proved that convincing. Whilst none of this means that the Orthodox churches present insuperable barriers to further democratisation – except perhaps in Russia where their attitude tends to reinforce elite suspicions of democracy – it does suggest that they are hardly going to be key contributors to any further deepening of democratisation processes.

The question of the political implications of the Pentecostal explosion ties in with a second issue which relates to what has been called the 'southernisation' of Christianity, as the traditional 'West' ceases to represent the core of the 'Christian world'.[3] The political consequences of this remain to be seen, but one obvious consequence has been a change in Christian public agendas and the re-assertion of traditional understandings of the family and personal morality. At the time of writing the Vatican retains a commitment to human rights but seems to have stepped back from more expansive visions of democracy – leaving aside individual bishops and priests who continue to speak up for the marginalised. With regard to the Pentecostal explosion some of the evidence suggests that the impact of this will be 'conservative' with a concern for social justice, shaped in part by the socio-economic position of many of these churches, but one tempered by explanations of this situation that are rooted in personal failings or demonic interventions rather than in analyses of structural inequality – though the example we gave of Mensa Otabil warns against any superficial generalisation on this score.

At the same time, in some situations participation in these churches does offer opportunities for social advancement, opens up space for the participation of women, and provides training in skills that might contribute to a broader opening up of political orders. And the very fact of religious pluralism and competition may also help to break up traditional hegemonies and contribute to the pluralisation of the wider society. Ultimately the jury remains out on the long-term political implications of this Pentecostal explosion (which also affects the Catholic and wider Protestant communities). Survey evidence remains inconclusive and, as Charles Taylor points out, will never be able to produce verifiable 'traceable correlations, say, between confessional allegiances and capitalist development'. He goes on to add that 'it is in the very nature of this kind of relation between spiritual outlook and economic and political performance that the influence may also be much more diffuse and indirect ... in fact the relationship is much more independent and reciprocal. Certain moral understandings are embedded in certain practices which mean both that they are promoted by the spread of these practices, and that they shape the practices and help them get established'.[4]

The overall conclusions of this study are modest. Over the last half century Christianity has had to engage with the democratic experiment as never before. Different traditions have responded in different ways: some have embraced pluralist politics enthusiastically, albeit aware that there will always be tensions between the 'two kingdoms', others have had to be dragged kicking and screaming into acceptance of democracy, whilst some remain sceptical about democracy's merits or see the whole political order as largely secondary to their primary mission of preaching the Gospel. Whilst we remain to be convinced that recent developments within Christianity will make a major direct contribution to liberalisation and democratisation, only in a few cases are they going to offer major obstacles to such change. We had hoped to conclude that the last fifty years had seen a shift whereby Christian churches and believers had ceased to become subjects and had become 'critical' participants – this might be true in some cases, but a more modest if dull conclusion might simply be that they have at least become participants in the democratic discussion.

Notes

1 A. Wolfe, 'Whose Christianity? Whose democracy?', in H. Heclo, *Christianity and American Democracy* (Harvard: Harvard University Press, 2007), p. 188.

2 For further confirmation of this see L. Stan and L. Turcescu, *Religion and Politics in Post-Communist Romania* (Oxford: Oxford University Press, 2007).

3 P. Jenkins, *The Next Christendom: The Coming of Global Christianity* (Oxford: Oxford University Press, 2002).

4 C. Taylor, *A Secular Age* (Harvard: Harvard University Press, 2007), p. 156.

Bibliography

Aguilar, M. *A Social History of the Catholic Church in Chile, Volume I: The First Period of the Pinochet Government, 1973–80* (Lewiston: The Edwin Mellen Press, 2004)

Alexander, J. (ed.), *Real Civil Societies: Dilemmas of Institutionalization* (London: Sage, 1998)

Anderson, A. *An Introduction to Pentecostalism: Global Charismatic Christianity* (Cambridge: Cambridge University Press, 2004)

Anderson, J. *Religion, State and Politics in the Soviet Union and the Successor States* (Cambridge: Cambridge University Press, 1994)

Anderson, J. *Religious Liberty in Transitional Societies: The Politics of Religion* (Cambridge: Cambridge University Press, 2003)

Anderson, J. (ed.), *Religion, Democracy and Democratization* (London: Routledge, 2005)

Anderson, J. 'Putin and the Russian Orthodox Church: assymetric symphonia', *Columbia Journal of International Affairs*, 61:1 (2007), pp. 185–201

Ash, T. Garton *The Polish Revolution* (London: Granta Books, 1991)

Aubert, R. *The Christian Centuries, Vol.5: The Church in A Secularised Society* (London: Darton, Longman and Todd, 1978)

Audi, R. and Woltersorff, N. *Religion in the Public Sphere: The Place of Religious Convictions in Political Debate* (Lanham: Rowman and Littlefield, 1997)

Bautista, *Cardinal Sin and the Miracle of Asia* (Manila: Vera Reyes, 1987)

Bebbington, D. *The Non-Conformist Conscience: Chapel and Politics, 1870–1914* (London: George Allen and Unwin, 1982)

Berger, P. and Huntington, S. (ed.), *Many Globalizations: Cultural Diversity in the Contemporary World* (Oxford: Oxford University Press, 2002)

Blachnicki, F. 'A theology of liberation – in the spirit', *Religion in Communist Lands*, 12:2 (1984), pp. 157–67

Blackburn, D. *The Fontana History of Germany, 1780–1914* (London: Fontana, 1997)

Bloom, I. , Martin, J. P. and Proudfoot, W. (ed.), *Religious Diversity and Human Rights* (New York: Columbia University Press, 1996)

Blythe, J. *Ideal Government and the Mixed Constitution in the Middle Ages* (Princeton: Princeton University Press, 1992)

Boesak, B. *Black and Reformed: Apartheid, Liberation, and the Calvinist Tradition* (New York: Orbis, 1984)

Bourdeaux, M. *Religious Ferment in Russia* (London: Macmillan, 1968)

Bourdeaux, M. *Patriarchs and Prophets* (London: Macmillan, 1970)

Bourdeaux, M. *Land of Crosses – The Struggle for Religious Freedom in Lithuania, 1939–78* (Devon: Augustine Publishing Co., 1979)

Brassloff, A. *Religion and Politics in Spain: The Spanish Church in Transition, 1962–96* (London: Macmillan, 1998)

Bromke, A. 'A new juncture in Poland', *Problems of Communism*, No. 5 (1976)

Brouwer, S., Gifford, P. and Rose, S. *Exporting the American Gospel – Global Christian Fundamentalism* (London: Routledge, 1996)

Bruce, S. *The Rise and Fall of the New Christian Right: Conservative Protestant Politics in America, 1978–1988* (Oxford: Clarendon, 1988)

Bruce, S. *Religion in the Modern World* (Oxford: Oxford University Press, 1996)

Bruce, S. *Fundamentalism* (Cambridge: Polity, 2000)

Bruce, S. 'Did Protestantism create democracy?', *Democratization*, 11:4 (2004), pp. 3–20

Bruneau, T. *The Political Transformation of the Brazilian Catholic Church* (Cambridge: Cambridge University Press, 1974)

Buchanan, T. and Conway, M. (ed.), *Political Catholicism in Europe, 1918–65* (Oxford: Clarendon Press, 1996)

Burns, J. (ed.), *The Cambridge History of Political Thought, 1450–1700* (Cambridge: Cambridge University Press, 1991)

Butt, R. *The Power of Parliament* (London: Constable, 1969)

Byrnes, T. and Katzenstein, P. (ed.), *Religion in an Expanding Europe* (Cambridge: Cambridge University Press, 2006)

Callahan, W. 'The evangelisation of Franco's "New Spain"', *Church History*, 56 (1987), pp. 491–6

Callahan, W. 'Church and state in Spain, 1976–91', *Journal of Church and State*, 34:3 (1992), pp. 503–19

Callahan, W. *The Catholic Church in Spain, 1875–98* (Washington DC: Catholic University Press of America, 2000)

Canning, J. *A History of Medieval Political Thought* (London: Routledge, 1996)

Casanova, J. *Public Religions in the Modern World* (Chicago: Chicago University Press, 1994)

Chadwick, O. *The Reformation* (London: Penguin, 1970)

Chazan, N. *et al.*, *Politics and Society in Contemporary Africa* (Boulder: Lynne Reinner, 1999)

Chrysoloras, N. 'Why Orthodoxy? Religion and nationalism in Greek political culture', *Studies in Ethnicity and Nationalism*, 4:1 (2004), pp. 40–61

Cleary, E. 'The Brazilian Catholic Church and church–state relations: nation building', *Journal of Church and State*, 39:2 (1997), pp. 253–72

Cleary, E. *The Struggle for Human Rights in Latin America* (Westport: Greenwood Press, 1997)

Cleary, E. and Stewart-Gambino, H. (ed.), *Conflict and Co-operation: The Latin American Church in a Changing Environment* (Boulder: Lynne Reinner, 1992)

Cleary, E. and Stewart-Gambino, H. (ed.), *Power, Politics and Pentecostals* (Boulder: Westview, 1998)

Comblin, J. *The Church and the National Security State* (New York: Orbis, 1979)

Cornwall, J. *Hitler's Pope: The Secret History of Pius XII* (London: Penguin, 2000)

Cowling, M. *Religion and Public Doctrine in Modern England*, (Volume II (Cambridge: Cambridge University Press, 1985)

Craig, G. *The Church and the Age of Reason, 1648–1789* (London: Penguin, 1970)

Cross, F. and Livingstone, E. (ed.), *The Oxford Dictionary of the Christian Church* (New York: Oxford University Press, 1985)

Cuneo, T. (ed.), *Religion in the Liberal Polity* (Notre Dame: Notre Dame University Press, 2005)

Cunningham, J. *A Vanquished Hope: The Movement for Church Renewal in Russia, 1905–1906* (New York: St Vladimir's Seminar Press, 1983)

Curry, T. *The First Freedoms: Church and State in America to the Passage of the First Amendment* (New York: Oxford University Press, 1986)

Daniel, W. *The Orthodox Church and Civil Society in Russia* (College Station: Texas A and M University Press, 2006)

Davis, D. 'Editorial: The Russian Orthodox Church and the future of Russia', *Journal of Church and State*, 44:3 (2002), pp. 653–70

Davis, D. and McMearty, M. 'America's "forsaken roots": the use and abuse of founders' quotations', *Journal of Church and State*, 47:3 (2005), pp. 449–72

De Blaye, Edouard *Franco and the Politics of the New Spain* (London: Penguin, 1976)

De Broucker, J. *Dom Helder Camara: The Violence of a Peacemaker* (New York: Orbis, 1970)

De Gruchy, J. *Christianity and Democracy* (Cambridge: Cambridge University Press, 1995)

De Tocqueville, A. *Democracy in America* (London: Collins, 1966)

Diamond, S. *Not by Politics Alone: The Enduring Influence of the Christian Right* (New York: The Guilford Press, 1998)

Dickens, A. G. *The English Reformation* (London, Fontana, 1964)

Dionne, E., Elshtain, J. and Drogosz, K. (ed.), *One Electorate Under God – A Dialogue on Religion and American Politics* (Washington DC: Brookings Institute Press, 2004)

Di Palma, G. *To Craft Democracies* (Berkeley: University of California Press, 1990)

Durham, M. *The Christian Right, The Far Right and the Boundaries of American Conservatism* (Manchester: Manchester University Press, 2000)

Dvornik, F. *Early Christian and Byzantine Political Philosophy: Origins and Background*, Volume 2 (Washington: Harvard University, 1966)

Elliott, J. *Europe Divided* (London: Fontana, 1968)

Ellis, J. *The Russian Orthodox Church: Triumphalism and Defensiveness* (London: Macmillan, 1996)

Epstein, J. *The New Argentine Democracy* (London: Greenwood Press, 1992)

Erickson, J. *Orthodox Christians in America* (New York: Oxford University Press, 1999)

Esposito, J. and Watson, M. (ed.), *Religion and Global Order* (Cardiff: University of Wales Press, 2000)

Ethier, D. (ed.), *Democratic Transition and Consolidation in Southern Europe, Latin America and Southeast Asia* (London: Macmillan, 1990)

Fedorov, V. 'Barriers to ecumenism: an Orthodox view from Russia', *Religion, State and Society*, 26:2 (1998), pp. 129–43

Feldman, N. *Divided by God: America's Church–State Problem and What We Should Do About It* (New York: Farrah, Strauss and Giroux, 2005)

Filatov, S. (ed.), *Religiya i politika v postkommunisticheskoi Rossii* (*Religion and Politics in Post-Communist Russia*) (Moscow, 1994)

Finke, R. and Stark, R. *The Churching of America, 1776–2005*, Revised edition (New Brunswick: Rutgers University Press, 2005)

Fitzgerald, F. 'The evangelical surprise', *New York Review of Books*, LIV:7, 26 April 2007, at www.nybooks.com/articles/20131 (accessed 6 August 2008)

Fleet, M. and Smith, B. *The Catholic Church and Democracy in Chile and Peru* (Notre Dame: Notre Dame University Press, 1997)

Fogarty, M. *Christian Democracy in Western Europe, 1820–1953* (London: Routledge and Kegan Paul, 1957)

Fowler, R., Hertzke, A. and Olson, L. *Religion and Politics in America: Faith, Culture and Strategic Choices*, 2nd edition (Boulder: Westview, 1999)

Frank, J. *The Levellers* (Cambridge, Mass: Harvard University Press, 1955)

Freston, P. *Evangelicals and Politics in Asia, Africa and Latin America* (Cambridge: Cambridge University Press, 2001)

Gallagher, T. *Theft of a Nation: Romania Since Communism* (London: Hurst, 2005)

Garrard-Burnett, V. and Stoll, D. (ed.), *Rethinking Protestantism in Latin America* (Philadelphia: Temple University Press, 1993)

Geffre, C. and Jossua, J.-P. *1789: The French Revolution and the Churches* (Edinburgh: T. and T. Clark, 1989)

Gibson, W. *Church, State and Society, 1760–1850* (London: Macmillan, 1994)

Gifford, P. *African Christianity: Its Public Role* (London: Hurst, 1998)

Gifford, P. *Ghana's New Christianity: Pentecostalism in a Globalising African Economy* (London: Hurst, 2004)

Gifford, P. (ed.), *The Christian Churches and the Democratisation of Africa* (Leiden: E. J. Brill, 1995)

Gill, A. *Rendering unto Caesar: The Catholic Church and the State in Latin America* (Chicago: University of Chicago Press, 1998)

Glazier, S. (ed.), *Perspectives on Pentecostalism* (New York: University of America Press, 1980)

Goeckel, R. *The Lutheran Church and the East German State: Political Conflict and Change under Ulbricht and Honecker* (Ithaca: Cornell University Press, 1990)

Graham, R. *Spain: Change of a Nation* (London: Joseph, 1984)

Greeley, A. and Hout, M. *The Truth about Conservative Christians: What They Think and What They Believe* (Chicago: Chicago University Press, 2006)

Green, J., Rozell, M. and Wilcox, C. (ed.), *The Christian Right in America – Marching to the Millennium* (Washington DC: Georgetown University Press, 2003)

Grell, O. and Scribner, B. (ed.), *Tolerance and Intolerance in the European Reformation* (Cambridge: Cambridge University Press, 1996)

Grugel, J. *Democratization: A Critical Introduction* (London: Palgrave, 2002)

Gutiérriz, G. *A Theology of Liberation: Liberation and Faith* (London: SCM, 1988)

Gvosdev, N. *An Examination of Church–State Relations in the Byzantine and Russian Empires with an Emphasis on Ideology and Models of Interaction* (Lewiston: Edwin Mellen Press, 2001)

Hall, J. (ed.), *Civil Society: Theory, History, Comparison* (Cambridge: Polity Press, 1995)

Hansen, H. and Twaddle, M. (ed.), *Religion and Politics in East Africa* (London: James Currey, 1995)

Harakas, A. *Living the Faith: The Praxis of Eastern Orthodox Ethics* (Minneapolis: Light and Life Publishing, 1993)

Harding, S. *The Book of Jerry Falwell* (Princeton: Princeton University Press, 2000)

Hastings, A. (ed.), *Modern Catholicism: Vatican II and After* (London: SPCK, 1991)

Hatch, N. *The Democratisation of American Christianity* (New Haven: Yale University Press, 1989)

Haynes, J. *Religion and Politics in Africa* (London: Zed Books, 1996)

Heclo, H. *Christianity and American Democracy* (Harvard: Harvard University Press, 2007)

Held, D. *Models of Democracy*, 1st edition (Cambridge: Polity Press, 1987)

Held, D. *Models of Democracy*, 2nd edition (Cambridge: Polity Press, 1996)

Hennelly, A. (ed.), *Liberation Theology: A Documentary History* (New York: Orbis, 1992)

Herbert, D. *Religion and Civil Society – Rethinking Public Religion in the Contemporary World* (Aldershot: Ashgate, 2003)

Hesli, V. Erdem, E. , Reisinger, W. and Miller, A. 'The Patriarch and the President: religion and political choice in Russia', *Demokratizatsiya, 7.1 (1999)*, pp. 42–72

Hewitt, W. *Base Christian Communities and Social Change in Brazil* (Lincoln and London: University of Nebraska Press, 1991)

Hewitt, W. 'The changing of the guard: transformations in the politico-religious attitudes and behaviour of CENB members in Sao Paulo, 1984–93', *Journal of Church and State*, 38:1 (1996), pp. 115–36

Heywood, P. *The Government and Politics of Spain* (London: Palgrave, 1995)

Hill, C. *The English Bible and the Seventeenth Century Revolution* (London: Allen Lane, 1993)

Hinchley, C. 'Tocqueville on religion and modernity: making Catholicism safe for liberal democracy', *Journal of Church and State*, 32:2 (1990), pp. 325–41

Hobsbawm, E. *The Age of Revolution, 1789–1948* (London: Abacus, 1993)

Hopko, T. 'Orthodoxy in post-modern pluralist societies', *Ecumenical Review*, 51:4 (1999), pp. 364–71

Hopko, T. 'The narrow way of Orthodoxy: a message from Orthodoxy in America to Eastern Europe', *Christian Century*, 15 March 1995, pp. 269–99

Hopson, R. and Smith, D. 'Changing fortunes: an analysis of Christian

Right ascendance within American political discourse', *Journal for the Scientific Study of Religion*, 38:1, (1999), pp. 1–13

Hunter, J. D. *Culture Wars: The Struggle to Define America* (New York: Basic Books, 1991)

Huntington, S. *The Third Wave: Democratization in the Twentieth Century* (Norman: University of Oklahoma Press, 1991)

Huntington, S. 'The clash of civilizations?', *Foreign Affairs*, 77 (1993), pp. 22–49

Huntington, S. *The Clash of Civilizations and the Remaking of World Order* (New York: Simon and Schuster, 1996)

Huntington, S. *Who Are We? America's Great Debate* (London: Simon and Schuster, 2004)

Ireland, R. *Kingdoms Come: Religion and Politics in Brazil* (Pittsburgh: University of Pittsburgh Press 1991)

Jeglinski, P. and Tomsky, A. '*Spotkania*: Journal of the Catholic Opposition in Poland', *Religion in Communist Lands*, 7:1 (1979), pp. 23–8

Jenkins, P. *The Next Christendom: The Coming of Global Christianity* (Oxford: Oxford University Press, 2002)

Johnston, D. and Sampson, C. (ed.), *Religion, The Missing Dimension in Statecraft* (Oxford: Oxford University Press, 1994)

Johnston, H. 'Towards an explanation of church opposition to authoritarian regimes: religio-oppositional sub-cultures in Poland and Catalonia', *Journal for the Scientific Study of Religion*, 28:4 (1989), pp. 493–508

Jones, M. *The Limits of Liberty: American History, 1607–1980* (Oxford: Oxford University Press, 1983)

Joseph, R. (ed.), *State, Conflict and Democracy in Africa* (Boulder: Lynne Reinner, 1999)

Kalyvas, S. *The Rise of Christian Democracy in Europe* (Ithaca: Cornell University Press, 1996)

Kaplan, E. *With God on Their Side: George W. Bush and the Christian Right* (New York: The New Press, 2005)

Karpinski, J. 'Poles divided over church's renewed political role', *Transition*, 5:4 (1996), pp. 11–13

Karpinski, J. 'The constitutional mosaic', *Transition*, 11 August 1995, pp. 4–9

Karpov, V. 'Religiosity and tolerance in the United States and Poland', *Journal for the Scientific Study of Religion*, 41:2 (2002), pp. 267–88

Keane, J. *Tom Paine: A Political Life* (London: Bloomsbury, 1995)

Keane, J. 'Secularism?', in Marquand, D. and Nettler, R. (ed.), *Religion and Democracy* (Oxford: Blackwell, 2000)

Kelly, P. *Politics and Religious Consciousness in America* (New Brunswick: Transaction Publishers, 1984)

Kingdom, R. and Linder, R. (ed.), *Calvin and Calvinism: Sources of Democracy* (Lexington: D. C. Heath, 1970)

Klaiber, J. *The Church, Dictatorships and Democracy in Latin America* (New York: Orbis, 1998)

Knox, Z. 'The symphonic ideal: the Moscow Patriarchate's post-Soviet leadership', *Europe-Asia Studies*, 55:4 (2003), pp. 575–96

Koumoulidis, T. (ed.), *Greece in Transition: Essays in Modern Greek History, 1821–1974* (London: Zeno Publishers, 1977)

Koyzis, D. 'Imaging God and his kingdom: Eastern Orthodoxy's iconic political ethic', *Review of Politics*, 55:2 (1993), pp. 267–89

Kritz, N. (ed.), *Transitional Justice*, Volume 1 (Washington DC: United States Institute of Peace, 1995)

Labaree, B. *Colonial Massachussetts – A History* (New York: KTP Press, 1979)

Lehmann, D. *Struggle for the Spirit: Religious Transformation and Popular Culture in Brazil and Latin America* (Cambridge: Polity Press, 1996)

Levine, D. (ed.), *Churches and Politics in Latin America* (London: Sage, 1979)

Lieven, A. *America Right or Wrong: An Anatomy of American Nationalism* (Oxford: Oxford University Press, 2005)

Linker, D. *The Theocons: Secular America under Siege* (New York: Doubleday, 2006)

Linz, J. and Stepan, A. *Problems of Democratic Transition and Consolidation* (Baltimore: Johns Hopkins University Press, 1996)

Lipski, J. *History of the Workers' Defence Committee in Poland, 1976–1981* (London: University of California Press, 1985)

Lunnon, F. *Privilege, Persecution and Prophecy: The Catholic Church in Spain, 1875–1975* (Oxford: Clarendon Press, 1987)

Luxmoore, J. 'Eastern Europe 1995: a review of religious life in Bulgaria, Romania, Hungary, Slovakia, the Czech Republic and Poland', *Religion, State and Society*, 24:4 (1996), pp. 357–66

McManners, J. *The French Revolution and the Church* (Westport: Greenwood Press, 1982)

Maddox, G. *Religion and the Rise of Democracy* (London: Routledge, 1996)

Madeley, J. and Enyedi , Z. (ed.), *Church and State in Contemporary Europe: The Chimera of Neutrality* (London: Frank Cass, 2003)

Mainwaring, S. *The Catholic Church and Politics in Brazil, 1916–85* (Stanford: Stanford University Press, 1986)

Mainwaring, S. and Wilde, A. (ed.), *The Progressive Church in Latin America* (Indiana: University of Notre Dame Press, 1989)

Marley, D. 'Ronald Reagan and the splintering of the Christian Right', *Journal of Church and State*, 48:1 (2006), pp. 851–70

Marsden, G. (ed.), *Evangelicalism and Modern America* (Grand Rapids: William B.Eerdmans, 1984)

Marsh, C. (ed.), *Burden or Blessing? Russian Orthodoxy and the Construction of Civil Society and Democracy* (Boston: Institute on Culture, Religion and World Affairs, 2004)

Martin, D. *Tongues of Fire: The Explosion of Protestantism in Latin America* (London: Blackwell Publishers, 1990)

Martin, D. *Pentecostalism: The World their Parish* (Oxford: Blackwell, 2002)

Marty, M. *Pilgrims in their Own Land* (Boston: Little Brown, 1984)

Marty, M. and Scott Appleby, R. (ed.), *Fundamentalisms Observed* (Chicago: Chicago University Press, 1991)

Maxwell, D. *African Gifts of the Spirit: Pentecostalism and the Rise of a Zimbabwean Transnational Religious Movement* (Oxford: James Currey, 2006)

Meacham, C. 'Changing of the guard: new relations between church and state in Chile', *Journal of Church and State*, 29:3 (1987), pp. 411–33

Meacham, C. 'The role of the Chilean Catholic Church in the new Chilean democracy', *Journal of Church and State*, 36:2 (1994), pp. 277–99

Merkel, W. 'The consolidation of post-autocratic democracies: a multi-level analysis', *Democratization*, 5:3 (1998), pp. 33–67

Michnik, A. *Letters from Prison and Other Essays* (London: University of California Press, 1985)

Michnik, A. *The Church and the Left* (Chicago: Chicago University Press, 1993)

Millard, F. 'The shaping of the Polish party system, 1989–93', *East European Politics and Society*, 8:3 (1994), pp. 467–94

Miller, D. and Yamamori, T. *Global Pentecostalism: The New Face of Christian Social Engagement* (Berkeley: University of California Press, 2007)

Mojzes, P. (ed.), *Religion and the War in Bosnia* (Atlanta: Scholars Press, 1998)

Molokotos-Liederman, L. 'The Greek ID card controversy: a case study of religion and national identity in a changing European Union', *Journal of Contemporary Religion*, 22:2 (2007), pp. 187–203

Morall, J. B. *Political Thought in Medieval Times* (London: Hutchinson, 1971)

Morgan, E. *Roger Williams: the Church and State* (New York: Harcourt, Brace and World, 1967)

Noll, N. *The Old Religion in a New World: The History of North American Christianity* (Grand Rapids: Wm. B. Eerdmans, 2002)

Osiatynski, W. *The Round Table Negotiations in Poland* (Working Paper No. 1 of the Centre for the Study of Constitutionalism in Eastern Europe)

Ozment, S. *The Age of Reform 1250–1555: An Intellectual and Religious History of Late Medieval and Reformation Europe* (New Haven: Yale University Press, 1980)

Papanikolaou, A. 'Bzyantium, Orthodoxy and democracy', *Journal of the American Academy of Religion*, 71:1 (2003), pp. 75–98

Parsons, G. *Perspectives on Civil Religion* (Aldershot: Ashgate, 2002)

Pennington, D. *17th Century Europe* (London: Fontana, 1970)

Pennington, D. and Thomas, K. (ed.), *Puritans and Revolutionaries* (Oxford: Oxford University Press, 1978)

Perez-Diaz, V. *The Return of Civil Society* (London: Harvard University Press, 1993)

Phillips, K. *American Theocracy: The Perils and Politics of Radical Religion, Oil and Borrowed Money in the 21st Century* (New York: Viking Books, 2006)

Philpott, D. 'The Catholic Wave', *Journal of Democracy*, 15:2 (2004), pp. 32–46

Porch, D. *The Portugese Armed Forces Movement and the Revolution* (London: Croom Helm, 1977)

Potter, D. *et al.* (ed.), *Democratization* (Cambridge: Polity Press, 1997)

Preston, P. (ed.), *Spain in Crisis* (London: Harvester Press, 1976)

Pridham, G. and Lewis, P. (ed.), *Stabilising Fragile Democracies: Comparing New Party Systems in Southern and Eastern Europe* (London: Routledge, 1996)

Prodromou, E. 'The ambivalent Orthodox', *Journal of Democracy*, 15:2 (2004), pp. 62–75

Prodromou, E. 'Religious pluralism in twenty-first century America: problematizing the implications for Orthodox Christianity', *Journal of the American Academy of Religion*, 72:3 (2004), pp. 733–57

Przeworski, A. *Democracy and the Market: Political and Economic Reforms in Eastern Europe and Latin America* (Cambridge: Cambridge University Press, 1991)

Quigley, T. 'The Chilean coup, the Church and the human rights movement', *America*, 11 February 2002), at http://web7.infotrac.galegroup.com/itw/infomark/624/3/60178090w7/purl=rc1_EAIM_0 (accessed 3 March 2005)

Radu, M. 'The burden of Eastern Orthodoxy', *Orbis*, Spring 1998, pp. 283–300

Ramet, S. *Nihil Obstat: Religion, Politics and Social Change in East-Central Europe and Russia* (Durham: Duke University Press, 1998)

Ramet, S. *Balkan Babel: The Disintegration of Yugoslavia from the Death of Tito to the Fall of Milošević*, 4th edition (Boulder: Westview, 2004)

Ravitch, N. *The Catholic Church and the French Nation, 1589–1989* (London: Routledge, 1990)

Rhodes, A. *The Vatican in the Age of Dictators, 1922–45* (London: Hodder and Stoughton, 1973)

Ricks, D. and Magdalino, P. (ed.), *Byzantium and the Greek Identity* (Aldershot: Ashgate, 1998)

Robinson, R. A. *Contemporary Portugal: A History* (London: Allen and Unwin, 1979)

Roudemetoff, V., Agadjanian, V. and Pankhurst, J. (ed.), *Eastern Orthodoxy in a Global Age: Tradition Faces the Twenty-First Century* (Lanham: Rowman and Littlefield, 2005)

Rude, G. *Revolutionary Europe, 1783–1815* (London: Collins, 1967)

Rudolph, S. and Piscatori, J. (ed.), *Transnational Religion and Fading States* (Boulder: Westview Press, 1997)

Sahliyeh, E. (ed.), *Religious Resurgence and Politics in the Contemporary World* (Albany: SUNY Press, 1990)

Sakwa, R. 'Christian Democracy and civil society in Russia', *Religion, State and Society*, 22:3 (1994), pp. 273–304

Sanchez, J. *The Spanish Civil War as Religious Tragedy* (Indiana: University of Notre Dame Press, 1987)

Schedler, A. 'How should we study democratic consolidation?', *Democratization*, 5:4 (1998), pp. 1–19

Schuck, M. *That They May Be One: The Social Teaching of the Papal Encyclicals, 1740–1989* (Washington: Georgetown University Press, 1991)

Scwab, P. and Frangos, C. (ed.), *Greece under the Junta* (New York: Facts on File, 1970)

Segers, M. and Jelen, T. *Wall of Separation? Debating the Public Role of Religion* (Lanham: Rowman and Littlefield, 1998)

Sells, M. *The Bridge Betrayed: Religion and Genocide in Bosnia* (Berkeley: University of California Press, 1996)

Shields, J. 'Between passion and deliberation: the Christiain Right and democratic ideals', *Political Science Quarterly*, 122:1 (2007), pp. 89–113

Sigmund, P. 'The Catholic tradition and modern democracy', *Review of*

Politics, 49:4 (1987), pp. 530–48

Sigmund, P. *Liberation Theology at the Crossroads: Democracy or Revolution* (New York: Oxford Univesity Press, 1990)

Skilling, H. Gordon *Samizdat and an Independent Society in Central and Eastern Europe* (London: Macmillan, 1989)

Smith, B. *The Church and Politics in Chile* (Princeton: Princeton University Press, 1992)

Smith, B. *Religious Politics in Latin America: Pentecostal vs Catholic* (Notre Dame: University of Notre Dame Press, 1998)

Smith, C. *Christian America: What Evangelicals Really Want* (Berkeley: California University Press, 2002)

Smith, C. and Prokopy, J. (ed.), *Latin American Religion in Motion* (New York: Routledge, 1999)

Snow, P. and Manzetti, L. *Political Forces in Argentina* (Westport: Greenwood Press, 1993)

Stacpoole, A. (ed.), *Vatican II By Those Who Were There* (London: Geoffrey Chapman, 1986)

Stan, L. and Turcescu, L. 'The Romanian Orthodox Church and post-communist democratisation', *Europe-Asia Studies*, 52:8 (2000), pp. 1467–88

Stan, L. and Turcescu, L. *Religion and Politics in Post-Communist Romania* (Oxford: Oxford University Press, 2007)

Steigenga, T. *The Politics of the Spirit: The Political Implications of Pentecostalized Religion in Costa Rica and Guatemala* (Lanham: Lexington Books, 2001)

Stepan, A. *Arguing Comparative Politics* (Oxford: Oxford University Press, 2001)

Stepan, A. (ed.), *Democratizing Brazil: Problems of Transition and Consolidation* (Oxford: Oxford University Press, 1989)

Sutton, J. and Van Den Bercken, W. (ed.), *Orthodox Christianity and Contemporary Europe* (Leuven: Peeters, 2003)

Swatos, W. (ed.), *Religion and Democracy in Latin America* (New Brunswick: Transaction Publishers, 1995)

Taras, R. *Consolidating Democracy in Poland* (Boulder: Westview Press, 1995)

Taylor, C. *A Secular Age* (Harvard: Harvard University Press, 2007)

Thompson, W. *The Political Thought of Martin Luther* (Brighton: Harvester Press, 1984)

Tokes, R. (ed.), *Opposition in Eastern Europe* (London: Macmillan, 1979)

Turcescu, L. and Stan, L. 'Religion, politics and sexuality in Romania', in *Europe-Asia Studies*, 57:2 (2005), pp. 291–303

Vardys, V. S. *The Catholic Church, Dissent and Nationality in Soviet Lithuania* (New York: East European Quarterly, 1978)

Vasquez, M. *The Brazilian Popular Church and the Crisis of Modernity* (Cambridge: Cambridge University Press, 1997)

Velikonja, M. 'The role of religions and religious communities in the war in the ex-Yugoslavia, 1991–1999', at www.georgefox.edu/academics /undergrad/departments/soc-swk/ree/2003/velikonja03.html (accessed 25 March 2006)

Wallis, J. *God's Politics: Why the American Right Gets it Wrong and the Left*

Doesn't Get It (Oxford: Lion, 2005)

Walshe, P. 'South Africa, prophetic Christianity and the liberation movement', *Journal of Modern African Studies*, 29.1 (1991), pp. 27–60

Watson, J. *The Christian Coalition : Dreams of Restoration, Demands for Recognition*, (Basingstoke: Macmillan, 1999)

Weigel, G. *The Final Revolution: The Resistance Church and the Collapse of Communism* (Oxford: Oxford University Press, 1992)

White, S. *et al.*, *Religion and Political Action in Postcommunist Europe* (Strathclyde: Studies in Public Policy, 307, 1998)

Whitehead, L. (ed.), *The International Dimensions of Democratization: Europe and the Americas* (Oxford: Oxford University Press, 2001)

Wilcox, C. and Jelen, T. (ed.), *Religion and Politics in Comparative Perspective: The One, the Few and the Many* (Cambridge: Cambridge University Press, 2002)

Witte, J. (ed.), *Christianity and Democracy in Global Context* (Boulder: Westview, 1993)

Witte, J. and Bourdeaux, M. (ed.), *Proselytism and Orthodoxy in Russia – The New War for Souls* (New York: Orbis, 1999)

Wolfe, A. *The Transformation of American Religion: How We Actually Live Our Faith* (Chicago: Chicago University Press, 2003)

Wolfe, A. 'Dieting for Jesus', *Prospect*, January 2004, at www.prospect -magazine.co.uk/printarticle.php?id=5804 (accessed 7 July 2008)

Wozniuk, V. 'Vladimir S.Soloviev and the politics of human rights', *Journal of Church and State*, 41:1 (1999), pp. 33–50

Wuthnow, R. *Communities of Discourse: Ideology and Social Structure in the Reformation, the Enlightenment and European Socialism* (London: Harvard University Press, 1989)

Zmirak, J. and Black, J. 'Problems of identity in America: two views', a review of Huntington's book in *Modern Age*, 47:3 (2005), pp. 278–84

Index